GARY YANKER'S
SPORTWALKING

GARY YANKER'S
SPORTWALKING

by Gary Yanker

CONTEMPORARY
BOOKS, INC.
CHICAGO ▪ NEW YORK

Library of Congress Cataloging-in-Publication Data

Yanker, Gary.
  Gary Yanker's Sportwalking.

  1. Walking.   2. Physical fitness.   I. Title.
II. Title: Sportwalking.
GV199.5.Y3625   1987   796.5'1   86-32960
ISBN 0-8092-4966-9 (pbk.)

Sportwalking™, Event Walks™, Travelwalking™, and
Walksports™ are trademarks claimed by *Walking World*.

Photography by Michael Bennett unless otherwise credited.

Published by Contemporary Books, Inc.
180 North Michigan Avenue, Chicago, Illinois 60601
Manufactured in the United States of America
Library of Congress Catalog Card Number: 86-32960
International Standard Book Number: 0-8092-4966-9

Published simultaneously in Canada by Beaverbooks, Ltd.
195 Allstate Parkway, Valleywood Business Park
Markham, Ontario L3R 4T8 Canada

This book is dedicated to the dynamic trio: Helen Thaman, and John and Virginia Rice who prove walking can be a lifetime sport.

CONTENTS

THE AUTHOR

GARY YANKER IS "the foremost authority on walking" and the "leader of the walking movement" in America according to *USA Today*, *American Health*, NBC's "Today Show," *The Miami Herald*, *Footwear Magazine*, and the *Frankfurter Allgemeine*. He has sportwalked in 30 countries on 4 continents and has been dubbed the "king" of sportwalkers by "Regis Philbin's Healthstyles."

After practicing corporate and intellectual property law for eight years, Yanker gave up his full-time career to make walking the number one sport and exercise in America. Fifty-five million Americans in the U.S. and 180 million worldwide now exercisewalk. His walking story has been featured worldwide in the media, including the CBS News with Dan Rather, *Time*, *Vital*, the *New York Times Magazine*, *Good Housekeeping*, "PBS Late Night," "PM Magazine," "Hour Magazine," and the CNN News.

Gary's first book, *The Complete Book of Exercisewalking* (Contemporary), started the walking boom (*Women's Sports and Fitness*) and is now the bestselling fitness walking book in the United States and worldwide. *Gary Yanker's Sportwalking* is his fourth walking book, his others are *Gary Yanker's Walking Workouts* (Warner), and *America's*

Greatest Walks (Addison Wesley). Gary is the national walking editor for *Prevention Magazine.*

Gary started his sportwalking career as a member of the world's oldest walking club, The Black Forest Wanderclub, founded in 1864. He has also helped to organize the *Prevention* National Walking Club, America's largest, with over 100,000 members, and serves as its chairman.

ACKNOWLEDGMENTS

FIRST, MANY THANKS to my editor, Nancy Crossman, and to one of my best sportwalking supporters, Hank Fisher of the Netherlands Board of Tourism. My special thanks go to the Sportwalking Staff and my special consultants from *Walking World* and Contemporary Books:

Research Directors:	Kelly C. Kane
	Catherine Gordon Ticer
	Liz Vinciguerra
Contributing	Carol Tarlow
Editors:	Shelly Branch
	Linda Filchev
	Donavan Vicha
	Liz Vinciguerra
Exercise Models:	David Balboa
	Mark Bricklin
	Sylvia Brown
	Andrew Crane
	Richard Goldman
	Richard A. Hudson
	Ingrid Jacobson

	Kelly C. Kane
	Deena Karabell
	Jody Lewis
	Mort Malkin
	Darielle Rayner
Exercise	Tom and Dina Orr
Consultants:	Andy Bostinto
	Kelly C. Kane
	Michael Bennett
Typists:	Maria Diaz
Photography:	Michael Bennett
	Virginia Rice
Technical Advisor:	Kelly C. Kane
Art and Design:	Joe Tully
	Mal Bessen
	Georgene Sainati
Volksmarching:	Dr. David Toth
	Charles Repik
Racewalking:	Richard Goldman
	Mort Malkin
	Henry Laskau
	Gus Krug
	Richard Charles
Long Distance Walking:	Dr. Warren Doyle
Mountaineering:	Jerry Gorman
Events:	Neil Finn
Medical:	Dr. Alan Selner
Podiatry:	Dr. Terry L. Spilken
Apparel:	Richard S. Polk

Special thanks to the following walking clubs and health organizations and their offices and members for assistance in preparing this book: Tom and Dina Orr, 21st Century Nautilus; Zina Lawrence, Charles D. Repik, and Dr. David Toth, American Volkssport Association, National Office and New York Branch; Cliff Harvey, Sylvia Brown, Jane Wescott, Appalachian Mountain Club; Ted Fields of The March of Dimes; Pam Shandrick of Mountain Travel; Madeline Dennis, NY/NJ Trail Conference; Dr. Warren Doyle, Appalachian Long Distance Hikers' Association; Rich Goldman of the Metropolitan Racewalkers; Verna Ness of The Mountaineers; Claire Huertel and Jake Steinem, City Sports; Mort Ament, John Byrnes, Pauline Miles, and Toby Karpel, Empire Blue Cross, Blue Shield; Gerd Pieper, International Volkssport Association; York Onnen, The President's Council on Physical Fitness and Sports; Bob Defer of the U.S. Orienteering Federation; and Susan "Butch" Henley of the American Hiking Society.

And finally, thanks to my advisors and supporters of walking throughout the world: *In the U.S.:* Mitch Douglas, Donna Adkins, Steve Marks, Alfredo Santana, Nancy Neiman, Nancy McCord, Shirley Davis, Ruth Tedder, Sandi Mendelson, Bill Reiss, Mysia Haight, Diane Hovenesian, Ellen Herrick, George Gibson, Susan Fisker, Mary Shapiro, Lisl Cade, Steve Conley, Bob Balzer, Anemika Wijn, Walter Sperr, Valerie DiMaria, Alison Ward, Mark Bricklin, Carol Baldwin, Maggie Spilner, Bob Teufel, Ben Dunlap, Dick Welsh, Anne Schwartz, Suzie Peterson, Jane Ayre, Barbie Glass, Jody Weiss, Paul McIntyre, Bill Hickman, Jerry Sharell, Jerry Petitt, Sue Dynerman, Gina Savoca Rose, Laura Alvord, Bruce Cohn, Ron Brody, Laurie Lico, Gina Rogers Gould, Harvey Plotnick, Ted Macri, Julia Pfieffer, Diana and Jean Marie Vogel, David Clow, Diana Adams, Karen Kreps, Jean McGuire, Paula Panich, Doug Milburn, Michael Teuschler, Will Rice, Thomas G. Murphy, Mary Jane Horton, Richard Hansen, Lynn O'Rourke Hayes, Gary Bitner, Peg Sinclair, T George Harris, Lynn Laurenti, Bill Reiss, Virginia Rice, Corinne Hoexter, Drew Mearns, Bruce Bassett, Tom Singleton, John Harris, Kristin Yanker, Carol Spina, Lisl Yanker, Helen Thaman, Bud Siemon, Tom and Kathy Owens, Foy J. Shaw, Larry Williams, Peter N. Yanker, Diane Adams, Betsy Livingston, Rachel Skolkin, Lee Kass, John Mantica, Karen Kreps, Steve Moergen, Karen Tompkins-Tinch, Bill Tinch, Sue Jones, Linda Kassens, Jim Hind, Sonny Seals, Dan and Leslie Killips, Judith and Brad Ryland, Reed Sparling, and the Powells: Nick, Jim, Jackie, and Molly. *Overseas:* Christina Oates, Gay Oughton, Hilary Rubenstein, Suzanne Palme, Hans Iliohan, Marcel Classen, Ingrid and Erich Schymik, Maria von Pawelcsz, Enrico Zuffi (Swiss National Tourist Office), Tony Haeusler, Paddy Derivan, Roy Murray, Bill Maxwell, Kevin Shannon (Irish Tourist Board), Roy Harvey, Ron Richardson, John Guerin, Brian Leverell, Bedford Pace (British National Tourist Office, Knut Blaetterman (German National Tourist Office), Tony Rothwell, James Farrow, Shin Hada, and Karl Harada.

Special thanks also to my *Sportwalking* Questionnaire Respondents: Gail Allen, Frank Alongi, Erika Archibald, Bob Carlson, Bill Chisholm, Edward Evangelidi, Lorraine Havens, Susan "Butch" Henley, Budd Herrman, Ron Laird, Henry H. Laskau, Linda Nelson, Dr. Howard J. Palamarchuk, Murray Rosenstein, Martin Rudow, Gordon Wallace, Alan Wood, and Colin Young.

PREFACE

I WROTE THIS PREFACE last because I couldn't give you my final word and overview of the *Sportwalking* book until I saw how it turned out. After seeing the whole picture, three major themes emerged:

A REGULAR EXERCISE

Before you start reading my book, let me put a potent idea into your head: Your body will not function properly, particularly after age 25, unless you exercise. Put aside the more controversial claims made for exercise that it will make you live longer, achieve more, or change your life forever. Just reflect on the basics: better shape, better feeling, and stronger body. That's reason enough to improve the quality of your life. But an exercise program is hard to get going and keep going. Exercise can become a habit, but it's easily abandoned because of boredom. Exercises which try to do too much of the same thing over and over in a short time burn out quickly (even some styles of walking can burn you out). Only exercise instructors and athletes are motivated to exercise the same way over and over again. But you and I won't last—that's why walking and the *Sportwalking* program, in particular, offers that opportunity to have fun with your exercise program while staying with it. I call *Sportwalking* an exercise system in the guise of a sports training system. The exercises train you for activities you like to do—the same sport activities that help you to reach your quota of exercise requirements.

REAL WALKERS

The exercise models you see in this book are real walkers, not models who are in shape because they diet, run, or spend four hours every other day bodybuilding as an integral part of making their living. From the photos and captions you can see how each model has developed different body part shapes as a result of their various walksports. For example, notice how Dick Hudson and Sylvia Brown's calf muscles are thicker from hiking and backpacking than Ingrid Jacobson's and Mark Bricklin's are slimmer from racewalking. But sportwalkers participate in a number of walksports. By practicing the different training techniques and exercises in this book, you too will be able to shape your body parts any way you want.

Like the walkers in *Sportwalking*, the fitness advice I give throughout the book is genuine, based on over a decade of real walking experience. Now that this sport has caught on it's amusing to observe "experts" who don't practice what they preach. Publicists, editors, writers, and doctors all give walking advice even though they don't walk for exercise and sport themselves. Anybody can call themselves a walker—almost all of us "walk" for some transportation—but "real" walkers say it honestly. The walking movement is substantial enough without having to adopt the trendiness of other sport fashions. Soon, the accomplishments and health benefits reaped by real walkers will force consumers to take a closer look at their own exercise programs.

A CLOSE-UP VIEW

Sportwalking is different from my other two exercisewalking books. It's more of an "inner game" book. You will learn and apply the training techniques and exercises while you are walking along, focusing on one body part at a time. You'll also be able to form a mental image of walking correctly, which will look a lot like the close-up photos of the exercises shown in this book. Because we tend to visualize walking techniques from a certain angle, many shots were taken from behind the models. These close-ups should help you to focus on individual exercises and techniques, as this is the best way to concentrate on your sports training.

The first national exercisewalking video: Gary Yanker's Walking Workouts.
(MCA Home Video)

INTRODUCTION

WALKING IS GOOD exercise, a great way to travel, and a fun sport. My first two walking books, *The Complete Book of Exercisewalking* (Contemporary Books, 1983) and *Gary Yanker's Walking Workouts* (Warner Books, 1985 and MCA Home Video), describe the biomechanics of walking and show how to use walking as a regular aerobic exercise program. My third walking book, *America's Greatest Walks* (Addison-Wesley, 1986) introduces "tour" or travelwalking as the best way to sightsee up close and identifies the 100 best walks in America.

With *Gary Yanker's Sportwalking*, my fourth walking book, I hope to make walking America's most popular participation sport. Since *sport* really means diversion, recreation, and fun, I hope sportwalking will contribute to a rejuvenation of the spirit of amateurism and noncompetitive sports participation to balance the scale recently tipped too far toward professionalism and highly competitive sports.

In other words, when you sportwalk, you should have fun. If sportwalking stops being fun, you should move on to something else. With sportwalking, the health and fitness goals should be second to the goal of recreation. In fact, if you are doing sportwalking correctly, better health and fitness will follow automatically because you will be more active and engaged.

Gary Yanker.

Sportwalking is really an exercise and diet book in disguise. In it you will learn how to practice easy sports-training methods to add variety to your exercise program. You will also learn how to enhance a regular year-round walking program with organized weekend sportwalks and how to incorporate sportwalking events into your vacation and business travel plans. *Sportwalking* not only gives variety to walking for exercise, it also makes it more fun because it shows you how to get together with other walkers to form clubs and organize special walking events.

For many athletes, competitive sport and exercise workouts have become a source of injury, concern, and anxiety. Sportwalkers are relieved of the pressures and anxieties that come from competitiveness. Today, many sports medicine specialists are recommending walking as the primary exercise program. It delivers cardiovascular benefits without the increased risk of injury. They benefit from the satisfaction of "completing the distance" *without* the pressures of competition. Sportwalks take place in beautiful surroundings in the company of friends and other walkers. They represent a rebirth of the amateur spirit in sports.

By the end of the 1980s walking as a sport will replace running as the number one participation sport, just as exercisewalking has already replaced running as the number one exercise. In Holland and other European countries, there are already large-scale walking events, with 15,000 to 50,000 participants. In the United States, these events are in their formative stages, some attracting about 3,000 to 8,000 participants.

I hope *Sportwalking* will influence the direction of these events by helping walkers keep their amateur spirit and dissuading them from being unduly influenced by sports promoters who are not really interested in walking or who do not walk themselves. In other words, I hope the emerging walking events of the 1980s do not become a carbon copy of the running events of the 1970s.

BENEFITS OF SPORTWALKING

The major benefits of sportwalking are recreation and enjoyment, with resulting better health and fitness. But there are other important benefits as well:

Today, many sports medicine specialists are recommending walking as the primary exercise program. It delivers cardiovascular benefits without the increased risk of injury. While there are no walking injuries *per se*, many people have biomechanical problems due to their structural anatomy. My podiatry consultant Dr. Terry Spilken says: "I never advise my patients not to walk, whereas I occasionally advise my runners to refrain completely from that activity because of their anatomy." Thus, for walkers, a podiatrist can help correct anatomical problems, allowing people with previous foot problems to enjoy the benefits of the information provided by this book. The major benefits of sportwalking are recreation and enjoyment, with resulting better health and fitness. But there are other important benefits as well:

1. *Safety*—Walking is not only the safest exercise, it is probably also the safest sport with the fewest injuries. The two biggest problems are blisters and falling down. The one is not serious, and with proper preparation can be avoided, and the other occurs in many sports and can be minimized with care and concentration.

2. *Longevity*—Like walking for exercise, you can practice the sport of walking throughout your whole life. Sportwalkers do not have to be young, and they are not limited to a short practice span of five to twenty years as are gymnasts, football players, even runners. You can practice sportwalking your entire life, and it will probably help make it a longer one at that.

3. *Challenge and Adventure*—Adventure sportwalks will take you to places you have never been before, where you will make discoveries about the world as well as yourself, meet new people, and face new challenges. Life for the sportwalker is never static.

4. *Sightseeing*—Because of its pace, sportwalking offers an opportunity to sightsee while you participate. Most sportwalks emphasize distance and endurance rather than speed, so you get to see the sights as you walk along.

5. *Companionship*—Sportwalking is the best excuse to be with friends and a great opportunity to make new friends. Participating in and organizing sportwalks gives you a chance to meet walking enthusiasts across the country and throughout the world.

WHO SHOULD READ THIS BOOK?

Sportwalking is intended for three audiences:

1. Advanced exercisewalkers (readers of my first two books who are now interested in broadening their walking horizons)

2. Beginning walkers who are interested in the sport and recreational aspects of walking rather than its pure exercise value

3. Practitioners of different sportwalking styles—volksmarchers, walkathon participants, hikers, wanderers, ramblers, backpackers, mountaineers, long-distance walkers, and racewalkers—as well as those who want to take up any of these activities.

Right now, each of these sportwalking groups constitutes a world unto itself, largely unaware of what other walkers are doing. *Sportwalking* is an attempt to universalize the specific sport form, incorporating all its divisions into one system of techniques and training. This will lead to one overall sportwalking system.

HOW THE BOOK IS ORGANIZED

Sportwalking is organized to inspire as well as to instruct. The choice of sportwalks is yours. My goal is to show you how they are interrelated and how you can use them all for year-round walking fun and fitness.

Part One, "Participating," introduces you to the history and variety of sportwalking. It shows you the excitement of the different walking sport styles by profiling the sportwalker and by giving a summary of the various sportwalks, including their purpose and training methods.

In Part One you will also read about Nijmegen, the "Olympics of Walking." My participation in this wonderful event, which takes place in Nijmegen, Holland, inspired me to write this book and organize walking events of my own in the United States. Few of us would ever dream of participating in the Olympics, but Nijmegen is "everyone's Olympics" where walkers from 25 nations walk together at their own pace.

Part One also includes a chapter that defines and grades, by level of challenge and fitness, the various types of sportwalks, showing you how each offers an opportunity for a different experience and challenge in walking and training.

Part Two, "Training," contains the core of the book—the exercises and routines needed to become a sportwalker. Included is an introduction to the theory behind sportwalking training and a training schedule for year-round sportwalking.

Also included are recommendations for specialized training for long- and short-distance sportwalks and speed events. The chapters on practice follow the order of an actual training program, with exercises and routines presented along with the schedules and charts you need. Of special note are the unique advanced walking techniques. These are presented according to body parts in action, and include the necessary exercises for building strength and flexibility. Within each training chapter are long- and short-form routines for seasonal and specific event training variations.

Part Three, "Preparing," tells you about special pre-event preparations and day-of-event strategies and tactics. Chapter 12, "WalkTech," provides information for selecting shoes and clothing, as well as ideas for selecting other items that will fit in your sportwalk pack. The training diet provides nutritional advice to enhance not only your performance but your enjoyment of sportwalking as well.

Part Four, "Organizing," covers the planning and organizing of large and small walk events as well as individual challenge walks. Here you will learn how to organize your own walking club and teach or coach other walkers, using the popular method of the walking clinic.

Finally, Part Five, "Events Calendar," provides you with a calendar of major walks in the United States and around the world, including a directory of clubs and organizations that sponsor them. Also included are sources for finding any of the 25,000 walking events held annually worldwide.

Sportwalking will help you decide whether you want to become a sportwalker. If you are already practicing one or more of the walking sports, it will tell you what's new and exciting in the others. Increasingly walkers are trying them all; they are mixing up their walking routines with all the different kinds of walking. The hikers are coming into the city. The racewalkers are going to the country. The mountain climbers are climbing the stairs of high-rise buildings. The walking sports are being synthesized into one large sports movement—the sport of walking.

GARY YANKER'S
SPORTWALKING

PART ONE
PARTICIPATING

1
WALKING: THE SPORT
OF THE EIGHTIES

BY THE TIME this book is published, America will be in the middle of an all-out walking boom parallel to the running boom of the 1970s. In America and Europe since 1980, walking as an organized sport and recreational pastime has surpassed all other national participation sports. No other sport—not jogging, baseball, bicycling, or swimming— approaches walking in terms of the sheer numbers of participants (40 million in the United States and 180 million worldwide).

Here are some highlights of the dramatic growth of walking since 1980:

- Data from the 1980 Bureau of the Census show that 5.4 million Americans (5.5 percent of the work force) walk to and from their workplace. This is an increase of about 15 percent over 1970 census figures.
- The 1983 Bureau of the Census Recreation Survey shows that 93 million Americans choose walking as their favorite recreation, making it the number one choice for sport, recreation, and tourism. An estimated 20 million hikers and backpackers use our national and state parks.

1

City Sports, San Diego Hill Stride.

- Five national sports polls—Gallup, Perrier, The President's Council on Sports and Physical Fitness, *Walking World*, and American Sports Data—estimate that 36 to 55 million Americans choose walking as their first sport or exercise.
- In Europe, the Ramblers Association of Great Britain grew from 26,000 to 51,000 members. Twenty percent of the British and 40 percent of the German population tell poll takers that walking is their favorite sport or exercise. Holland holds more than 900 sportwalks annually. New Zealand has marked over 1,000 trails and walkways. There were 29,000 walkers marching in the four-day international walk tour in Nijmegen, Holland, and 32,000 in Augsburg, Germany.

- The total number of walking clubs and chapters worldwide increased from 12,000 in 1976 to 25,000 in 1986. The number of U.S. walking clubs and chapters jumped from 1,000 in 1976 to 6,000 in 1986, including 300 new corporate walking clubs. The number of volksmarch clubs in the United States grew from 17 in 1978 to 500 in 1986. And the number worldwide increased from 2,000 to 4,000, with nearly 14,000 separate volksmarches scheduled in 15 countries for 1987.
- The number of competitive racewalkers has tripled from 1980 to 1986, from 10,000 to 30,000. The number of racewalking clubs has jumped from 17 to 50.
- In 1984, 528,000, and in 1986, 605,000 walkers participated in the March of Dimes WalkAmerica program. The number of walkathons went from 1,100 in 1983 to 1,400 in 1985.
- *Prevention* magazine's national walking club grew from 0 to 55,000 members in six months in 1986.

The March of Dimes Walkathon.

- Since 1978 at least six major exercise and weight-control programs have adopted walking as their primary exercise: Weight Watchers, Pritikin, Palmaire, Canyon Ranch, Duke University, and Vanderbilt University weight-management programs. Yearly graduates total over two million.
- Fifty shoe manufacturers produced over 100 new walking-style shoes since 1980.
- The Boy Scouts of America now have five merit badges for hiking, backpacking, and fitness walking.
- The President's Council on Physical Fitness and Sports has instituted walking fitness awards.

You may have been wondering why I call walking a "sport." Many people think of it as a means of transportation—slow transportation. Others view it as an enjoyable, relaxing pastime or diversion, and still others as a stress-free form of exercise. Yet the sport of walking involves many sporting events, clubs, races, clinics, and coaches. Furthermore, walking has four separate sports divisions: wandering/hiking, marching/striding, long distance walking, and racewalking. Over 30 different walking sport activities are of a competitive or participatory nature. Racewalks, scrambles, and challenge walks, and the most dramatic and fastest growing "volkmarches" and "strides" see an annual turnout of tens of thousands of walkers. Sometimes walking bands provide musical entertainment at these international walking events.

WHAT IS A SPORTWALK?

The word *sport* means a diversion, game, or recreation; it also means athleticism or competition. A "sportwalk" is an organized walk for fun—recreation, diversion, adventure, and, of course, competition. "Organized" means advanced planning of a sportwalk event according to the specific goals of terrain, time, distance, and speed. Walksports contribute to a common pool of scientific research, practical experience, training methods, and technical refinements which make the walking a dynamic and universal sport and exercise form.

Sportwalking is different from exercisewalking or travelwalking. *Exercisewalking* is a regular walk done briskly or against resistance for health maintenance and fitness. When you train for a big sportwalk, you apply exercisewalking techniques by gradually increasing your weekly walking mileage and walking practice over the weeks and months preceding the event. *Travelwalking* (also called "tour walking") is done at a stroller's pace for sightseeing and discovery. Sportwalking's difference lies in its incorporation of groups and clubs for diversion and recreation, more important elements to sportwalking than exercise and discovery.

Of course, these three types of walking are interrelated. For example, you can't help but be a tourist when you participate in one of the international walks in Holland, Jerusalem, Wales, or Ireland, because these walks take you through historical places, over green hills, and into grand cities.

Sportwalkers will become the mainstay of the new active Americans, because walking stands at the center of a new people's sports movement and represents a sport that can be practiced consistently throughout one's lifetime. If you are already one of the millions of sportwalkers, this book will give you the complete picture of what walkers in the other divisions of the sport are doing and how you can join in. The book tells you where to go to organize a walk or walking club in your community and how to train for any sportwalk coming up in the next 12 months. If you are not already a sport- or exercisewalker, or do not now exercise but are curious about walking, this book will bring you to the head of a network of trails branching out to the walking sport just right for you.

WALKING AND JOGGING

Ironically, the main stimulus for the new walking sports boom of the 1980s is the jogging boom of the 1970s. The parallels between the growth of jogging and walking are intriguing; jogging showed adult Americans the way back to fitness, which most had lost since their high school or college athletic days. Running races gave them the opportunity to train and compete in sports again and to achieve a high level of physical fitness. Road races also brought out large numbers of Americans, not as spectators, but as participants. These races marked the beginning of the mass-participation sport in America and Europe. Since the beginning of the jogging or running boom in 1972, the number of joggers and runners grew to between 25 and 34 million Americans.

It has been speculated that jogging's popularity had a number of causes: Frank Shorter's 1972 Olympic victory in the marathon, Jim Fixx's *Complete Book of Running*, and Dr. Kenneth Cooper's recommendation of running as the best means to aerobic fitness. The special-interest magazine *Runner's World* and the growth of a "fitness consciousness" among Americans also contributed to the popularity of running.

Jogging also spawned a series of booms in other participatory sports—bicycling, aerobic dancing, cross-country skiing, roller skating, and even swimming. Among all of these, running remained the leader in participation, shoe sales, and media attention. Why? Perhaps the best explanation is jogging and running's accessibility, convenience, low cost, and efficiency in producing aerobic fitness. Doing the other sports almost always requires special equipment, pool or court time, or snow.

All the factors that contributed to jogging's popularity were also present in walking, except one. Initially, walking received a bad grade for its seeming inability to produce aerobic fitness. Nevertheless, while jogging and the other sports gained visibility throughout the 1970s, the sport of walking also grew, albeit less visibly, at the grass-roots level. Now walking, with its own magazines and newsletters, including *Walking World*, is growing into the leading role in mass participation and moderate activity.

For a time, the broad base of walkers were content to remain anonymous and practice their sport in a personal, unorganized way in parks, on city streets, and on wilderness trails. Although walkers knew about the "aerobic question," they didn't really care because they walked first for the fun and second for the exercise. Meanwhile, aerobics testers, such as Dr. Michael Pollack, determined that walking speeds in excess of 3½ miles per hour in fact produced aerobic fitness. Dr. Ezra Sohar determined that walking with a weight-loaded backpack also produced aerobic fitness. Finally, Dr. Lenore Zohman showed that climbing stairs or walking on hills involves aerobic conditioning too. Most of these tests were made in the late 1970s and enhanced the reputation of walking as an efficient exercise form, in preparation for the boom of the 1980s.

BOOKS STIR UP INTEREST

A series of walking books were published at this time, some extolling the exercise benefits and the joys of walking, while others recounted the adventures of long-distance walks. The first walking books, like the first running books, predated the boom and were written by authors who lacked the enthusiasm for walking that Fixx had for running. A close reading of these books shows that most of the authors were not really passionate recreational walkers, let alone sportwalkers. However, these books contributed to walking, and many are still in print. Still other writers did an outstanding job of introducing readers to certain aspects of walking sports, such as racewalking, backpacking, and fitness walking.

Interestingly, none of these walking books have become best sellers, even though their authors might have hoped for this in the wake of the success of the running books. None, that is, except Peter Jenkins's *A Walk Across America*, which was not an exercise book or even a sport book, but a personal adventure book about a discovery trip of self and culture accomplished on foot. It's amazing how a diary of a long-distance walker is impossible to put down. Such is the power of walking, even if only experienced vicariously!

In the spring of 1979, while the Jenkins's book was still on the best-seller list, 200 hikers set out to walk across the United States, though not primarily for a personal adventure. Instead of roads, these hikers used old pioneer trails whenever they could. In the spring of 1980, 50 hikers finished, including a small child and a 70-year-old couple. They had accomplished their purpose—to bring attention to the need for building and maintaining a national trail system for hikers, using the now-neglected pioneer trails of early America. The next year the Mellon Foundation granted the Appalachian Mountain Club $950,000 to institute a national trail-building education program. Many other events during the period of 1978 to 1986 acted as harbingers of the walking boom.

In 1983, walking reached a turning point with the first exercise book, *The Complete Book of Exercisewalking*, and its successor, *Gary Yanker's Walking Workouts*, which broke the sales barrier of 15,000 copies over other walking books and sold over a quarter million copies worldwide. The walking boom began.

CLUBS AND EVENTS

Perhaps the most remarkable parallel between the walking and running movements is the growth of the system of sports clubs and organized events, which did not reach a feverish pitch until the end of the 1970s and the beginning of the 1980s. Road Runners clubs founded throughout the United States in the early 1970s have influenced the formation of the new local and national walking and hiking clubs. Added to five separate walking club systems already in existence were 15 new ones (see Appendix C).

However, while the parallels of the walking and running movements are certainly remarkable, important differences stand. For example, in walking, competition is secondary to participation, almost the reverse of running. The boom in walking sports is not just the replacement of the primacy of one sport for another; rather it is really a shift in the whole sports philosophy from professionalism (athleticism) and competition to amateurism (sportsmanship) and participation.

Walking's inheritance of the place in the sun as the mass-participation sport is not the demise of running; insiders in the sport predict that running too will regain visibility, though not as a spectacle of a mass of competitors. These insiders predict that running will regain strength in the professional sphere, where the sport is watched on television by millions of sports fans, like football or baseball. Already, many race organizers have put a cap on the number of participants, and some races even require a qualifying time. Most running publications are becoming increasingly oriented to the serious runner, and sports merchandisers hope the media will concentrate on elite runners, giving them the superstar attention of their athletic brethren in other competitive and professional sports. Increasingly, the running establishment will focus more on the Bill Rodgers type of runners rather than the Jim Fixx type. So, while running will not decline, its growth rate and potential for further dramatic growth seem doubtful.

Running-shoe sales are flat; as running becomes more serious, fewer amateurs will find a common interest for the events. And as a mass sport, running has been brought into question by doctors who observe that its high intensity and high injury rate are not suited to the masses of amateur athletes in America. Thus, as the glory and excitement of running faded, the light of walking intensified. Those who did not like high-intensity exercise went straightaway to walking without even giving running a try. People who take running seriously now also walk—to work, on vacation treks, and on weekend hikes and strolls.

THE STORY OF SPORTWALKING: ANCIENT TO MODERN HISTORY

The history of walking long precedes the 1980s boom. While walking as an exercise activity goes back over 2,000 years to the ancient Greeks, throughout most of history, walking was the basic mode of transportation. It was a functional activity, as most of the world traveled on foot for tourism, commerce, and religious pilgrimages. Walking transportation predominated until the adoption of wheeled transportation about 200 years ago. Interestingly, at the same time walking also became a *widely* practiced sport. What had been the serious business of getting around on foot became a game, a diversion.

One of the first sportwalks was held in England in 1589, when Sir Robert Carey walked 300 miles from London to Berwick for a wager. King Charles II of England, also a sportwalker, racewalked from Whitehall to Hampton Court. Racewalking was born.

Throughout the 1700s, many other feats of walking long distances—from 100 miles in 24 hours to 700 miles in 14 days—were accomplished. Some of the fast walking races involved distances of more than 300 miles, qualifying them as tests of endurance more than speed. Brisk, even slow walking was used to go the distance. When Capt. Robert Barclay in 1801 walked 1,000 miles in 1,000 hours, he went only 1 mile per hour, walking not for speed but endurance.

These long-distance walkers became our first professional athletes, because they competed for wagers. They were called "walkists" or pedestrians, and they constituted a new sportwalking division: long-distance walking. From 1860 to 1903, long-distance walking had its heyday, and the era was called the Pedestrian Age. Walking was then probably the leading sport in Europe and America. But the sportwalking story did not end there.

Back in the 1700s, a noncompetitive, or recreational, division of sportwalking developed that advocated an easy pace for long, enjoyable walks. The walks had to be done in natural settings on trails, not on tracks or roads. The walk or wandering itself was the goal, rather than the walking speed or walking distance. Wanderers, or wanderbirds, completed long walks for tourism, discovery, reflection, and inspiration. They were poetic about their walking, calling it an art rather than a

**Capt. Robert Barclay:
1,000 hours in 1801.**

**Mary Marshal, Champion Lady Pedestrian:
50 miles in 12 hours in 1877.**

science and saying that the journey (the walk) was more important than the destination. Wanderers often had no specific destination.

Wandering spawned many natural outdoor sportwalks; hiking, bird-walking, backpacking, mountaineering, and trekking are offspring of the wanderbirds. It also strongly influenced the noncompetitive and tourist aspects of the other walking divisions. But, from the 1800s on, sportwalking broke down into three divisions: wandering or hiking, racewalking, and long-distance walking. The racewalkers continued to narrow their field and became part of the track and field division of Olympian sports in 1896 and 1908. The Wanderers went on to found thousands of walking clubs and to organize weekend walks. The oldest surviving walking club, the Black Forest Wanderverein, began in 1864. The long-distance walkers continue today with individual feats of distance, ranging up to 15,000 miles, and also with some 6-day walking events.

**Edward Payson Weston:
America's Father of Sportwalking.**

The early 1900s saw the birth of sportwalking's fourth division: marching (or striding). This was about the time that racewalking became an Olympic event. Marching revolutionized not only sportwalking but also the concept of sport itself. It converted sport from merely a competitive and spectator event to a popular mass-participation activity. The walking marches started as military training in a little town in Holland near the German border called Nijmegen (pronounced "Nye-maygen"). The marching type of walking was brisk and sharp. It came from taking a longer stride.

The march training exercise was originally designed to test physical fitness. However, civilians picked up the exercise and turned it into a sport. As a result, Nijmegen spawned modern fund-raising walkathons, volksmarches, and now in the 1980s, hill strides. Now, 15,000 marching or striding sportwalks are held every year throughout the world.

Before you learn more about sportwalking's four divisions in Chapter 3, "Choosing Your Walksports," you'll read about my personal experience as a participatant in sportwalking's greatest international event, the Nijmegen Four Days' March.

11

Chuck Repik has logged over 15,000
miles at volksmarches around the world.

2
NIJMEGEN: THE SPIRIT OF SPORTWALKING

NIJMEGEN, HOLLAND, IS the home—really the Mecca—of sportwalking. And "Vierdaagse Nijmegen" ("Four Days' March"), held there every year on the third weekend in July, is the Olympics of sportwalking, the premiere international sportwalk, and an inspirational model for sportwalkers worldwide. The Dutch may have been the first to make walking into a sport; perhaps they even coined the word *sportwalking*. (They have over 200 different words for walking, including "sport wandeln," or sportwalking.)

Imagine an Olympic event in which you, the average person, can participate. The only qualifications are that you be fit enough to "walk the distance" and that you register by the deadline (see Appendix 000 for information on registering). There are no qualification meets, no pressure to win or to place in the top three; you receive a gold medal just for finishing.

Nijmegen also symbolizes the best in amateur sports. It's called the Four Days' March, but it's really a walk. The word *march* is a term carried forward from the Nijmegen event's origins as a military exercise. Today, only a third of the participants are marching soldiers; most participants walk Nijmegen at their own pace. You may not compete;

racewalking and running are prohibited. Your goal is to walk the distance, because you have to finish to get the gold medal.

You should, but don't have to, train for the event. If you're fit, you can try finishing the four-day walk without special training, as I did, but it will definitely challenge the soles and the heels of your feet, as well as your leg muscles. And you may not make it. There were moments during the first two days when I thought I wouldn't be able to finish. But I did, and the "Four Days" became the single best sportwalking experience I have ever had. Nijmegen inspired me to write this book and to organize my own sportwalks throughout the United States. I hope America will someday have an international walking event like Nijmegen.

I love Nijmegen. It's where modern sportwalking began, and it remains the international capital of the sport. *Nijmegen* is the one foreign word walkers all over the world should have in their vocabulary.

The pictures shown here are from my 1983 trip. The following description of the event is in chronological order to give you a better idea of how it unfolds.

THE NIJMEGEN EXPERIENCE

I first learned about Nijmegen from Chuck Repik, Chairman of the Northwest Chapter of the American Volkssport Association, who broke a sportwalking record by completing over 14,000 miles of walking events. I was interviewing Chuck for my walking column, "Gary Yanker on Sportwalking," when in passing I asked him what the largest walk event was that he had ever completed. He said the Nijmegen Four Days' March and began to describe an absolutely incredible walking event. Chuck called it a "military march," but to me it sounded more like a walkathon with as many spectators and more individual participants than the Olympics. According to Chuck, it even had its own opening-day ceremony. Chuck said Nijmegen was the largest sportwalking event in the world, with over 20,000 participants and about 300,000 spectators.

I could hardly believe it. If it was that big, why hadn't we heard about it in the United States? Chuck said that GIs and their families stationed in Europe were the only Americans he saw participating in Nijmegen, even though 70 percent of the total participants were civilians. He told me that troops and civilians from 30 different countries travel to

As day breaks I see hundreds of walkers behind and in front of me.

Nijmegen every year on the third weekend in July to walk for four days in a row.

Participants walk at their own pace and follow one of three circular courses—the white course, which is 20 kilometers per day, the blue course, which is 30 kilometers, or the red course, which is 50 kilometers (about 31 miles). Participants begin walking at 4:00 and 9:00 A.M. and finish anytime before 4:00 P.M. Each day the walk begins from the same area, but walkers head out in a different direction so that each day's route, starting and finishing at the same point, forms one leaf of a clover.

Chuck first walked Nijmegen when he was an American soldier stationed in Europe. I asked him if he had to specially train to complete the 120-mile (Chuck took the red course), four-day walk. He said that it was a good idea but not absolutely necessary if you did a lot of walking anyway. According to Chuck, it was more important to have good foot protection than training, because most people who didn't finish had problems with blisters and leg cramps. Chuck said that he used resin to protect his feet.

I was intrigued and right then and there decided that I, too, would walk Nijmegen. My trip was arranged by Hank Fisher, the Director of the Dutch National Tourist Office in New York. Although Hank is a walker himself, he had never walked Nijmegen, and he was curious why an American would be interested in going all the way to Holland for a walking event. The Dutch consider their country to be for bicycling, he reminded me, not walking. I assured him that my preliminary research had shown that Holland was probably the premiere walking country in the world, with over 900 organized walks a year. I would be wearing two hats in Nijmegen, one that of a participant, the other that of a journalist reporting on the "world's greatest walk event."

Once the trip was set, I began to have second thoughts. It was a month away, really too little time to raise my walking mileage level from the 21 miles per week I was doing to the 31 miles a week or longer that I thought I should be at least able to do, to complete the distance at Nijmegen. From information I received from the Nijmegen organizers, I learned that the prescribed training for the event was at least four months of weekend walking. I thought that even though I was generally fit enough, my feet and leg muscles might not hold out. I was also concerned that, because I would be arriving in Holland only two days before the event, there would be insufficient time to recover from jet lag. Finally, I was concerned about sleeping quarters. I had registered late and discovered that the only space available was a bunk on a cruise ship pulled dockside. I worried that that would not be comfortable enough to allow for recuperative sleep. But Chuck thought I could do it, so I stopped worrying for the moment and started preparing for the trip.

I arrived in Amsterdam in the morning (still the night before in New York) and was picked up by my friends Hans and Jena, who led me on

I do my warm-up stroll in Amsterdam two days before the event.

a walking tour of the city. Amsterdam is a great city for sightseeing on foot, because there are miles of walkways along the canals. You should take a walking tour if you travel to Nijmegen or any other international sportwalk from another time zone. It not only limbers you up but also helps you stay awake until it's bedtime at your destination.

The next day we did some more touring of Amsterdam on foot and by car before I took the train to Arnheim, where I spent the next night. I learned that many walkers stay in Arnheim and each day commute by train for an hour to and from the event. Since the walk starts at 4:00 A.M. every day, this means getting up at around 2:00 A.M.

The anticipation started to build, and I again grew anxious. Knowing that I was about to walk 31 miles a day for four days in a row, I wanted to be nearer to survey the walking area. If you are going to Nijmegen or any other international walking event for the first time, try to arrive at least 24 to 48 hours before the event starts, so that you can familiarize yourself with the surroundings and reduce your pre-event anxiety level. I arrived a couple of hours and one night short of that goal.

THE DAY BEFORE

I woke up early the next morning in order to be the first in line when the banks opened, so I could change more dollars into Dutch guilders and catch the train to Nijmegen.

During the hour-long train ride, I began to wonder what I'd find at Nijmegen. How could they build a four-day event around walking? Why would people travel from other countries to attend a *walking* event? Surely there must be only a handful of international participants. I thought a lot of exaggeration was probably mixed in with the praise for this event.

It was late morning by the time the train pulled in to Nijmegen. Hundreds of people were milling about, many of them military personnel carrying duffel bags. I heard several languages being spoken other than Dutch. The soldiers were dressed for walking, in leather pants and hiking boots or jogging shoes. Many wore medals, including a gold medal prominently displayed on their jacket or hat. I guessed this was the medal received upon completion of the four-day walk. These must be the previous veterans of Nijmegen that Chuck had told me about.

The scene at the train station reminded me of a community festival.

People were shouting and singing in an atmosphere of gaiety. Were these people ready to walk for four days? They lacked the serious look of the professional athlete ready for competition. But from the large, well-defined calf muscles exposed on those who wore walking shorts, I inferred that many had done some serious walking training. These were not fat tourists ready to embark on a holiday weekend.

I then realized that much of the smiling and laughing really looked more like grinning and sounded like joking—the kind you might expect from a smart aleck who knows he's going to win a bet. These people knew something I did not: the Nijmegen experience. Were they grinning at me and all the other rookies attending this event for the first time? The grin seemed to say, "Boy, just wait; something's in store for you."

In English (which most Dutch people speak), I asked a station guard for directions to the registration center and asked sheepishly whether it was too far away to walk. He pointed to a stream of walkers and said they were all headed there and to follow them. "You can make it on foot; it's better than having to wait in line for the bus." So, I backpacked it to town, slightly worried that I'd be using up too much energy before the walk itself, which was scheduled to start the next morning at 4:00.

HISTORY OF THE FOUR DAYS' MARCH

I walked to the restaurant that served as the staging area to check on my registration and search out the events personnel I would be interviewing. I was surprised at how little attention officials gave this journalist walker from America. A press conference was just breaking up as I arrived in the press room. The organizers were on a tight schedule readying for the event, but I finally caught up with some of them, including Marcel Claasen, who, over coffee, filled me in on the history of the event.

Marcel, who speaks good English, is Nijmegen's historian. He believes that Nijmegen and other noncompetitive sports-touring circuits began in Holland with the 11-city ice-skating tours. Skaters would skate from town to town along the canals and verify their passage through checkpoints in each town. The first Four Days' March was held in 1909, Marcel told me, with approximately 138 participants. It was sponsored by the Dutch League for Physical Education and grew out of a military training exercise similar to those still used in basic military training in many parts of the world. In 1916, at the end of World War I, civilians began participating as well. A gold medal was introduced in 1926, awarded to every participant who completed 10 walks. In 1928, the year the International Olympics was held in Amsterdam, the four-day walk event went international. I learned from Marcel that there was no exaggeration in what Chuck had told me. Nijmegen now has 25,000 participants from 30 countries. A ceremony, called the "Parade of Flags," opens the event the evening before.

Marcel apologized that he would not be walking this year, but he wished me luck on my marches, and I headed off on foot to find my "boatel." As I walked through Nijmegen heading for the river, it became clear that the whole town had been decorated for the event. Bars and restaurants had set up tables on the sidewalks and halfway into the street. Many of the walkers I'd seen at the train station were now drinking beer and having sandwiches in the afternoon sun. Every third restaurant had a live band, and people everywhere were dancing and laughing and singing—they didn't seem the slightest bit concerned about the next day's very long walk. What chutzpah, I thought.

I found my boatel, parked my belongings, changed clothes, and went up on deck for an early dinner. I met a group of American soldiers, who were also staying on the boat. This was unusual because most soldiers were bivouacked in a special camp outside the city. They told me they had been specially selected by their military commanders to participate in the four-day march and that they had trained for four months, marching every weekend with full military gear. The American military wanted to be sure they made a good showing. For the unit to qualify for a medal, they explained, each team member had to finish the walk. And they had to carry a rifle and a 20-pound pack the whole route.

THE PARADE OF FLAGS

After dinner I headed back to the train station to catch a bus to the stadium for the Parade of Flags ceremony. When I arrived, I joined a long line working its way into the stadium. I noticed thousands of soldiers practicing with flags, rifles, or musical instruments in drill teams around the stadium, and I was struck by the large proportion of female soldiers represented in each national unit.

Once inside the stadium, I roamed about for a few minutes, looking for the press section, which was right down at the "50-yard line." The stadium filled up fast, and an announcement that the ceremony was about to commence was repeated in Dutch, English, German, French, and other languages.

With the striking up of the marching music, a parade of walking groups carrying flags streamed into the stadium and passed the reviewing stand as an announcer called out each country's name in Dutch. I learned that all the paraders were teams of walkers who would be participating in the four-day march. Some countries were represented by military teams, others by police and fire departments, and still others by gymnastics clubs.

The Parade of Flags was certainly colorful. It was modeled after the opening-day ceremony of the Olympics. Scots marched in their kilts, playing bagpipes; the British bobbies in uniform; and the U.S. Army contingents in full military gear. The marching groups were from 30 different countries, too many for me to recognize all the flags, but certainly noteworthy were those from Japan, Israel, Poland, and Scotland. The sports club teams wore their workout clothes and carried bouquets of flowers. The Japanese sports club drew the most applause from the stands. They were the most cheerful and the shortest of all the paraders.

I thought, these people really are taking this event seriously. I asked some of my fellow journalists in the reviewing stand if they were also going to walk. I was told that I would be the only journalist trying to complete the whole walk. Gulp.

After the parade was completed, Dutch gymnasts put on a display of floor and acrobatic exercises. There were also clowns, who mimicked them and entertained children in the stands. The ceremony ended with 20 parachutists dropping into the stadium in multicolored parachutes. A spectacular sight.

THE NIGHT BEFORE

I took Chuck's advice and double-checked my gear before going to sleep. I made sure I had a couple of pairs of socks, Band-Aids, blister tape, a water canteen, sunglasses, and a hat. It was still light out when I got into bed, so I drew the curtains and closed the window to block out the noise from the other passengers on the ship. I was concerned that I might not sleep because of nervousness, but the gentle rocking of the boat was like a sedative. I fell asleep by 9:00 P.M., just a little later than I had planned.

THE FIRST DAY'S WALK

When I awoke at 2:00 A.M. it was, of course, still dark. I was comforted somewhat when I realized I was not the only one awake at this hour; I could hear noises in the hallway, and I met up with the soldiers in the dining area, where a half-asleep cabin boy prepared some tea and coffee and put out bread, butter, and jam for us. In the hurry to get up, I forgot my canteen. I went back to my room at about 3:00 A.M. to retrieve it and then hurried off the boat to wait for the taxi I had ordered the night before to take me to the starting area.

The taxi did not show. I looked for a pay phone to call; there was none. I started up the hill and ran into some bar patrons who were on their way home. All the bars and restaurants were closed. No telephones were available anywhere. I grew nervous and began to doubt that I would make it to the start on time. If I missed the start, I would not have a chance to qualify for the gold medal. There were later starts for walkers doing the 20- and 30-kilometer courses, but I had not registered for those. So, I decided I had better walk to the start area and walk fast. As I ascended toward the center of town, I headed in the direction of what I remembered to be the hotel area.

I walked faster and faster, wondering where all the marchers were. It was now 3:30 A.M. I moved faster. The streets had emptied; not even a bar patron was to be seen. It seemed I was the only one awake in all of Nijmegen. Could I have miscalculated the start time? Did my watch not set properly? Perhaps that's why there was no taxi driver. I broke into a run, hearing my footsteps echoing on the cobblestone street.

At last a person! I asked the old man, "Vier Daagse March start?" He did not understand me. I repeated my question, using a throatier sound. He nodded and pointed ahead. Did he understand my question? I had no choice; I kept moving. The time was 3:45. Finally I saw some shadowy figures moving ahead at a brisk pace. Were they part of the event? I hurried in their direction. They looked like walkers; they were wearing hiking boots and bicycle caps.

I addressed them in English: "Where is the start of the marches?" They pointed down the boulevard in the direction we were walking.

"Are you marching today?" They nodded yes. I felt relieved. But, just to be sure, I asked if the marches had started yet. "At 4:00 A.M.," they said. I looked at my watch; it was 3:50. I heard voices and recognized the outline of the hotel. I had made it. But now I was in for some *real* walking, I thought.

Inside the courtyard were hundreds of marchers jammed together shoulder to shoulder, waiting and talking loudly, some laughing, others complaining about the early hour. My walk/run to the site had awoken me, but I had to shade my eyes from the strong spotlights that lit up the courtyard. I was surprised to see many smokers among the participants. There were no soldiers in this group of starters. I remembered that they would start out from their camps. I also saw no women; they would start later with the 20- and 30-kilometer groups. We were the group walking 50 kilometers a day. I slowly worked my way to the front of the line, moving into empty spaces in the crowd.

The voice over the loudspeaker announced in Dutch that the marches would soon begin and that we should move on in an orderly fashion to the starting chutes in front of us. Despite these instructions, the crowd started pushing forward. As I approached the starting gate, I saw a number of little chutes, like turnstile aisles at a supermarket. We were funneled through these, our route tickets punched as we went through. We walked out into what was still a pitch dark chilly morning.

MY WALK PLAN

I stepped out quickly, turned left, then right, and started walking briskly, passing many marchers on my way to the front of the pack. My walk plan was to start out briskly so I could achieve a position near the front. According to the rules, we were forbidden to racewalk or run the event, so I kept my pace at about 4¼ miles per hour, or 120 steps per minute.

The walk route led from narrow city streets to open boulevards. The marchers stayed on the sidewalks except to pass. It was Tuesday; the town of Nijmegen was just waking up to begin the work day. A few cars approached with drivers and passengers on their way to early morning jobs; they all took the time to roll down their windows and cheer us on. We also began hearing cheers from the windows of the houses along the street: "Good luck! Good luck! [in Dutch]." I felt encouraged. I was with fellow walkers.

We made a number of left and right turns, crossing major intersections where police groups intermittently stopped traffic to allow groups
of marchers to cross. I passed marchers whenever I could, because the
route narrowed and widened and passing was not always possible. From
previous long-distance walks, I had learned that my energy level is best
at the beginning of the day, with a renewed burst coming again
sometime toward the end of the day. I wanted to take advantage of this
energy cycle to do my best and fastest walking when my energy was
highest. Also, I realized that it was better to be with the walkers at the
front, because they helped me keep my pace brisk and even. There were
also fewer walkers at the front, so if you wanted to pick up your pace,
you didn't have to fight your way through a crowd.

As we crossed the bridge leading out of town, it grew lighter. The sun
was rising. I now began to see the faces and the numbers of my fellow
marchers. I tried to take a sunrise picture, but the light meter on my
camera showed I didn't have enough light. Even though we were
stretched out along miles of streets and boulevards, we seemed a large
group. I learned later from officials that 23,000 walkers were walking
with me this day. As it grew lighter I would walk backward from time
to time, looking at the marchers behind me and taking photographs of
them. Most looked pretty much like I did, but two walkers were
particularly memorable. One wore wooden shoes (and finished the
whole 120 miles without changing them); the other carried a brush and
canvas and painted a Dutch windmill scene while walking.

**He painted while
he walked.**

It was exciting; never had I been in the presence of so many walkers from so many different countries. I overheard many foreign languages being spoken and tried to guess which country the walkers were from. Distinguishing between Swedish, Danish, Finnish, and Norwegian was my greatest challenge, but I had help. I studied their dress and mannerisms and occasionally recognized a flag patch they wore on their shirts.

Off and on, my thoughts returned to my walk plan. Having trained too little, I worried that I would not be able to complete the 31 miles of walking each day. I remembered Chuck's warning: To finish, you have to protect your feet. So, as a precautionary measure, I had inserted padded insoles in my walking shoes as extra foot protection, and I carried extra pairs of socks and a pair of jogging shoes to switch off with during the day.

As daylight broke, we turned off the road onto a pathway that ran along a canal. It became difficult to pass walkers because the path was full of them in columns four deep. You had to pass in the embankment leading into the canal; it was hard going. At this point (about 7:00 A.M.), the marchers I had started with had steadied their pace. Many started singing and chanting cheers and march slogans. At the end of the canal path was the first refreshment area, where sandwich and soda vendors had pulled up. I was ready for a second breakfast, so I purchased a sandwich and lemonade and kept walking. Other walkers had stopped to eat and drink and raise their feet along trees and fences. I passed up this rest stop.

Once we had turned off the canal path onto a dirt road, the line of marchers began to grow longer and thinner. We had left Nijmegen's city limits and were heading out into the Dutch countryside. I saw my first windmill of the day. The road wound and turned so you could look back and see a long line of walkers stretching and winding around the countryside.

The route went on and off country and dirt routes. We were following the red pointers that were now stacked with blue and white ones, indicating that the 20- and 30-kilometer walkers had joined us along the route. I didn't notice when this happened because I was still plowing forward. I did notice, however, when the military marchers joined us. Theirs was a definite pace with march leaders calling out cadences.

The soldiers did not join the civilian marchers right away; we saw

Walking the Dutch countryside.

them off in the distance, moving parallel to us down another road. Occasionally, one unit would pass another, shouting a special greeting, "To your left, to your left, passing on your left, right, left." I was surprised to hear many of the European units calling out their cadences in English. I learned that these were NATO troops who took their training with American soldiers stationed in Europe and that the Americans had a greater variety of cheers and march songs. Eventually the soldier and civilian routes intersected, and the soldier units filed in between us.

Once we were walking with the soldiers, the pace of the civilian marchers picked up. It was helpful to walk with a military unit, which steadied the pace. I stayed with them for 15 to 30 minutes and then begin moving forward again. I realized that other walkers were doing the same but for different reasons.

SOCIAL EXPERIENCES

Jacky is a thirty-year-old window dresser from Liverpool who told me she had already walked Nijmegen three times as a British soldier. This time she had a week's vacation from her job and was "walking it for a lark." Back in England, she trained for the marches by walking or running an average of 10 miles a day. She also trained to control her weight because she loved to eat and drink. Jacky told me she was going to party every night during the four-day walk with members of her former military unit and that she would probably average only four hours of sleep. I asked her whether this would be enough sleep. She said she'd catch up when she got back home.

Jacky kept a steady pace that first day and seemed unaffected by her social "walk plan." I pulled ahead of her, and she gave me a friendly smile. I had observed her walking and talking with many different men. There were other single women in the marches too. Some of the Dutch women marched along with soldiers, either old friends to whom they were giving moral support or recently acquired friends.

The march was a great opportunity to meet new friends and visit with old ones. I observed many new friendships being formed among marchers; walking with a partner makes the time go by faster. I also observed many family groups walking together. But there were also individual marchers who were out on a personal challenge, cheered on from the sidelines by family and friends or even total strangers.

Jacky, the window dresser from Liverpool, trained for Nijmegen by walking 10 miles a day.

I kept rough track of our mileage by the number of control points we passed (one every five kilometers, or three miles). At these points, event officials took our route cards and punched them with a specially coded punch hole. Back on the road in the afternoon, civilians started joining the soldiers in singing and cheering. The walk route passed many villages along the way. We knew we were approaching a town because we could hear the town band playing. As we entered, we would pass a reviewing stand and would be cheered on by the local citizens who crowded the streets. If you felt tired, the band and the cheering quickly straightened you up and put new energy into your step.

When I felt fatigued, I used the band music and singing to keep up my walking pace. I wanted to finish before 4:00 P.M. so I would have plenty of rest time before the next day's walk. To keep up my own pace, I hooked up with marching teams who called out cadences and kept a brisk steady pace. The Dutch soldiers and fire brigades seemed to be the fastest. The sun was still out, and it was a breezy summer day. I felt as though I might make it.

Cheering on family and friends from the sidelines.

THE FINISH LINE

I arrived at the finish line at about 2:45 P.M., over an hour earlier than my plan, but I was sore and limping as I came through the chute. I did not sit down on the grass like other walkers. Instead, I got myself a soda and headed back to the boat for an early dinner and a long night's sleep. I wanted to ensure that I would be fully recuperated by the next day. I would not be joining Jacky on the dance floor tonight; I was dying to get my shoes and socks off and my feet elevated.

Walkers resting at the finish line.

DAYS 2, 3, AND 4

The pattern of walking and resting on the other three days was similar to day 1, but the routes differed. Each day it became more and more difficult to get up early and finish early. I remembered to do my stretches (mostly because of painful memories of long-distance walks where I didn't stretch) both during and after the walk, but I never did get to the dance floor.

Although I felt stiff each morning and limped the first couple of miles, I soon warmed up to the walk and was in high gear by midmorning. It didn't last though; by midafternoon I had to fight to keep up with the faster walkers. Each day I lost a little ground, finishing later and later as I took more frequent rest stops, finally one every hour, to soothe my aching feet and muscles. I tried to keep the rest stops short, because if I rested too long, the stiffness would set in and it would be a mile or two before I was limbered up again. Eating and the lunch stop became big events of the day. I was burning more than 3,000 calories, two to three times what I would burn on a normally active day. So I ate small but frequent portions and particularly enjoyed an occasional chocolate bar or piece of fresh fruit. Caffeinated beverages were also helpful to jump-start my sore body after longer rest stops.

Through shaded streets.

Young people walk, too.

I passed up the first-aid and massage stations, except once for journalistic reasons. While a massage and professional foot care might have been necessary, it was agony standing or even sitting to wait for these. The rhythmic action of walking provided more relief. Also, the psychological relief of knowing you were getting closer to the finish line and wasting less time doing it was important.

I was taking relatively good care of my feet by changing my socks and shoes two or three times during the walk day, but I did not escape some heel blisters. So, I had these and more sore muscles fixed once at a first-aid station. The first-aid people provided superb blister care. They created a second skin on my heel with *dachbau* (see Chapter 12 for an explanation). But the sport massage hurt so much that I have since pronounced the term using only a German accent—"Schport maas-saage"—to emphasize its torturous effect. You can create it for yourself by pressing down the length of your quadricep muscle after you have

Resting for lunch.

Day 3 involved some hills.

walked thirty miles. But I must confess that when I left the first-aid station, my leg muscles felt more limber.

There was only one point when I again had thoughts of being unable to finish: in the afternoon of the second day. Pride and the fact that I had come this far moved me forward. I learned that my body could do more than my mind thought it could, but I vowed then to train more for my next Nijmegen. I observed that walkers with more training finished each day more relaxed, and, of course, if I was ever to join Jacky on the dance floor, I would need to train more.

The third day was our hill day. While Holland is flat and most of our walking was on flat surfaces, every year the event organizers managed to find some hills to give the route extra challenge. I have to say the hills were a relief, because they changed the walking pattern so you were able to use different muscles and different foot surfaces. This effect also came from switching from road walking to walking on the grass.

THE FINAL FINISH LINE

It was the afternoon of the last day. As we turned back toward Nijmegen, we were guided not to the chute area but onto the main street. I knew a ceremony was afoot because many walkers had worn funny costumes and were carrying stretchers with worn-out-looking stuffed animals.

nishers get bouquets of flowers.

The Nijmegen Gold Medal can be earned by finishing the four-day walk.

The final day became a rowdy festival, similar to the final day in school after all exams have been taken. Beer drinking, usually reserved for the end of the walk day, began at lunchtime. All the walkers were in a good mood, but it was a particularly hot day, and I soon realized I should have stopped for a soda before we entered the city. The vendors had all sold out, and a crowd of 300,000 spectators lined the streets, so it was impossible to pull over and stop. You had to keep walking to the finish, which was in the center of town. There was some comfort in the cheering of the people who made you feel like you had just won the Olympic gold medal. Families came out to cheer on their relatives, calling out names of walkers as they recognized them. It was clear that for many, finishing this walk was the fulfillment of a personal challenge. There were many young people, but I also saw 70-, 80-, and 90-year-olds, who were advertising that age is not a barrier.

The spectators handed walker-friends bouquets of flowers. I started to feel a little left out until a perfect stranger handed me a bouquet, too. Then I noticed that Nijmegen's townspeople were cheering for all of us, a community of walkers. I finished. I picked up my gold medal and certificate at the registration center. For me, a new sport was born, as I hope it will be for you, too.

I have described Nijmegen because it reveals a lot about the spirit and organization of walking events (the agony and the ecstasy). My Nijmegen experience also offered a lesson: You can bluff your way through, but, for maximum enjoyment and satisfaction, you should train properly.

Nijmegen is the granddad of sportwalks and among the most challenging. It is also the best organized sportwalk and can serve as a model for how to train for, participate in, and start your own sportwalk event. It represents, in effect, a quick course to a new sport.

3
CHOOSING YOUR WALKSPORTS

SPORTWALKING OFFERS THE greatest variety of any sports form, with over 30 different activities to choose from. Use this chapter as a menu for planning your walking. I recommend sampling a number of sportwalks before deciding on a favorite; choose sportwalks based on your level of interest and your ability to do them.

Consider first whether you want to practice long walks (over 12 miles) or short walks (under 12 miles). A continuous 12-mile walk determines a sportwalk's status, whether it is for a moderately fit or a highly fit walker. Unfit walkers should not try a continuous walk of more than three miles. A continuous walk is defined as one you can do without resting more than 15 minutes every hour of walking.

I find that the best way to choose a sportwalk is to match your personal profile to the profiles of other walkers and walks in each sportwalking division. This involves matching your weekly training program to a sportwalk's grade, distance, and pace and your personality to the walk's sportstyle. Also consider other factors, such as "access" or how far you have to go to walk.

Of the four sportwalking divisions profiled in this chapter, each has its own sportstyle, historical profile, celebrated walkers, walk groups,

I reach the top of Ireland's Mt. Torc.

and sportwalks. The sportwalks are graded from I to V according to the level of training required; the fitness grades will help you compute the exercise values of the sportwalks so you can use them to stay in shape. The walks are also listed in order of increasing challenge or difficulty. The five grades correspond to six degrees of difficulty, A through F, that are used by mountain climbers and hikers for terrain and weather conditions. Here, in brief, is my grading system.

- Grade I—Easy corresponds to Fitness Level I—Poor and Difficulty Level A.
- Grade II—Moderate corresponds to Fitness Level II—Fair and Difficulty Levels B and C.
- Grade III—Moderately Difficult corresponds to Fitness Level III— Good and Difficulty Level D.
- Grade IV—Very Difficult corresponds to Fitness Level IV—Very Good and Difficulty Level E.
- Grade V—Extremely Difficult corresponds to Fitness Level V— Excellent and Difficulty Level F.

The accompanying chart provides more details on the training requirements and participation levels for each of these grades.

CHART 1
SPORTWALK GRADES AND TRAINING FITNESS LEVELS

Grade I—Easy Sportwalks

Sports Training

Related Fitness: Level I—Poor
Average Weekly Training Mileage: 1½ to 7 miles
Average Training Pace: 1 to 2 miles per hour (mph) (30- to 60-minute
      mile [m/m] pace)

Sports Participation

Terrain: (A) Easy, flat, or slightly undulating in any weather, altitude
      changes less than 250 meters
Half-Day Sportwalk Distance: 3 miles or less
Whole-Day Sportwalk Distance: 6 miles or less
Consecutive Walking Days: 2 days or less
Daily Average: 6 miles or less

Comments: If you have never done any long walks, start with Grade I
sportwalks.

Grade II—Moderate Sportwalks

Sports Training

Related Fitness: Level II—Fair
Average Weekly Training Mileage: 14 to 21 miles
Average Training Pace: 2 to 3½ mph (17 to 30 m/m pace)

Sports Participation

Terrain: (B & C) Moderate, mostly flat, or moderately hilly with altitude
      changes less than 500 meters but not higher than 1800 meters,
      avoiding extremely bad weather
Half-Day Sportwalk Distance: 6 miles or less
Whole-Day Sportwalk Distance: 12 miles or less
Consecutive Walking Days: 2 to 4 days
Daily Average: 12 to 20 miles

Comments: You can attempt a 24-mile walk in 2 days when you have
trained the 6 weeks needed to take you to the top of Level III. At the
bottom of Level III, it will take 4 days to comfortably complete the
distance.

Grade III—Moderately Difficult Sportwalks

Sports Training

Related Fitness: Level III—Good
Average Weekly Training Mileage: 22 to 28 miles
Average Training Pace: 3½ to 4¼ mph (14 to 17 m/m pace)

Sports Participation

Terrain: (D) Flat or moderately difficult hills with sections that can be steep, rocky, or marshy
Racewalk Pace: Short (3 km or less), 8 to 12 m/m; long (more than 3 km), 12 to 14 m/m
Half-Day Sportwalk Distance: 12 miles or less
Whole-Day Sportwalk Distance: 13 to 25 miles
Consecutive Walking Days: Intermediate distance, 4 to 7 days; long distance, 8 to 45 days
Daily Average: 13 to 25 miles

Comments: With Level III, any long-distance walk is possible, if you start within your daily mileage range and increase your daily distance 2 to 5 miles every 7 days.

Grade IV—Very Difficult Sportwalks

Sports Training

Related Fitness: Level IV—Very Good
Average Weekly Training Mileage: 29 to 49 miles
Average Training Pace: 4¼ to 5½ mph (11 to 14 m/m pace)

Sports Participation

Terrain: (E) Steep mountains, climbs and descents, rugged surfaces, thick underbrush or snow, or map and compass needed
Racewalk Pace: Short distance, 7 to 11 m/m; long distance, 8 to 12 m/m
Half-Day Sportwalk Distance: 20 miles or less
Whole-Day Sportwalk Distance: 26 to 34 miles
Longest 24-Hour Walk: 50 miles
Consecutive Walking Days: Intermediate, 50 to 75 days; long, 300 to 1,000 miles
Daily Average: 25 to 31 miles

Comments: Level IV is the grade and the required training fitness level for the Nijmegen Four Days' March described in Chapter 2.

Grade V—Extremely Difficult Sportwalks

Sports Training

Related Fitness: Level V—Excellent
Average Weekly Training Mileage: 50 to 125 miles
Average Training Pace: 4¾ to 7½ mph (8 to 13 m/m pace)

Sports Participation

Terrain: (F) Steep hills and mountains, can require scrambling (hands and feet), maps in some cases
Racewalk Pace: 20 km, 7 to 8 m/m; 50 km, 8 to 9 m/m
Half-Day Sportwalk Distance: 25 to 35 miles
Whole-Day Sportwalk Distance: 35 to 75 miles
Longest 24-Hour Walk: 75 to 100 miles
Consecutive Walking Days: Intermediate, 4 to 21 days; long, 22 to 360 days
Daily Average: 31 to 50 miles

Comments: You need peak training levels to master the endurance, speed, and terrain difficulty of Grade V.

In the remainder of this chapter, the four sportwalking divisions are grouped into two categories, mass-participation and special sports, and have modern names representing the most current or widely practiced sport form in that division. Group 1, mass-participation sports, consists of hiking/wandering and marching/striding, and Group 2, specialized sports, consists of long-distance walking and racewalking. These rankings and groupings reflect not only the number of participants and organizations, but also the likelihood that you will be able to practice these sports as an amateur athlete.

THE MASS-PARTICIPATION SPORTWALKS

HIKING/WANDERING

The hiking/wandering division has 40 million participants in the United States and 120 million participants worldwide, making it the largest of the sportwalking divisions. It includes wandering (the German version), rambling (the British version), hiking (the American version), and their various derivatives: backpacking, walkabouting, mountaineering, and trekking. Though they are related by history and sportstyle, these sportwalks are not all the same in their levels of intensity, which range from moderate to vigorous.

The hiking/wandering division has the greatest number of organizations with the largest total membership. It is also the oldest division, with organized walking clubs established as early as 1864.

Sportstyle. If you like the outdoors, claim a philosophical or artistic bent, or just desire relaxation, you will enjoy most elements of the hiking/wandering sportwalks. If you are unfit or unsure where to start in sportwalking, hiking/wandering (let's call it hiking for short) serves as a good entry point, because you can start slow and set your own pace. I call hiking self-paced walking; the pace varies with each walker and ranges from a stroll at 1 mile per hour to a brisk walk at 3½ miles per hour. Your step length varies from 1½ to 2½ feet; your legs are not stretched out, so it is comfortable. The pace really depends on your mood, the surroundings, and the walking speed that you perceive as comfortable.

The hiking style is closely linked to nature, because those who hike generally stay off paved roads and highways, prefering dirt trails reserved for pedestrians. Most hiking sportwalks work point-to-point through the woods, though they are developing into circular walks and organized tours.

Historical profile. Hiking originates with the ancient Greeks, who considered walking to be healthy for both the body and the mind. The Greek doctor Hippocrates declared walking the best medicine. Socrates and Plato practiced walking to stimulate thinking. Their peripatetic school flourished with the art of thinking and discoursing while walking up and down the paths of Athens' Lyceum (*peripaton*).

The Roman walking scholars (*ordo vagorum*) continued this reflective tradition until it was later adopted as wanderwalking in the 16th through 18th centuries by European and American poets, artists, and writers, including Emerson, Goethe, Thoreau, and Coleridge. Wanderwalking acquired the reputation as a thinking person's recreation and sport. Because it was also closely linked to nature, wanderwalkers were called "wanderbirds" (*wandervoegel*). They founded the original walking clubs, called *wandervereins*, and their membership included ordinary citizens who loved nature and wanted to preserve it. These clubs, as the wander art traveled from the lowlands to the highlands (Alps), inspired a system of hiking and mountaineering clubs and later trekking groups to travel to areas of the world where the terrain was exotic, remote, or special, as in India and Peru.

A new phenomenon called "urban hiking" broke the wanderverein tradition in the 1970s, though most wanderers and hikers still prefer to do their walking in the country or wilderness. Urban hiking is done in city parks, suburban streets, and nearby nature areas, and has expanded to include neighborhood walks or walkabouts. City walking clubs, like Walkabout International and the Shorewalkers Club, follow walking routes that take them on and off city streets. However, the hiking division of sportwalking will continue to make the greatest contribution to the fun of walking by ensuring that sportwalking courses follow the most scenic routes and remain primarily noncompetitive and recreational.

Groups.   Wanderers and hikers are a community of walkers related by their love of walking and the great outdoors. Groups include the walking clubs and organizations devoted to walking and other outdoor recreation, such as wander clubs, hiking clubs, walkabout clubs, and mountaineering and trekking tour organizations. Most hiking groups develop and maintain walking trails as part of a conservation effort and view themselves as outdoor and conservation clubs first, hiking clubs second.

Each country has its own set of local, regional, and national walking clubs, among which are many independent clubs and tour groups not part of a national system. Appendix 000 lists these major clubs by country.

In the United States, the walking groups are represented by six large regional and national walking club systems such as the American Hiking Society and Walkabout International. Outdoor and conservation groups such as the Sierra Club, Appalachian Mountain Club, and the Mountaineers lead hikes.

Founded in 1876 as an outdoor and conservation society, the Appalachian Mountain Club (AMC) is the oldest U.S. hiking club, with 40,000 members (up from 17,000 in 1976), and it has the largest endowment for public service and trail conservation ($4.5 million).

Since its formation, the AMC has spawned other regional outdoor clubs, such as the Mountaineers, the American Alpine Club, and the Colorado Mountain Club, all of which are mountaineering clubs that plan hiking, backpacking, and mountaineering weekend outings and trips. These mountaineering clubs, in turn, have inspired mountain walking and trekking organizations like Mountain Travel, Sobek Tours, and the Sierra Club Outing Committee.

Walkabout International, founded in 1982, holds walks in city and suburban areas and treats them as "natural" (albeit existential) settings. Walkabout International is the urban counterpart of the Wanderbirds. In San Diego, the headquarters city, Walkabout International sponsors an average of 750 walks a year, with more than 5,000 walkers at each. I joined some Walkabouters on a midweek walk through a local San Diego neighborhood and was impressed by how much there is to see and discover in an ordinary suburban neighborhood, particularly if the walk leader can point out and explain sights like back yards of interesting residents.

In Europe, national and continental federations of walking clubs are known as the European Rambler's Association, the German Mountain and Wanderclub Federation, The Ramblers Association of Britain, Federation Française de la Randonnee Pedestre in France, and Spain's Federacion Española de Montanismo.

The Rambler's Association (with 51,000 members) is the British equivalent of a wander club. Its members walk in nature, building and maintaining long- and short-distance paths. Consequently, they have established the longest and the best-marked system of walking trails in the world—emulated by Europeans, Americans, and New Zealanders—and have written thousands of walking guidebooks. In Germany, Der Deutsche Gebirg und Wanderverein (the German Federation of Mountain and Walking Clubs) has over one million members in 50 regional and 2,600 city clubs. It is probably the largest and oldest of all national walking club systems, sponsoring 75,000 "wander days" (*wandertag*) a year. It contains the world's oldest walking club, the Schwarzwald Wanderverein (translated as the Black Forest Wander Club), founded in 1864.

I didn't find out that I learned my walking from the oldest walking club in the world until 25 years after I had done it. Wandering on many Sundays with members of the Neustadt branch of the Black Forest

Wander Club was like a Sunday walk in the woods with friends. We usually headed out on a Sunday morning and didn't return until late afternoon. On each outing, we followed a different path and had a midday lunch or tea break at an inn along the way. Sometimes we'd picnic in the open and save our inn meeting for a late-afternoon beer or an early-evening meal. The wandering pace varied from slow to brisk, depending on how we felt. We always took time to stop and study plants and observe the habits of wild animals. If we didn't make it every weekend, we at least participated in one wandering with the change of each season. Winter wandering in the Black Forest was probably the best of all.

Sportwalks. The sportwalks in this division are usually point to point, starting and ending in a different place, offering constant diversion and discovery.

Wandering (Grades I to III). Wandering (akin to rambling) means to walk slowly without a destination. It is walking for its own sake where the journey is more important than the destination; the wanderer and rambler's pace has been likened to a meandering river. Wandering is a walking trip where the arrival time does not matter. You would be hard-pressed to plan a walking trip with wanderers or ramblers in a big city, because they associate "walking" with getting out of the city and into nature. Wander variations include *berg wandern* (mountain wandering or walking on high alpine ways), *eis wandern* (walking on glaciers in winter or over snow fields), *rundwandern* (roundabout walking, completing a circuit), and *nachtwanderung* (night hiking).

Rambling (Grades I to III). Rambling, the British term for wandering, means to stroll or roam about idly without any special goal. The typical ramble is on a country path.

Walking touring (Grades I to III). Local area walks are called "walking tours." They include architectural, historical, and nature studies.

Walkabouts (Grades II to IV). A walkabout is the Australian version of a discovery trip in a wilderness area. It has been Americanized to include city and suburban walking, and is also called neighborhood walking.

Tour walking (Grades III to IV). I coined the term "tour walks" to include touring an area while walking. These walks are for large-area sightseeing, done with inn-to-inn and hut-to-hut stops at a moderate pace. Tour walking is like the rally in sports-car events.

Inn to inn (Grades II to III).   Lowland walking from inn to inn requires forwarding supplies and baggage inn to inn so that the walker can carry a light pack. "Strategic transportation" is sometimes used to pick up and deliver walkers to and from the walking route and the inn. Daily mileage ranges from 6 to 15 miles.

Hut to hut (Grades III to IV).   Hut-to-hut mountain hiking uses a network of mountain huts, refuges, and inns for overnight accommodations.

Hiking (Grades III to IV).   Hiking is akin to tramping. In America, the word *hiking* is widely used for all walking forms. Hikes are long, vigorous walks through woods and over rugged terrain. The hiking step is about a half foot longer than that of the wandering or rambling step because of the unevenness of terrain.

Hiking includes day hikes varying from 4 to 20 miles a day and long-distance hikes averaging 6 to 30 miles a day. The 50-mile hike (Grade IV) is an all-day hike requiring 10 to 24 hours to complete. It was popularized during the presidency of John F. Kennedy. Urban hiking (a misnomer) is the city version and means walking in city parks and nearby nature areas. Area hikes lead out from and return to the same lodge or base camp each day. This is practiced in lodges in Oregon (Salmon River Lodge) and Mt. Kenya (Jungle Top Mountain Lodge), among other exciting places.

Backpacking (Grades III to IV).   Backpacking means to walk in the wilderness or the woods with a knapsack on your back, usually overnight. In your pack, you carry everything you need to survive in the wilderness.

Day packers carry a light knapsack with one or two meals and a change of clothes.

Trail walking (Grades III to IV).   A trail walker follows almost exclusively marked or unmarked dirt trails. In Europe, a network of over 200,000 miles of these trails connects towns and cities to the country-side. Most have signs at the beginning of the trail that indicate walking time and distance.

Tramping (Grades III to IV).   Tramping means to walk with heavy steps. It is the New Zealand and Australian name for hiking and trekking. When I traveled to New Zealand's South Island, I discovered a tramper's paradise. The South Island has what are called tracks

I walk to the top of Scotland's Ben Nevis in the Scottish highlands, a 3½-hour climb from sea level to over 4,000 feet, 9 miles round-trip.

(Milford Track, Holly Ford Track), which may be the world's finest trail walks because of the great variety of scenery. One walk encompasses several geographical zones, such as deserts, tropics, and mountains.

Voyageuring (Grades III to IV). This is walking while carrying a canoe. It is popular in lake districts like the Boundary Waters of Minnesota.

Orienteering (Grades III to IV). Developed in Sweden, orienteering literally means cross-country competition following a course while finding your way by maps and compasses. Half of the orienteering events are now done walking instead of running, so it becomes a mix of hiking and bushwacking.

Hill walking (Grades III to V). Hill walking is a British term for walking up mountains under 4,000 feet in height. Americans call it nontechnical climbing or mountaineering. Germans call it *bergwandern.* Hill walking is popular in Scotland, where mountains over 3,000 feet, called "Muros," are climbed. I walked to the top of Ben Nevis, Scotland's highest mountain at 4,900 feet. It was a 9-mile hill climb that took 3½ hours. This is a good example of a mountain where one side is a challenging mountainous climb and the other an easy walk up. Throughout Scotland, but especially in the highlands and on the Isle of Skye, hill walking is practiced as a serious walking sport.

Trekking (Grades III to V). The word *trekking* comes from the Dutch word *trekken*, meaning to take an arduous journey. In the 1960s and 1970s, trekking was adopted by adventure groups to mean a long pleasure or adventure walk over high terrain like that found in Peru and the Himalayas. Trekking is pleasurable because pack animals and

Sportwalking exercise model Dick Hudson reaches the top of Mt. Whitney, one of the 100 peaks he has "peak bagged" in North America.

porters carry all the gear and supplies needed for the journey.

Bushwacking (Grades III to V).   Bushwacking is walking over land, off the trail or beaten path. Walking through low underbrush and climbing over and under logs make this walksport quite strenuous. Orienteering is an organized form of bushwacking.

Mountain climbing (Grades III to V).   Mountaineering means to climb mountains for sport. Nontechnical climbs are unaided by gear except for, at most, an ax or pick. Many large mountains, like the Matterhorn and Ben Nevis, have a walkway up them.

Peak bagging (Grades III to V).   Peak bagging is a challenge walk where a hill walker tries to climb a certain number of hills and mountains over a certain height in a set period of time. For example, the record in Great Britain is 276 conquered in under one year. In the United States, peak bagging is practiced in Colorado.

Scrambling (Grades IV to V).   Scrambling means to climb or crawl over rough terrain. It is also mountain climbing that involves using your hands and feet at times, particularly near the top portions.

Celebrated walkers.   Role models, past and present, for wanderers and hikers include actors, poets, writers, and journalists (Emerson, Dickens, Finley, John Chancellor); scientists and philosophers (Farrady, Russell, Santayana); artists and musicians (Brahms, Van Gogh, Doc Severenson); actors (Walter Matthau, Woody Allen); politicians (Truman, Douglas); and naturalists, who bring speed into harmony with nature and help walkers find the most beautiful walking routes (Muir, Thoreau).

MARCHING/STRIDING

Fifteen million people in the United States and 50 million worldwide participate in marching/striding, the second-largest but fastest-growing division of sportwalking. Presently, clubs and groups—about 6,000 worldwide—in this division organize the greatest number of new sportwalks (15,000 annually). Major sportwalks include international marches, volksmarches, walkathons, and hill strides. The groups concentrate on sponsoring, organizing, and sanctioning walking events, and work to affiliate established clubs with these events. Most of their sportwalks are organized along a circular route, rather than point to point.

Sportstyle. If your purpose is to participate rather than compete, and scenery is not a priority but keeping track of the miles is, then marching or striding (let's call it striding) is for you. Walk event organizers usually certify your miles at the end of each event, and some organizations, like the International Federation of Popular Sports, give you lifetime mileage awards. The striding style is a brisk walk achieved primarily with a step longer as opposed to faster than that used in racewalking.

Racewalking is discouraged, often prohibited, at striding events because the pace of each individual sportwalk ranges from moderate (3 miles per hour) to brisk (4¼ miles per hour). Distance is emphasized over speed or difficulty of terrain. "Marching" does not mean you have to walk in formation; just walk briskly and rhythmically, with a long stride. Enough sportwalks in this one division are held annually to offer sportwalk weekend opportunities and certify your miles walked in any of 17 industrialized countries.

Historical profile. The striding style originated at Nijmegen in 1908 as a military training exercise. In 1928, Nijmegen, the first international sportwalking event, was converted from a march-training exercise into a civilian walking event.

From its inception, march training was designed to teach soldiers how to walk long distances briskly. The Romans are best known for introducing the 21-mile-a-day march to conquer and patrol their extensive land-based empire. In fact, the word *mile* came from the Roman *mille* and meant a thousand military paces, each representing two steps. The Romans walked throughout Britain, Europe, North Africa, and the Middle East on many long marches. Emperor Hadrian, known as the wandering emperor, toured his whole empire on foot, marching the 21 miles a day in full armor.

Nijmegen spawned more than 15 international two- and four-day marches in Ireland, Wales, Israel, Japan, and Denmark, and it inspired the walkathons in North America and the "volkssport" movement in Germany. The emphasis in the volkssport movement is on a series of organized 6- to 12-mile noncompetitive walks.

In the years since 1968, the volksmarch movement helped spread the concept of circular march walking to 17 countries and more than 5,000 sanctioned walking events, and along with Nijmegen, helped shape sportwalking into a primarily noncompetitive sport where finishing first is less important than going the distance at any speed. The walkathons and volksmarches in turn influenced the further development of new circular walking events, including the hill strides.

The marchers probably are the best organized of all the walking groups and have influenced the development of walking events in other divisions. This division probably contributes the most to the method of organizing the sport of walking.

Groups. The walking groups in this division stress organizing and sanctioning walk events more than recruiting walking club members. They encourage participation of other walking clubs and groups in their events. There are three basic major event organizers: The International Two and Four Day March Groups, the International Volkssport Verein (IVV), and the March of Dimes. The 10 International Two and Four Day March Groups emulate each other but are not affiliated. The IVV (translated International Federation of Popular Sports) probably has the largest system of sanctioned events (6,000 worldwide); 500 events in the United States draw a half-million registered walkers, and 6,000 events worldwide draw 15 million participants. The March of Dimes is a national fund-raising organization whose annual WalkAmerica program includes 1,400 walkathons throughout the United States.

Sportwalks. Sportwalks are done primarily for exercise and fitness training and emphasize distance over terrain or speed.

Walkathon (Grades II to IV). The purpose of a walkathon is to raise funds for charities by soliciting money pledges from sponsors for completing sets. However, fund-raising is gradually becoming secondary as the walkathon takes primacy. Walkathons range from 5 miles to 35 kilometers (kilometers are preferred to miles as the distance measures, because pledges total greater amounts).

The first U.S. walkathon was held in 1970 in Columbus, Ohio, by a chapter of the March of Dimes. Today, the March of Dimes WalkAmerica program attracts up to 23,000 walkers in 60 U.S. cities for a total of over 500,000 walkers in communities nationwide. New York holds the largest walkathon, with over 23,000 participants.

The American Heart Association holds walkathons called Turkey Walks. The American Lung Association calls its walkathons Treks for Life. Many political groups, like World Hunger and World Peace Council, use walkathons to raise funds and create public awareness.

Pep Stepathons (Grades III to IV). The Pep Stepathon walkathon was developed by Weight Watchers to help participants reduce weight. It shares aspects of long, brisk walks.

Retro-walking (Grades III to IV). These are backward sportwalks, where you use a mirror to find your way. This not only requires balancing skills, but also trains your leg muscles in a more balanced manner.

Volksmarches (Grades III to IV). Translated literally from German, *volksmarch* means "people's march" and mostly follows a circular route of six or twelve miles. Participants win merely by completing the course; it doesn't matter whether they ran or walked it. Volksmarching clubs and events were founded throughout Germany to

The start of a Danish Volksmarch.
(Photo by Gerhard Bromberger)

rebel against professionally organized running events that offered money prizes to top athletes only and ignored the amateur participants. Subsequently, they were organized to allow the widest possible participation without head-to-head competition. However, walkers could go through checkpoints to accumulate medals and mileage awards.

Volksmarchers count their mileage in sportwalks. Many have reached cumulative totals of over 12,000 miles. In 1967, volksmarching was introduced into the United States by American servicemen returning from military tours in Germany. Volksmarches were first held on U.S. military bases, but the movement spread to civilian life, where suburban, country, and city routes replaced the bases. Today, 500 volksmarches are held in the United States.

Volksmarches also include swimming, cross-country skiing, and bicycling, and are part of a citizen amateur sports movement spreading rapidly through other countries, including Germany, Austria, Switzerland, Lichtenstein, Luxembourg, Denmark, Norway, Sweden, The Netherlands, Great Britain, France, Belgium, Italy, Ireland, Canada, Spain, Israel, Greece, and Turkey. (See Appendix for the address for the International Volkssport Events Directory.)

I attended my first organized volksmarch, which was one of four marches held at the national conference of the American Volksport Association, in Norfolk, Virginia. Both the 6- and 12-mile courses wound through all of Norfolk, from the harbor front deep into the neighborhoods of Norfolk, and passed through quiet and busy streets, some pretty, some quite neglected. Since then, I've noticed that not all volksmarches are as scenic as hikes and wanderwalks are.

Strides (Grades III to IV).   Striding began in 1984. A stride is a long, sweeping, and measured step like a march step. *Hill strides* are newly invented fitness walks challenged by brisk walking and hilly terrain. The invention of hill strides is really a testimony to the dynamism of walking as a sport form, because many sportwalks represent some creative combinations of distance, speed, and terrain. I have made my training and organizing guidelines as universal as possible in anticipation of the establishment of new sporting activities.

I walked my first hill stride in San Francicso. It was a seven-mile course that covered the city's seven hills. The top of each hill offered a different panoramic view of the San Francisco Bay Area. Despite the walk's short distance, walking up and down steep hills increased the challenge. Similar hill strides held in other U.S. cities, like San Diego

San Francisco Hill Stride 1986: 8,000 participants.
(Photo by Jeff Reinking)

My finish at the First San Francisco Hillstride, attended by 3,000 walkers.

and Boston, use nearby hills as control points. Rewards include the best views of the city.

Event walks (Grades I to V).   Event walks follow a circular route that starts and finishes in the same area and have interval checkpoints. I coined the term "event walk" to refer to any organized sportwalk that follows a circular course controlled by points. This concept of noncompetition derives originally from the marching division, but now represents a more generalized approach applying to all divisions, such as the tour walk and challenge walk.

Two to four days' marches (Grades III to IV).   The Four Days' March in Holland started as a military training exercise and evolved into a civilian walking event. Thereafter, it was adapted in many industrialized countries as either a two or four days' march, where the two day march is a miniature version of the four day march that is easier to organize and to attend. Countries that hold international marching events include Israel, Ireland, Wales, Germany, and Switzerland. Daily walk lengths include 12, 20, and 31 miles. These distance distinctions are based on age and sex. Fourteen- to-fifteen year-olds can go 12 miles, 16- to 18-year-olds can go 20 miles, and 18-and-over males can go 31 miles per day.

Marathon marches (Grade IV).   A marathon march covers the distance of the marathon running route: 26.2 miles.

Death marches (Grades IV to V).   Death marches are 5- to 7-day point-to-point marches covering 300 miles. The number of participants is limited because of logistics. Vibourg, Denmark, to the German border is the most famous death march.

SPECIALIZED SPORTWALKS

Racewalking and long-distance walking constitute the specialized divisions of sportwalking with few but committed participants. Their overall sizes probably will not increase dramatically because it takes so much time to train and participate, but their technical and training contribution to the mass-participation walksports is crucial to the ongoing development of sportwalking.

LONG-DISTANCE WALKING

Long-distance walking has 5,000 U.S. and 20,000 worldwide participants. Long-distance walks are usually individualized and more specialized walks going point to point. A long-distance walk can be any walk over 50 miles in one day, or any multiday walk that averages more than 12 miles a day. Walks at shorter distances fall into the other sportwalking divisions.

Sportstyle. If you like to go slow, achieve a high level of endurance, lose weight, invent your own sport challenges, or want to get your name in the record books, then long-distance may be your walking sport. Generally speaking, the long-distance walk is not a race but a walk of endurance. The long-distance walker uses a variety of speed and step lengths—from 1 to 5 miles per hour and 1½- to 3-foot steps—to fit the terrain and the length of the sportwalk. Long-distance road walkers go farther than long-distance trail walkers, because the step length ranges from 2 to 3 feet.

Slow long-distance walking is like wandering, and fast long-distance walking can involve striding and racewalking. As I reported in the preface of my *Complete Book of Exercisewalking*, preparing for slow, long-distance weekend walks acted as the impetus to get me back into shape after a 60-pound weight gain and back into an exercise habit. These walks are great ways to catch up with your exercising on weekends and vacations.

Long-distance walking is also based on the different types of walking surfaces. Long-distance roadwalks average greater speed and longer daily distance. Because of the smooth surface, you can walk faster, sometimes more than 50 miles per day. Long-distance trailwalks rarely exceed 31 miles because of the slower speed on dirt trails. The average should not fall below 12 miles; otherwise it is standard hiking.

Historical profile. Long-distance walking has religious and commercial roots. The Crusades and other marathon-like religious pilgrimages represented a physical sacrifice and a test of the will. Long walking pilgrimages are still practiced today by monks in Japan and by worshipers in Ireland (annual pilgrimages up Croagh Patrick). Marco Polo may have walked 25,000 miles to trade with the East. Lewis and Clark did many of their Northwest expeditions on foot.

The earliest long-distance sport roadwalk was that of Sir Robert Carey in 1559. He walked a 300-mile course from London to Berwick on a wager. In 1762, John Hague walked 100 miles in 23 hours, 15 minutes. There were also long-distance wanderings, more of an adventure than a race. Johann Gottfried Seume walked from Germany to

Sicily and back (1801–1802) and from Germany to Russia, Finland, and Sweden (1805–1807). He wrote and had published a book on each one of these walks.

Long-distance sportwalking did not come into its own until the mid-1800s during a period known as the Pedestrian Age (1860–1903). In the United States and Europe, sportwalkers—called "walkists"—were the first professional athletes competing for prizes in excess of $25,000 for walking around a track or back and forth on a plank. Twenty-four-hour, 72-hour, and six-day races were held in stadiums like Madison Square Garden, formerly called the Crystal Palace. Some events drew as many as 60,000 spectators. Other wager events were held on the open road.

Edward Payson Weston, America's first nationally recognized professional athlete (1860–1907) walked 1,226 miles from Portland, Maine, to Chicago in 26 days. Weston emphasized techniques like heel-toe movement and the brisk walking pace to cover long distances. For the next 40 years, he made a career out of long-distance walking both in the United States and in England. He walked across the United States a number of times, including a walk at age 72 from Los Angeles to New York. He also held the record for the six-day race for a time, though he never beat Captain Barclay's 1801 record of 1,000 miles in 1,000 hours.

As competition progressed, both the pace and the length of long-distance walking increased. Those who picked up the pace became the racewalkers. Those who continued to increase the distance remained members of the long-distance walking division.

Groups. Clubs in the long-distance groups are generally small because long-distance walking is a sport with only a few hardy individuals. Every year around the world there are probably 500 or more complete long-distance sportwalks in excess of 1,000 miles each. An additional 10,000 walkers do between 500 and 1,000 miles, and 20,000 do long-distance challenge walks in the 50- to 300-mile range. Long-distance clubs sponsor about 100 "challenge" walks, where groups of walkers go long distances of 100, 300, and 500 miles without much rest or sleep.

Britain has a Long Distance Walkers Association, which awards certificates to those who can complete 100 miles in 24 hours. The Long Distance Hikers Association (600 members) in the United States organizes hikers who walked the Appalachian trails. Groups like the

Here I am finishing my 1,100 mile roadwalk from New York City to Jacksonville, Florida.
(Photo by Marilyn Tanner)

American Hiking Society's Hike-a-Nation or Hike-a-State Programs range in size from 50 to 400 walkers. Finally, clubs like the Appalachian Trail Conference, the Pacific Trail Club, the NY/NJ Trail Conference, and the European Long Distance Trails Association build and maintain long-distance trails. The United States is in the process of reviving its national system of pioneer trails for walking by building new trails which will link up the pioneer trails of old into a national network of trails.

Sportwalks. Training and participation in long-distance walks beyond 100 miles require the greatest·time commitment of all the walking sports. The sportwalk grades range from II to V, depending both on the distance and completion time. This group combines distance with terrain, time, and speed to test endurance. At one end of the long-distance spectrum are sportwalkers who strive to walk thousands of miles. At the other end are walkers who set distance and endurance records; they often go 24 hours straight with little or no sleep.

Long-distance trail walks or hikes (Grades III to IV). Long-distance trail walks or hikes follow dirt paths and hiking trails, avoiding cities and roads. A regular hike is distinguished from a long-distance walk by an average of more than 12 miles a day on multiple days or more than 30 miles per day.

Long-distance road walks (Grades III to IV). In a long-distance road walk, nature is less important than the challenge of going the distance, so these sportwalkers stay on roads. Long-distance road walks average more than 15 miles per day on multiday walks and 26 miles on one-day walks.

Ultra-distance walks (Grades IV to V). Ultra-distance walks cover in excess of 100 kilometers in one day.

Twenty-four-hour walks (Grades III to V). A 24-hour walking event must be completed within 24 hours. Distances range from 50 to 100 miles, sometimes more. You sleep very little or not at all during the walk. A British walking club, Centurions, admits only those who can complete 100 miles in 24 hours. You prepare by first completing 50- and then 75-mile walks in 24 hours.

Six-day races (Grades IV to V). Six-day walking events have been revived since their heyday in the 1800s by long-distance walking and marathon running clubs. Try to walk or racewalk as far as you can around a track with a stopwatch. The record for men is over 600 miles and for women is over 300 miles. The most famous is the Sir John Astley Belt Six Day "Go As You Please" race. Eventually this became a running event held in the United States and England.

Walking feats (Grades III to V). LDWs often want to make history and get themselves in the record books. These individual record-setting walks take months and years to complete, going cross-country or cross-continent. Part of the long-distance walk feat is to create your own sportwalk, one that has never been done before. Categories include historical, geographical, or political boundary routes preferably never traveled before on foot. Age, sex, and handicaps are also factors that can make an LDW feat. Walks around the world, the perimeter of the United States, the Pacific Crest Trail, West Coast of the United States, and the length of the Mississippi have now been done.

Challenge walks (grades IV to V). These are single day (10- to 24-hour day) continuous walks over 20 miles and up to 100 miles or multiday walks in excess of 1,000 miles. They are not so much tests of speed or distance as they are tests of endurance. I have adopted the term *challenge walk* to refer to any long-distance walk that is point-to-point and practiced by individual walkers or small groups of walkers.

Cross-country walks (Grades III to V). These long-distance walks travel end to end, north to south, or east to west across a state or nation.

Cross-continental walks (Grades III to IV). These long-distance walks cross whole continents.

Perimeter walks (Grades III to IV). These long-distance walks follow a coastline around a country, continent, or body of water.

Celebrated long-distance walkers. Capt. Robert Barclay and Edward Payson Weston are the most famous long-distance walkers from the Pedestrian Age. Famous Lady Pedestrians include Madame Anderson who completed 2,700 quarter miles in 2,700 hours, and Bertha von Burg who walked 372 miles in 6 days. The longest walk reported to date was 62,137 miles in 1910 by Dimitri Dans of Rumania. In the 1960s and 1970s, the Gormley family of Rhode Island walked the perimeter of the United States, John Merrill walked Britain's perimeter, and John Hillaby walked across Europe. Peter Jenkins and Gary Moore have walked across America, David Kuntz walked around the world, and David Meeghan walked from the tip of South America to the tip of North America. Betty Tucker walked the length of Death Valley alone, the 30 members of the Hike-a-Nation team walked across America following pioneer trails, and Eugen Llianis walked 6,800 miles on the streets of Newburgh, New York; Pleny Smith walked backwards across the United States and Europe.

RACEWALKING DIVISION

Racewalkers compete against each other or the clock: speed is paramount over distance. Racewalkers' training methods resemble those of running clinics and programs.

Racewalking is sportwalking's "competitive" division and has 30,000 U.S. and 90,000 worldwide participants. Still, it probably makes the greatest contribution to training techniques used in all the walking sports. Racewalkers practice walking fast along shorter courses and train for their own Olympic events (20km and 50km), making them part of the track-and-field athletic division along with running. America, Great Britain, Mexico, East Germany, Italy, Sweden, and Russia have the largest and strongest number of racewalking participants.

Sportstyle. If you are competitive and like strenuous exercise, this division will appeal most to you.

Racewalkers focus on physical development and competition by applying special walking techniques such as increasing the length of their steps and moving their legs faster. With hip extension and leg straightening they are able to achieve 106 percent of their hiking step length, about eight inches longer, in order to average a three- to four-foot step length range. They race on smooth and generally flat terrain, and

Racewalkers finishing at the annual Metropolitan Racewalk sponsored by the Metropolitan Racewalkers' Club led by Richard Goldman, one of my sportwalking exercise models.

their speed ranges from 11- to 8-minute miles. Walkers set speed records and require the highest form of cardiovascular fitness. Competitive training schedules require a time commitment of two to four hours per day.

Historical profile. Even though early Greek marathons were a mix of running and walking, racewalking's roots are imbedded in the science of walking. Starting with Leonardo da Vinci, walking was studied anatomically. It became the base for the science of biomechanics because it represents the most complex human movement. Because of racewalking, the whole concept of walking acquired a technical attitude about efficiency and the best way to achieve speed and endurance. In the 1500s British royalty waged purses with carriage footmen, who had to keep up with horses and coaches by walking along, and messengers, who carried letters and documents great distances, in walking footraces. At first fast walkers raced as long as 1,000 miles. As the "heel toeing" technique became more precise and training methods improved, racewalk distances narrowed to between 3 and 50km, and the speed increased to between four and seven mph. Racewalking did not become an Olympic sport until 1896, when the first 1,500-meter walk race, and 1908, when the London Olympics introduced longer distances of 20 and 50km. In 1911 the first U.S. racewalk was held on Coney Island and has since been an annual event. The future for racewalking: will it surpass running? While racewalking in the United States has grown by a multiple of three times in five years, there are still only 20,000 racewalking participants and 10,000 real competitors.

Groups. Racewalking is growing fast in America and Europe as a network of teams, clubs, and clinics become organized by former Olympians under two umbrella organizations: The Walkers Clubs of America and the Racewalking Association in Great Britain. Independent racewalking teams and clubs such as the Metropolitan Racewalkers in New York City, however, also exist.

Sportwalks. Racewalks are part of the track-and-field division of the Olympics and other sports federations. Most sportwalks in this division are competitive.

Developmental walks (Grades III to IV). These racewalks are timed but not sanctioned by an athletic authority. They are designed to introduce sportwalkers to the racewalking field.

Funwalks (Grades I to III). These one-mile walks are often made part of a running race.

Sprintwalks (Grades III to V). These racewalks range from 1 to 3 miles.

Marathon racewalks (Grades IV to V). These long-distance racewalks range from 25 miles upward and include 50km and 100km events. They are the walking equivalent of a marathon run and are often more strenuous.

Health walks (Grades II to III). These racewalks are for exercise and fun, not competition.

Racewalks (Grades III to IV; 20 km to 50 km are Grades IV to V). The racewalk events include 1 mile, 3km, 5km, 10km, 20km/26 miles, and 50km as events. One to 12 miles (20 km) is average.

Celebrated racewalkers. Henry Laskau (Dean of American Racewalking); Howard Jacobson (racewalking fitness guru); Larry Young, American Bronze Medalist; Steve Hayden, leading contender; and Ron Laird, most-titled racewalker.

FUTURE SPORTWALKS

As I said, walking is a growing and dynamic sport form with many new events which can still be invented. Here are some of my ideas for future sportwalk events, challenges, and races:

Mall walkathons (Grades III to V). These indoor walks are great over holiday weekends and last 6 to 12 days. Shoppers can watch a hardy group of walkers go round and round on an indoor mall track like the pedestrians once did in Madison Square Garden.

Walk relays (Grades III to V). Walk teams will pass a torch as they travel sections of a route stretching over thousands of miles.

Weekend walkathons (Grades II to V). Walkers will choose routes and distances which start and end up in the city in one or two days; held in a festival atmosphere.

Walk days (Grades I to V). National and local days declared by public officials to be set aside to walk and celebrate.

Walk week (Grades I to IV). A whole week of city and nearby country walking including clinics, workshops, and other activities.

Walk networks (Grades II to IV). Walkers can be certified for long-distance walks by walking through a marked trail and roadway route with permanent checkpoints located at inns and restaurants along the way.

EXERCISEWALKING AND SPORTWALKING

Many exercises have spun off from the various walksports, and about 55 million Americans practice regularly (two or three times a week) some form of these healthful activities.

The four sportwalking divisions have produced a variety of related exercise routines. Wandering/hiking and long-distance walking are practiced for both exercise and sport by increased distance and frequency. Striding and marching have produced a variety of briskwalking exercise routines. In the 1950s, Truman popularized a briskwalking form called *constitutional* walking. In the 1960s, Harry Kaufman introduced Swedish walking, and John F. and Robert Kennedy introduced 50-mile hikes as a physical fitness test. In the 1970s dancer Cyd Charisse and others introduced a form of briskwalking called *wogging*

**My sportwalking exercise models, Darielle Rayner and
Sylvia Brown, are hike leaders for the New York Chapter
of the Appalachian Mountain Club and average 50
miles of walking per week. Here they get ready to walk.**

(interspersed walking and jogging), and Weight Watchers introduced
pepstepping. In the 1980s, Steve Reeves (the actor who played Hercules)
introduced *powerwalking* and Dr. Leonard Schwartz introduced walking with hand-held weights. Also, wrist and ankle weights were used to
walk with. Fitness walking has been advocated as an alternative to
jogging. Weight Watchers walk fast to raise their aerobic capacity.
Briskwalking speeds range up to five mph and do not require any special
techniques, just motivation to step out as if you were rushing to an
appointment in the 1980s.

PART TWO
TRAINING

TRAINING IS THE core of sportwalking. Chapter 4 introduces you to the theory behind sport training; the other chapters in Part Two present specific training components in the sequence in which you should actually practice them. Practice charts show you how to progress and distribute the different types of training by week in each seasonal walking period. If you are a beginner, the off-season training routines will help you get back in shape for serious training.

4
TRAINING THEORY

THE TRAINING APPROACH to walking is different from the exercise approach. Exercise is for developing walking fitness. Training is for developing and improving sportwalking performance. Exercise is still part of training, but it is a means to a different end: preparing to perform well at one or more sportwalking challenges or events. Performing well means completing the event in a specified reasonable amount of time without overexerting yourself by growing too tired before the end of the walk and pulling muscles. It really means "going the distance."

If your goal is completing one particular sportwalk or a series of sportwalks, you should work out a personal training plan many weeks or months before the actual event. Although you should *exercisewalk* regularly year-round, *sportwalking* has a training cycle related to the best seasons for walking and walking events. Often, participation in shorter sportwalks is part of the process of building up to the longer ones.

This chapter indicates how you should vary your training methods to fit the requirements of the different sportwalking styles. For example, there are specialized training requirements for hiking, hill walking, volksmarching, and long-distance walking as well as various speed- and terrain-oriented events. In this chapter, the word *event* applies to all types of sportwalks.

TYPES OF TRAINING

Sportwalking training includes five components. Ranked here in order of importance, they are:

1. Technique training
2. Endurance training
3. Mobility training
4. Strength training
5. Speed training

Each particular type of training includes a series of exercises, which are practiced according to a routine. All the exercises progress to increasingly higher training levels measured in distance, speed, and repetition. You will practice all five during a training week, varying the amount and using a shorter or longer form of training regimen. Many of the training methods overlap, sometimes playing a primary role, at other times playing a secondary or supportive role.

All training forms are progressive, that is, designed to produce a *training or conditioning effect*. This means that if you train your body, gradually increasing the number of exercise repetitions—the time and rate of work (speed) and the work load—your body will adapt by becoming stronger and more efficient. Likewise, when you maintain a level of training, you also maintain a constant level of conditioning. The progressive increases in body development also apply to the sports skills and technical development.

TECHNIQUE TRAINING

Technique training includes individual technical stretching and strengthening exercises to improve your sportwalking skills and at the same time develop exercise skills which you will use to make you more fit or better conditioned for sportwalking. Technique training makes your walking more efficient; you get more speed and distance out of each step you take. Walking is a technical sport, much like gymnastics and golf, so technique training can affect your performance.

All training systems contain a skill in addition to a conditioning component. A training skill is the knowledge and experience of a training exercise and walking technique. Exercise and walking skills are especially important in technique, mobility, and strength training.

ENDURANCE TRAINING

In sportwalking, the distance you travel is more important than the speed. That's why speed training ranks number five in the training priorities, below endurance and mobility training. Endurance is the ability to last longer and to recover from fatigue faster once it has set in. Endurance in sportwalking is like fitness in exercisewalking, but it is more sport-specific.

The major goal in sportwalks is not to win the walk but rather to finish or go the distance. To do this, you need both "general" and "specific" endurance. General endurance is cardiovascular fitness. It is your body's aerobic capacity for working long periods before the onset of fatigue, for keeping you as a sportwalker out of the "breakdown lane," where you are in the middle of a long walk and can't go on any further. Specific endurance combines aerobic and muscular endurance. It is your body's capacity to work at a more intense level—to maintain a high speed continuously or to walk up a long, steep hill without resting.

The signs of improved general endurance are a lower resting pulse rate and a faster rate of recovery to a resting pulse rate after exercise. The sign of specific endurance training is reaching the performance level you had hoped to achieve at the sportwalk event itself.

For sportwalking, you can raise your level of general endurance through other aerobic exercises such as running, cross-country skiing, skating, swimming, and bicycling. This adds variety to your training program. You will develop both types of endurance from many miles and hours of walking and from practicing the special sportwalking exercises. You'll develop both general and specific endurance through continuous walking—long, slow repetitions progressively increasing over time at 50 to 75 percent of maximum effort. You will also achieve increases in specific endurance through interval walking. This consists of shorter walks at a given speed, or on terrain similar to that of the upcoming sportwalk event.

Endurance is related to the overriding principle of all sports: specificity of training. To improve performance in a sport, you have to practice the sport itself. Any exercise is not an adequate substitute. To do a three-mile mountain sportwalk, you have to practice on a mountain. To do racewalking, you have to practice at a racewalker's speed and distance. To complete a 100-mile, 24-hour walk you have to complete a 50- and a 75-mile walk in 24 hours.

To improve specific endurance, gradually maintain your level of effort while increasing the time and speed of training with interval exercises. These are shorter, more intense efforts of up to 100 percent, with more frequent rest-recovery periods of 1 to 5 minutes or until your pulse rate goes below 120 beats per minute. Before you begin interval training, you should become minimally conditioned (Level III), and you should use continuous training first. This book uses the same fitness or aerobic conditioning levels (I through V) used in my other walking books, so you can correlate your exercisewalking fitness with your sportwalking conditioning. For this purpose, fitness levels equal conditioning levels.

MOBILITY TRAINING

Except for perhaps racewalking, mobility training ranks number three in the sportwalking training hierarchy. While the technique training helps a walker improve mobility or range of joint and muscle motion, more specialized and continuous flexibility and rotation exercises can have a significant effect. In exercisewalking you stretch muscles to avoid injury. In sportwalking you stretch joints and muscles to significantly improve your performance, specifically the power of your leg drive, the range of your hip and arm movement, and the length of your stride.

A limited number of flexibility exercises are introduced in connection with technique training. With mobility training, these are expanded into a series of stretching and rotating maneuvers in a separate routine that becomes more than half your training period.

STRENGTH TRAINING

Strength training, like endurance training, helps you lay the foundation for a good sportwalking performance. Muscular strength in walking is dynamic rather than explosive. The sportwalking strength training is a routine split between calisthenic and weight-training exercises. Both involve adding resistance work to muscles used for walking. Calisthenics, with lower resistance or weight, allows for more repetitions to develop muscular endurance. This serves as the basis for developing general strength, to which more specific strength-training exercises can be added in the weight-training segments.

Weight training enables you to isolate and strengthen specific muscles used in walking, such as calf and deltoid muscles, to a more measurable and higher degree of resistance than can be achieved by just using gravity and your own body weight. You do more strength training in the build-up period (three times a week) than in the event-participation period (once a week). Strength training is more important if you are training for a walk over rugged or sloped terrain; it can substitute for lack of this kind of terrain to practice on. For example, the extra strength gained from weight training your quadricep muscles can make a big difference in mountain walking.

SPEED TRAINING

Speed training will help you develop a more rapid leg action as well as help develop specific endurance for shorter-distance fast walking. But the contribution of leg speed to overall walking speed is not as important as increases in stride length and leg strength. That's why overall or long-distance walking speed increases come as much as from technique, mobility, endurance, and strength training. Each contributes to a wider stride and a more powerful leg drive. A trained sportwalker can improve his or her walking speed from 20 minutes a mile to 8 minutes a mile! It is difficult to improve your raw walking speed or the speed of your leg repetitions over a short distance. Leg-speed increases take years, while stride-length increases take only months and add significantly to your overall walking speed.

There are few walking events where leg speed makes a difference. That's because most events are longer than a mile and are, therefore, in the nature of endurance events rather than speed or sprint events. The "walker's dash," or walking at flat-out speed, is not an event but a trial walk that helps establish the top walking speed. This is determined by walking as fast as you can over 200 to 300 yards.

Speed training itself has limited use. It is limited to interval training in distance ranges of 400 to 1,200 yards. Improved short-distance walking speed will help you break away, especially on uphill and downhill sections, to catch up when you've fallen behind. It will also help you improve your ability to make a show with a strong finish.

THE TRAINING YEAR

Most walks take place in the six-month period from May through October. This leaves November and December for rest-up and January through April for build-up.

REST PERIOD

The off-season, or rest period, usually corresponds with the cold weather and the holiday season, when time commitments to training are understandably lower. The off-season can also be any period when you are burned out on sportwalking and seek rest and recuperation. Even sportwalkers may burn out and welcome a change of pace.

However, you should not make the mistake of becoming totally inactive during this period; continue to maintain a minimum level of activity (200 to 300 calories of exercise and activity a day). You can achieve this with recreational or exercisewalking or by participating in other sports such as skiing or indoor sports. Many sportwalkers stay active with cross-country skiing and shorter walks.

THE BUILD-UP PERIOD

The build-up period starts after the holidays. Begin by identifying and planning for the year's upcoming sportwalks. Then you can begin a week-to-week progressive build-up, increasing your walking miles and walking speed and emphasizing endurance training and strength training according to a plan. The build-up period should start with a broad range of exercises, avoiding intense training until the last quarter of the period.

TRANSITION PERIOD

The transition, or pre-event, period is the one-month transition period before the event or challenge walk. During this period, the walker tries to complete a trial walk similar to the one he or she has been training for. A trial walk is a walk at a pace and a mileage level at least three-quarters of the event or challenge walk itself. The training levels by now have all reached their highest points. The sportwalker may also be concentrating on walking itself, having put aside auxiliary training methods like weight training and special flexibility-training sessions.

The pre-event period also includes a final *week before the sportwalk*. This time is devoted to moderate practice of both speed and endurance. You are resting up for your first sportwalk event.

SPORTWALKING SEASON

The events-participation period is a four- to six-month period when the sportwalker participates in a series of walks sometimes scheduled only one week apart. If the sportwalks are of long distances, they will take up a lot of the weekly walking training time and become part of the training program itself. Therefore, you should not overtrain between sportwalks but keep your cumulative mileage levels complementary to those in the long-distance walks. Also keep your speed and effort levels below 75 percent of the maximum effort.

Concentrate instead on technique and flexibility exercises along with some speed training, depending on the nature of the sportwalks. During this period, your strength training should also be kept to a minimum, perhaps one session per week. If your planned sportwalks are short distances (under 12 miles), maintain your general endurance while practicing mobility and specific endurance training. Specific training will vary depending on whether the purpose is completion or participation. If you are racewalking, emphasize speed training. Otherwise, keep your weekday mileage levels constant by distributing walking every day or every other day.

After each challenging sportwalk (more than 20 miles), there will be a recovery period of one or more days. During this recovery, you should

Period	Months	Training Efforts
Rest period	November–December	Moderate
Build-up period	January–February	High
Transition period	March–April	Highest
Sportwalking season	May–October	Highest

not stop your activity altogether, but keep moving with easy walking so your muscles don't grow stiff and your blood doesn't pool. You may be limping a little after multiple-day events. I find that once you get moving, your muscles warm up and the limping goes away. Psychological factors also affect your recovery period. If you performed well, the recovery seems to go faster; if you did not do so well, it may go slower. It helps to be aware of this so you can overcome depression more quickly.

TRAINING PLAN

Before starting a *training program* you need a *training plan*, and before you can construct a personalized training plan, you need a goal. For sportwalkers, the goal varies from participating in regular weekend walks to completing one or more major long-distance events. These can include major group events, challenge walks, vacation tours near and abroad, treks, and perhaps a long-distance or multiple-day walking circuit.

SELECTING EVENTS

Your calendar is the start of your training plan. Put on your calendar the dates of walking events you want to enter. Make a note of the number of weeks to the first event as well as how subsequent events are spaced out. Indicate next to the entry the distance of the sportwalk and any special features such as terrain, weather, competitiveness, number of days, and number of participants. If you are a casual walker or a beginner, selecting events may take more time. Start small with your own weekend sportwalk and do research on the type of walks that interest you the most. Check Appendix A for a list of major events and sources of information about smaller events. These will give you some ideas.

In fashioning your training plan, focus on distance, speed, terrain, and the number of days of participation required for each event. In general, select a sequence of events that gradually increases the distance and speed as well as the difficulty of terrain, so you can prepare for them properly. For volksmarching and long-distance walking, choose events so that the length gradually increases over the season, with the longest occurring in the second half. For hill walking and trekking, choose walk events that are at intermediate distances and levels of terrain difficulty. For hiking, wandering, and rambling, you can vary your walking distances from weekend to weekend, only occasionally taking a really challenging walk.

For racewalking, you will probably specialize in short- or long-distance events. Racewalking or competitive walking has special training needs tailored to the competitive and record-breaking events. For short-distance events (three and five km, 10 and 20 km), racewalkers can prepare with a number of practice trials that are similar to the event itself. If you walk fewer races, it is possible to maintain a high performance level for each one. Otherwise, training will vary, depending on the importance of the race; you may want to target "big races" for special efforts and all-out performance. If you are trying to qualify for a team or special championship event, you might reach one peak for qualification and a still higher peak for the final.

Training for multiday walking events gives the build-up period a different structure: intermediate distance points (or shorter walks) during the preparatory period. The sportwalk events on your calendar will determine your final mileage goals as well as walking time goals (for the longest event and the most difficult or competitive event). Once your goals are set, the charts on page 000 will show you the intermediate training points or steps toward reaching these goals and methods for adapting the training regimens to fit them.

Long-distance road walking or hiking events may last for weeks or months, with daily walking averages of more than 15 miles. In this case, event participation becomes part of the training program itself. You can build up your daily distance average over weeks of long-distance walking.

SPORTWALKING OBJECTIVES

While in exercisewalking the build-up period is more related to general endurance and fitness, in sportwalking it is related to both general and specific. It is oriented toward reaching the mileage and speed levels of the events that lie ahead. Event participation in sportwalking can be used for maintenance *or* for progressive conditioning, whereas in exercisewalking it is used to maintain a certain plateau or fitness level throughout the year.

Depending on the type of sportwalk events you choose, you will be concentrating on more or less endurance, strength, or speed training, but for all events you will train with a portion of each.

If you count all its divisions, you'll see that sportwalking is a year-round sport and, therefore, a reliable exercise. The training gap can be filled with winter walking events scheduled in the snow. Keeping a steady pace, walkers generate enough body heat to stay comfortably warm staying outdoors during a whole winter day. If you want to participate in moderately challenging or maintenance-level activities, there are weekend walking events ranging from 3 to 15 miles, which can serve you all year.

If you are planning one or more long walks or multiday walks (treks, inn-to-inn tours, challenge walks), a build-up period is necessary. If you plan on participating and competing in racewalks and challenge long-distance walks, give more care and attention to your training schedule.

As you get more involved with the sport, you will probably adopt a mixed training schedule that allows you to participate in some long and some short events, varying the distance and the terrain. The universal training program presented here allows you to maintain a basic foundation of walking sports fitness from which to branch out into more specialized walking as your time and interest expand. Despite the year-round availability of walking events, most sportwalkers settle into an up-and-down training cycle that reflects their other sports interests. Thus, you can tailor the training cycle, with its off- and on-season, to your individual interests.

TRAINING SCHEDULES
THE TRAINING WEEK

Regular sportwalk training sessions are a minimum of three times a week, while specialized training can add on an additional two or three days, bringing the total to six or seven days a week. At least two days, usually Monday and Friday, are light training days, especially when you are engaging in long weekend training or weekend sportwalks. The weekend becomes the focus of most of the walking training, and walking events themselves are counted as part of the training program.

With exercisewalking, the effort is more evenly distributed among weekdays. Exercisewalking emphasizes a steadier work effort every other day with a rest day or strolling walks in between. Sportwalking substitutes rest days with light training or specialized training other than endurance training. In the build-up period, strength and mobility training are performed on the days opposite endurance training days.

You need both heavy and light training days for sportwalking. Weekend days are best for the heavy, high-mileage training because you have the time and energy to do it. Saturday or Sunday should be the peak performance day, the day you log in your longest or fastest walk. If you are training for multiday sportwalks, you might train equally hard on both days. Tuesday and Thursday are also heavy walking training days. This leaves Monday, Wednesday, and Friday for light walking and more in-depth strength and mobility training. Your training level and the number of training hours will determine whether you use the long or short version of a training component.

TRAINING PATTERNS

As a sportwalker you should adjust the way you train based on both your long-term (the big event) and short-term (intermediate event) goals. Generally you should have a mix of hard and easy days, with one or more rest days. The weekly training pattern will also change during the various training periods. To maintain your interest and the level of fun and enjoyment, it is important to vary the training places, types of exercises, and type of event participation.

TYPES OF SCHEDULES

There are basically three types of training schedules within a training period: short-distance, long-distance, and racewalk. These are geared to the basic types of sportwalks. Many sportwalkers will shift from one schedule to another to fit the changes in planned events during the season.

Within the three schedule types, the five physical fitness levels are also reflected, depending on the physical challenge of the event(s) being trained for. These fitness levels affect the amount of training time, miles, and the intensity of the training effort. The three training schedules correspond with the sportwalking styles as follows:

1. *Short-Distance Schedules* (Levels I to III)—Backpacking trips, hikes, rambles, volksmarches, one-day tour walks, walkabouts, racewalks.
2. *Long-Distance Schedules* (Levels III to IV)—Two- to four-day

continuous walks, treks, hikes, mountain scrambles, hill walks, racewalks.

3. *Racewalk Schedules* (Levels III to V)—Short walks (20 km or less) and long walks (more than 20 km up to 50 km).

THE TRAINING SESSION

The typical sportwalking training session is organized like the exercise-walking session, with a warm-up and cool-down as well as strengthening and stretching exercises. The session is dominated by an aerobic or endurance-training portion where you walk continuously at a 75 percent effort level.

With exercisewalking, the length of the sessions stays constant, usually about an hour or less, while the work effort increases. With sportwalking, the sessions may go into overtime. In addition, sportwalking involves more specialized and concentrated training efforts.

Each type of training has a short and long version. The short version consists of a selected group of exercises, usually not more than three. These can be practiced during any training session for 5 to 15 minutes. The long version consists of a complete set of exercises (not more than eight), which are practiced from 15 to 30 minutes. These become part of a special or in-depth training session. A special training session may combine two types of special training, with the short version used as complementary exercises. A general training session involves a variety of short-version training exercises, with only one special-training portion, which now is used in a complementary role.

REGULAR TRAINING SESSION

The regular walk-training session contains a mix of all the training programs in short form, with the long-form endurance or distance training.

The organization of a regular sportwalking training session resembles an exercisewalking session, except that techniques are practiced while walking rather than as a separate standing exercise session. Flexibility exercises are also interspersed throughout the session rather than just at the beginning and the end. The outline that follows also features a regular or combined training session routine, with actual walking done in a session separate from the routines for strengthening and mobility training.

ALTERNATIVE #1
Regular Training Session   **60 minutes**
Warm-up   5 minutes
Stretching exercises   5 minutes
Strengthening exercises   5 minutes
Distance walk   35 minutes
Speed exercises   5 minutes
Cool-down   5 minutes

ALTERNATIVE #2
Special Training Session   **60 minutes**
Warm-up   5 minutes
Weight training—long form   35 minutes
Mobility training—short form   5 minutes
Distance walk   10 minutes
Cool-down   5 minutes

ALTERNATIVE #3
Split Training Sessions   **60–120 minutes**
First Session   *30–60 minutes*
Warm-up   5 minutes
Distance exercises (continuous walk)   12 minutes
Stretching   5 minutes
Distance exercises
   (second continuous walk)   12 minutes
Speed exercises   5 minutes
Cool-down   5 minutes

Second Session   *60 minutes*
Warm-up   2 minutes
Strength training (short form)   20 minutes
Mobility training (long form)   30 minutes
Cool-down   2 minutes

You'll be able to go further if you take rest breaks in between training sessions. Have a seat.

SPECIAL TRAINING SESSION

For two to three days a week when you are not doing a regular walking training session, you will be doing special or in-depth training. Typically you will spend the whole period on one type of training with a warm-up and cool-down session before and after the period. If you are planning a mixed training schedule, you might split the period among two special training areas that complement each other (such as strength with mobility training).

SPLIT TRAINING SESSION

You can incorporate regular training and special training into one training day (usually a weekend day) by splitting them up into a morning and afternoon session.

5
WARM-UP EXERCISES

You SHOULD PRECEDE and conclude every training session and walking event with warm-up and cool-down exercises. Warm-up and cool-down can be the same procedure just done in reverse, increasing or decreasing the amount of work effort.

Skipping the warm-up or cool-down is the most common and the most serious mistake a sportwalker can make. You should do them even before and after technique, mobility, and strength training.

WARM-UPS
LIMBER UP (2 TO 5 MINUTES)

Start your warm-up exercises by limbering up the whole body. You increase your heart rate, blood circulation, and the muscle-pumping action to your major muscle groups by moving your arms, legs, and torso. A walk that increases from a moderate to a brisk pace is the most common method. Do this for two to five minutes, whatever it takes to break a slight sweat.

Practice an extended warm-up half an hour or more before a sportwalk, racewalk, or long-distance walking event. During the warm-up period, also check that both your body and equipment systems are in working order.

You do not have to walk to limber up. Before practicing strength or techniques, you can limber up in place by doing a series of calisthenic exercises slowly and in wide or long, continuous movements. Sessions of walking and calisthenics to limber up should come before you do any flexibility exercise sessions. Your joints and muscles have to be warmed up before you stretch them.

STRETCH OUT AND ROTATE

After limbering up, you are ready to stretch out muscles and rotate joints you will be using in your training session. If you are doing mobility training, you can skip this stage and go right into the mobility-training routines, since the stretching and rotating exercises in the warm-up are really a microcosm of the mobility training.

But do the flexibility exercises before strength, speed, and endurance training. In this case, do not hold your stretches as long or rotate your joints as many times. Do only one flexibility exercise for each muscle

Darielle and I demonstrate warming up in place with exaggerated arm swings, trunk rotations, and sidebends.

Walker's Jumping Jacks: Front and back, another form of exaggerated arm swinging. In the Sportwalker's version you jump, reversing the position of your front and back legs. Swing your arms forward and back, in opposition to your legs.

Side-to-side bending with arms on your hips.

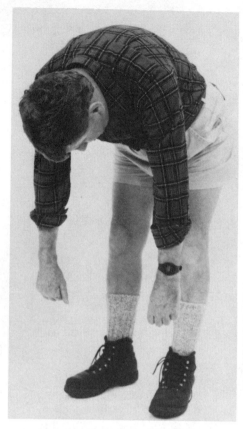

Dick Hudson demonstrates the Hangover Stretch, a good finish for the cool-down stretches. Dick has hiked the whole length of the Appalachian trail and has bagged a hundred peaks.

group. Otherwise, you may be doing too much exercise, thus straining your body before you start the major part of your training session.

COOL-DOWNS

Immediately after your training session, you should slow down the pace of your exercise in graduated stages (the limbering up in reverse) and then stretch and rotate the joints and muscles you used during your training. Remember to stretch every muscle you strengthen; the two exercises go hand in hand.

Choose cool-down stretches and rotations from the mobility training routines that are done sitting or lying down, since they will help you relax as well.

6
TECHNIQUE TRAINING

AFTER ENDURANCE TRAINING, technique training is perhaps the most important area for sportwalking. Technique training is the means by which you learn the proper biomechanics for walking. I like to tell my students that walking is not simple, but complicated. It's a technical sport like golf or gymnastics, more technical than its sister sports, running and biking. Technique training is the process of learning how to put more into walking, so that you'll get more out of it. This applies to exercisewalking as well as sportwalking.

Although the walking techniques presented here are highly developed and advanced, they still build on what you already know and do every day with ordinary walking. You already know how to walk (but you have probably developed some serious walking faults). This chapter will show you some technical refinements to improve your walking and help you become an "advanced walker."

Walking and training techniques will help you walk longer, farther, and faster. Each type of sportwalk performance includes all these elements, but emphasizes one or two of them over the others.

Longer refers to the sportwalker's ability to conserve energy and keep walking without getting tired. Conserving energy means minimizing

unnecessary movements and learning to relax body parts not needed during specific walking actions.

Farther refers to the sportwalker going the distance and building up mileage or reaching intermediate distance points on any sportwalk or sportwalk training schedule.

Faster refers to the time component in any sportwalk, not just in a racewalk. Going faster enables you to finish sooner and allows more time for rest and recuperation.

To do exercisewalking, you learn walking techniques to make your walking more dynamic, thereby increasing its exercise value or the number of exercise calories you put out per minute, as well as the number of muscles you tone and strengthen. With sportwalking, walking and exercise techniques take a different direction; they are more specific to the type of walk you are preparing to do and they are oriented to efficient performance, or maximizing speed and distance covered, while minimizing the amount of work and fatigue. These walking techniques help you store and conserve energy during a sportwalk. Where the exercisewalker would accept sloppy form in favor of more exercise calories burned, the sportwalker learns to conserve calories.

For a more detailed explanation of basic walking techniques for use in daily walking or in making walking into a dynamic workout, read my first books, *The Complete Book of Exercisewalking* and *Gary Yanker's Walking Workouts*. *Sportwalking* covers only the basics of walking as they relate to sportwalk training.

Technique training can be done in short form as selected technical exercises, as part of any walking-training session, or in long form as a special technique-training session lasting up to 60 minutes.

TYPES OF EXERCISES

The techniques-training section is divided into middle-, lower-, and upper-body actions so you can concentrate your practice, integrating a number of technical refinements at a time. Technique exercises are necessary for developing a fast, efficient, and powerful walking action through exercises for proper biomechanics and improved flexibility and strength.

BIOMECHANIC EXERCISES

The biomechanic exercises show you how to move body parts and hold them in proper position for the most efficient walking action. You improve your walking technique by repeating and correcting movement patterns while you are walking rather than while exercising in place as you do in beginner exercisewalking. But proper movements must also be supported by improved strength and flexibility. Repeating the technical exercises will not only help you master them, but also improve your walking performance.

FLEXIBILITY EXERCISES

Flexibility exercises help extend the range of motion of your joints and the muscles that operate them. The joints are the ankles, hips, shoulders, and spine. In all flexibility exercises for the joints, you should move the joints slowly through their full range to the extreme position.

In flexibility exercises for the muscles, you should stretch them out slowly and completely, holding the stretch for 10 to 30 seconds, depending on the degree of your flexibility.

For joints *and* muscles, avoid jerking and bouncing. Abrupt movements make your muscles contract and resist the stretching. As you practice flexibility exercises over the four-month build-up period (December to March), you will gradually increase the amount of time you spend stretching, say, from 5 minutes a session to 20 minutes. Vary the stretching exercises in order to maintain your interest as well as to concentrate on areas where you need more improvement.

STRENGTH EXERCISES

Strength exercises improve the ability of the muscles to produce a force against resistance. Sportwalking requires dynamic strength, meaning the ability to perform a large number of repetitions, rather than an infrequent number of explosive bursts. Strength exercises concentrate on the "walking muscles" (deltoids, pectorals, quadriceps, hamstrings and calves, obliques, hip flexors, and lower back).

A sportwalker should devote extra sessions to flexibility exercises two to three times a week during the build-up period. Each stretching period should be preceded by warm-up exercises for 2 to 10 minutes.

THE WALKING ACTION

The walking action is simply the movement of the muscles and limbs used in walking. The body is broken down into upper, middle, and lower body parts. Here, they are defined in terms of forward progression of the body; the walking action is analyzed in the context of one step forward, with the rear leg moving past the forward leg from the double-support phase stance (legs splayed). In the continuous phase of the movement, the leg formerly in the rear steps forward to become the forward leg, completing a walking action. The walking cycle is defined in terms of a cycle of three walking steps, starting with one foot, going to the other, and finishing on the one you started with. *One foot is always on the ground.*

The best way to develop your walking technique is to practice the technique exercises in three parts according to your upper, middle, and lower body. Each technique is described as a body action of a specific body area.

For each technique, this chapter gives the why and how of the

Ingrid Jacobson walks 35 miles per week,
sustains a terrific 9½-minute-mile pace, and
qualified for New York's Empire State Games
racewalking competition. Andrew Crane, her
partner in their fitness business Body and Soul,
tries to catch up with her on the right. On the
next two pages Ingrid demonstrates the
walking cycle for women.

technique exercises. Specifically, a biomechanics section describes in
detail the proper movements for a specific body area. Flexibility
exercises show you how to improve mobility range and fluidity of
movement for that specific body area. The strengthening exercises show
you how to strengthen the muscles used in that action. Finally, the
benefits section shows how the technique will improve the variety of
sportwalking styles.

A greater emphasis is placed on the training you do when you are *not*
walking, with strength (including weight training) and flexibility
exercises, which prepare you more quickly for a better sportwalk and in
some cases cut down on the need for high training miles.

The single-support phase (left foot on ground).

The double-support phase (right foot forward).

The single-support phase (right foot on ground).

The double-support phase (left foot forward).

Back view close up.

Back view.

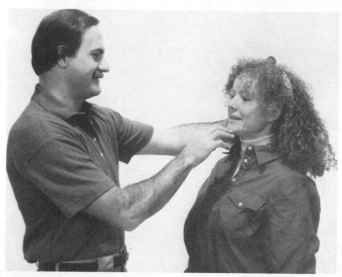

I show Sylvia how the chin and, ultimately, the head, control your whole body posture. Maintaining proper body alignment while walking, not just standing still, is the real challenge.

POSTURE IN ACTION

"Posture in action" means that your body is in the best and strongest position while you are walking, so limbs and torso can move within and around their joints with the least amount of resistance, affording fluid forward motion. Maintaining a fully aligned body while walking reduces fatigue and enables you to take longer steps. Good posture is good balance; you will be better able to maintain and increase your forward progression if you walk with proper posture.

It's easy to stand erect for a few seconds; the challenge is to maintain a properly aligned *posture in action*. It's called "walking tall." You need form, strength, and flexibility to walk tall. Walking tall gives you a higher center of gravity from which to take longer steps. It also holds your posture erect so your body weight rests on your bones and joints, giving your muscles the best possible chance to relax when they are not working. The posture exercises that follow integrate biomechanics with stretching and strengthening exercises.

BENEFITS

Posture techniques improve racewalking speed by helping to raise the body's center of gravity from which to take a longer stride. Variable posture positions expand the number of body positions for hiking, backpacking, and mountaineering to help you adjust to terrain changes. Posture techniques help conserve energy by eliminating the use of muscles that are not needed at a given time. This makes volksmarching, wandering, hiking, and long-distance walking more relaxed, increasing walking distance especially on multiple-day walks.

BODY ANGLE

The proper standing or erect body alignment is important in most sports training, but particularly in walking. The angle at which you hold your upper and lower body affects how well you will perform and how fatigue-free you will remain throughout the walk. Proper posture helps you relax the muscles of your body until you actually need them. You will learn how to disengage and engage muscles when they are needed and how to shift from working your body part to letting your muscular skeletal system support you. Improper posture unnecessarily strains muscles you do not need for walking, causing tiredness and tension early on.

Your body angle will be affected by the terrain angle and your walking speed. With exercisewalking you strive to keep an erect posture, a 90-degree angle from the ground; with sportwalking you take a more variable approach to posture. In other words, you have to lean your body forward when you accelerate or go up steep terrain for short periods of time and then return it to the upright position when you stabilize your speed or return to flat terrain.

POSTURAL MANEUVERS

When you notice that your walking posture is out of whack, try this three-part postural correction:

1. Stretch out your torso and limbs so they are at 90-degree angles in reference to the ground and your direction of travel.
2. Stretch out tense muscles that affect your posture position; stretch in the opposite direction from which they are pulling you.
3. Strengthen any muscle areas that are weak, causing poor posture from lack of muscular support or because of a muscle imbalance.

Backpackers like Dick have a tendency to lean too far forward in order to balance out their pack weight.

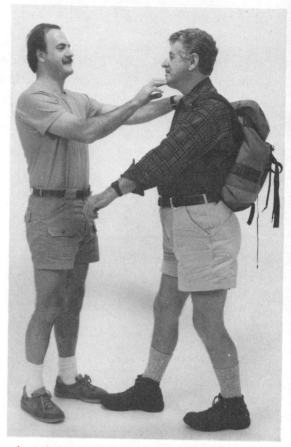

I push Dick's chin in a bit to straighten out his posture.

Now Dick holds his chin properly tucked in.

Use this three-part postural correction:
Establish your 90-degree angles with the
ground by holding your arms straight out . . .

. . . to your sides, shoulder high . . .

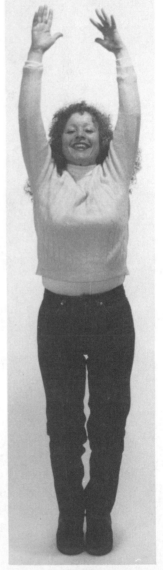

. . . and straight up.
Flat surface posture,
leaning from the heels.

93

Uphill posture.

POSTURAL STANCES

Posture in action means holding yourself in three proper positions while walking and being able to shift positions when needed. On flat surfaces it is important to generally maintain an erect or upright upper body so as not to upset the balance and coordinated movements of the walking action.

The flat-surface posture is really a balance act. With each step, you fall slightly forward, catching yourself with your forward stepping foot so that the forward lean does not exceed 5 degrees. Also, with each step your rear leg pushes you so you rotate on your forward foot. But you

Too far forward.   **Downhill posture.**

should keep the leaning within 5 degrees forward and 5 degrees backward. Be sure to lean from the heels, keeping your body in a straight line and not bending at the waist. If you lean too far forward, your body will rotate too far to the left or right, making you lose extra time or energy. If you lean too far back, it will make it more difficult to accelerate your body with each step.

The hilly-surface posture allows more leeway for leaning. When going uphill or downhill, these guidelines change, but you must still control the leaning and backward motion. If you lean too far forward, you'll have trouble bringing your rear foot forward, as illustrated. If you lean too far back on the downward slope, you'll slow down your pace and will probably overrotate your swing.

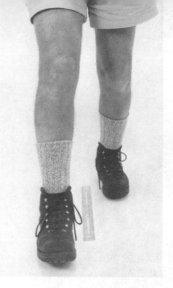

Feet should be 3 to 5 inches apart (front).

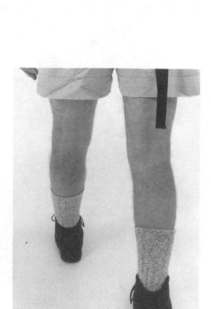

Feet should be 3 to 5 inches apart (back).

POSTURE PHASES

Apply upper, middle, and lower posture exercises during each of the four phases of the walking action:

- Phase #1: *Feet Side by Side*—Stand with your feet three to five inches apart, one foot raised, one foot anchored on the ground, overlapping the line of gravity.
- Phase #2: *Stride Stance*—Place one foot in front of the line of gravity, one foot behind the line of gravity. Both feet are on the ground and equidistant from the line of gravity.
- Phase #3: *Rear-Leg Push-Off*—Rear leg moves in an intermediate range between phases #1 and #2.
- Phase #4: *Front-Leg Extension*—Rear leg continues to move forward between phases #1 and #2.

Sylvia demonstrates the stride stance of the hiker with feet 24 to 36 inches apart.

RELAXING MUSCLES

Sportwalkers should practice relaxing and stretching different parts of the body. The best way to relax a muscle is to contract it further so that it will release. You will develop the ability to engage and disengage muscles as they are needed during the walking action. Your arms and trunk (including most of the shoulder and back muscles) should remain relaxed most of the time. Try to imagine that your upper body is sitting quietly on your hips. This relaxed state is selective, because you have to work the muscles you need to propel you forward, namely deltoid, hip, abdominal, quadricep, and calf muscles.

UPPER-BODY POSTURE

BIOMECHANICS

Your head and spine should be erect as if a string were running through your spine, pulling you skyward from the ground. People tend to hunch their shoulders or lean their head forward when they are tired or want to go faster or have to go up a steep incline. Keep your chin pulled in as shown; don't let it jut out.

The position of your head will affect how you hold the rest of your posture. For example, if you look down at the ground too close to your feet, you will have to tilt your head, which in turn will bend your spine. Therefore, use your head to effect posture corrections by pulling in the chin and tilting forward, backward, or side to side until it is properly centered over your chest, back, and shoulder girdle. From the side, your ears should look centered with your shoulders.

On the walking trail, you will notice your head tilt forward when you are getting tired. Use the position of your head as a barometer for your level of fatigue as well as your posture level. Your shoulders follow your head as it leans down toward your chest, rounding them. Your shoulders should remain relaxed (not raised) when you are not using them to swing your arms. If you notice your shoulders rounding, pull them back in military fashion to overcorrect this tendency.

Darielle shows how to stretch arms and shoulders while walking in bent fashion.

Ingrid demonstrates how you can stretch the arm and shoulder by swinging your arm up and over your head.

Sylvia demonstrates a single-arm windmill for a third shoulder stretch you can do while walking. In Chapter 9, Kelly Kane shows how you can stretch out your arms, to the front, up, side to side, and back, while walking with a backpack on.

FLEXIBILITY

Stretch out muscles that you feel are tensing and growing tight. Otherwise, they will pull your body away from a good posture in the direction of the tense muscle. For the upper body, stretch out neck, chest, shoulder, and back muscles while standing or walking. This relaxes tense muscles and at the same time corrects the position of your slumped head and shoulders.

I practice this posture-correction exercise on long walks when I can't take a rest or when the last rest stop doesn't completely relax me. It is important to make postural corrections on the go; otherwise tension and fatigue accumulate.

STRENGTH

Strengthen postural muscles before or after walking sessions to help you hold your upper body erect. Your postural muscles are your shoulder, chest, and upper-back muscles. Strong shoulder, chest, and upper-back muscles are less likely to tire from the arm-pumping action of walking.

Strengthening exercises for the upper-back area are:

- Rowing exercises
- Bent-over flye

Strengthening exercises for the shoulders and chest are:

- Overhead presses
- Push-ups
- Chest presses

The best approach is to develop a balanced set of upper-body muscles, so that stronger muscles will not pull or work against weaker muscles.

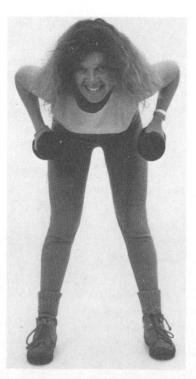

Darielle demonstrates bent-over rowing: keeping the back flat, using hand-held weights while pulling both arms to the sides of the chest, then lowering. This strengthens arms, shoulders, and back.

Bent-over flyes: keeping your arms straight and back flat, lift the arms to shoulder height. This strengthens the shoulders and outer arm muscles.

Overhead presses: From this position, push the weights straight up, overhead, but do not lock the arms. Lower slowly to the starting position. Repeat the exercise 6 to 12 times.

Chest presses: From this position, push the weights straight up, overhead, but do not lock the arms. Lower slowly to the starting position. Repeat the exercise 6 to 12 times.

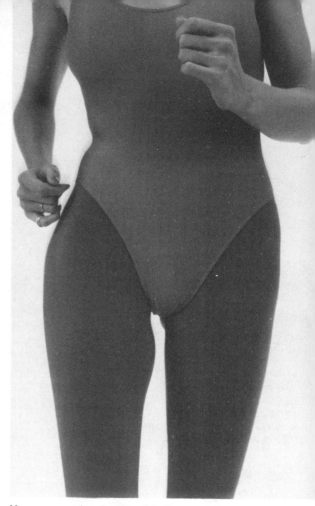

While walking, your upper body should not lean forward or side to side.

Your upper body should sit directly over your hips and start square.

THE MIDDLE POSTURE

BIOMECHANICS

Your torso should feel like it is sitting directly over your hips. Your hips should start square, that is, perpendicular to the direction of travel. Your torso should remain upright between walking steps as it moves parallel to the line of travel.

Keep your lower back flat by tucking your buttocks under your spine and pulling in your abdominal muscles. Do not arch your lower back when you lean forward. (The photo on page 102 shows incorrect back arching.) Maintain a flat back posture throughout the walking course.

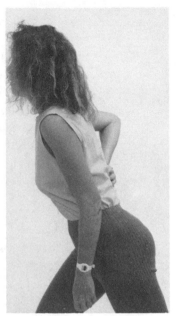

Your rear end sticking out is an indicator that your back is overarched while you walk.

Flatten your back by pulling under your buttocks. Reach back with your hand to check that you have accomplished this.

Radically lean, up to 15 degrees, on very steep inclines.

Arching your back will strain it and cause early fatigue. An arched back makes you stick out your rear end; in this position, it is difficult to take longer steps.

The photos on page 103 show the proper posture for flat-terrain walking. Note that the body leans slightly forward, about 1 to 3 degrees, when you accelerate walking speed or maintain your speed over 3½ miles per hour, but the back still stays flat. The photo on page 103 shows the proper flat-back posture for walking up moderate inclines. Note that you lean forward up to 5 degrees. Be sure you lean forward from the heels, keeping your back straight; return to erect posture when coming back to flat terrain or walking downhill. The photo on page 103 shows a radical forward lean of up to 15 degrees when on steep inclines. Remember to resume a moderately forward lean when the terrain angle decreases.

FLAT-BACK EXERCISE

Practice keeping your back flat, starting in the upright or erect position and bending forward at three degrees. Continue to bend to five degrees, then 15 degrees, 45 degrees, and finally 90 degrees. Note how you can prevent your back from arching at the various angles by not raising your head above your shoulder line.

Now, try the same flat-back positions while walking a few steps forward. This exercise is especially good for walking up very steep terrain—for example, when hill walking, where you should avoid arching your back when you lean into the hill.

FLEXIBILITY

The lower back and the hip joints and muscles take the most stress from walking. Stretch out your lower back by bending fully forward from time to time and also by arching your back. Stretch from side to side to stretch out hip and abdominal muscles while walking.

45 degrees.

90 degrees; upper body is perpendicular with lower body.

**Back arch prone:
use arms to gently lift
torso up to stretch,
strengthening the back.**

Torso raising and lowering while you walk.

STRENGTHENING

Strengthen your abdominal and lower-back muscles to help you keep
your middle body erect. Sit-ups or short-range abdominal curls will do
the trick. Strengthen your lower back with back lifts from the prone
position or by raising and lowering your torso as you walk.

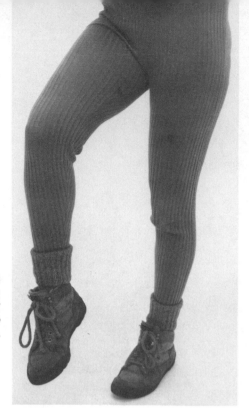

Point your feet in the direction of travel to maintain proper leg and hip position. Raise or lower your leg to accommodate the ruggedness of the terrain.

LOWER POSTURE

BIOMECHANICS

Keep your feet pointed in the line of travel, moving them parallel on rugged terrain—the photo on page 96 shows parallel foot placement—or overlapping them slightly, one over the other, on flat smooth surfaces, as shown in the photographs.

You can control your lower posture with the position of your feet, just as you guided your upper-body posture with the position of your head. Direct your feet forward, up, or down to maintain the proper leg and hip position.

If your feet and ankles do not flex fully (that is, do not achieve their full range) to accommodate your uneven terrain, you will employ other parts of your body unnecessarily and, therefore, feel unnecessary fatigue and muscle strain in your lower-leg muscles. Also, if you lift your legs too high off the ground when swinging them forward, you lean your upper body too far forward. If your legs do not bend and straighten fully with each walking step, you will feel more tension and fatigue in your front and back thigh muscles. Therefore, full flexing and extension are the goals in each of the posture stances.

FLEXIBILITY

Stretch out muscles by bending and fully straightening them before, during, and after the walk by working them to their full length. On short, stepping walks such as those on mountains, you can compensate by taking longer steps or by stretching out the muscles before and after the walk.

STRENGTHENING

The stronger your leg and hip muscles are, the less work will be shifted away from them onto your shoulders and back. Leg extensions with weights strengthen your quadricep muscles. Step-ups strengthen your quads and buttock muscles. Heel raises strengthen your calf muscles. These exercises will help you hold your leg posture, particularly when going up steep inclines.

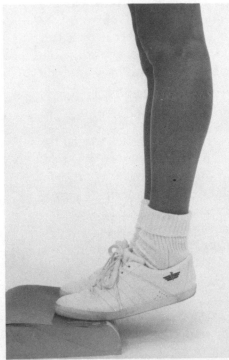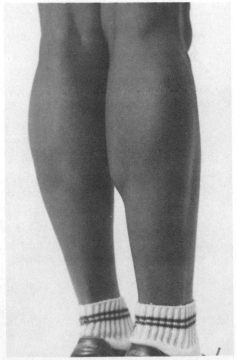

Heel raises strengthen and better define your calf muscles.

BODY PARTS IN ACTION

Whereas posture exercises show you how to hold your body in proper position as you walk, body-part exercises show you how to move your limbs and torso quickly, efficiently, and powerfully. This will help conserve energy while minimizing fatigue and maximizing work output.

The walking action affects three body areas:

1. Middle—Hip and torso action
2. Lower—Leg and foot action
3. Upper—Arm and shoulder action.

Biomechanical, flexibility, and strengthening exercises are integrated into each area.

HIP AND TORSO ACTION

Increases in walking speed are both a function of increased leg repetitions and increased stride length, with the greater gains coming from the latter. Walking with your hips increases your stride length and therefore your walking speed. With beginner walking, you keep your hips square to the line of travel throughout the walking cycle. By letting your hip follow through behind your forward moving leg (down and forward) you can extend the length of each walking step by six to eight inches. Hip extensions can increase your stride length significantly over the square-hip walking style.

If your stride length were limited by the length of your leg, a full stride would not exceed 3½ feet for the average person, no matter how far the legs were extended or spread out. The limit seems to be about 50 degrees. If, however, one hip advances in front of the other, an extra six to eight inches of stride length can be achieved, and the degree of raising and lowering the body with each step can be reduced. This up-and-down motion is wasted energy and can also cause you to lose your balance as you change the center of gravity.

BENEFITS

For hiking, mountaineering, and backpacking, eliminating bobbing will give you more stability on rugged terrain. Hip extension will also give

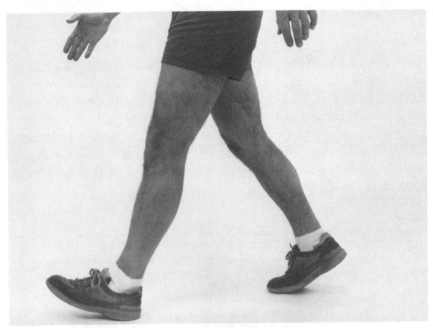

Hip extension: before.

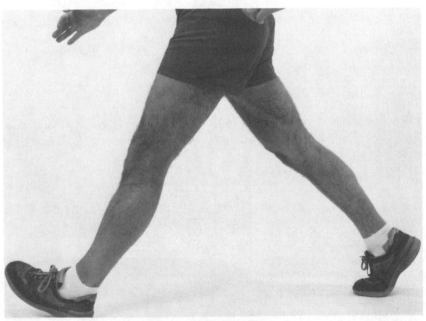

Hip extension: after.

Hip extension is used by hikers like Sylvia because it gives additional stretching and a variety of step lengths to the hiking regimen.

you the capability of stepping over logs, rocks, and crevices, eliminating intermediate positioning steps as well as stretching out hip and upper-leg muscles with a full leg-hip extension from time to time. For long-distance walking and volksmarching, hip extension will conserve your energy for walking more miles without fatigue. And, for racewalking, the hip extension assures maximum walking speed while still complying with racewalk rules (no lifting or bouncing, and no loss of ground contact, or running).

BIOMECHANICS

As your back foot starts to leave the ground and begins to swing under your body, your hip sinks downward, reaching its lowest point when

David Balboa shows the incorrect way; too much side-to-side motion of the hips. David teaches correct racewalking form and has developed Samba Walking: rhythmic walking to a dance beat. He also incorporates walking into his psychotherapy practice.

Darielle shows a skating exercise that helps extend
your hips more forward, rather than side to side.

your leg passes your supporting leg. Now, your hip moves forward and
back up to its normal height as it passes your supporting leg.

Avoid letting your hips sway from side to side in a primarily
horizontal, rather than vertical, forward motion. You'll lose balance and
waste energy. The photo on page 110 shows too much hip swaying,
resulting in a loss of forward motion. The best way to practice walking
with your hips is to imitate the sliding forward of a skater or cross-
country skier, as shown in the photos on page 111. As you step forward,
let each leg slide a few extra inches forward, giving it an extra push with
your hips. Both raising your hips walking in place and stretching your
stride help you to walk using your hips more. Be sure to flatten your
back and tuck your buttocks under your pelvic bone so that you can
better extend your hip with your forward- or upward-moving leg.

Ingrid demonstrates the lunge stretch: the best hip-stretching technique and all-around exercise for walkers.

The hip reaches the lowest point when it passes under the body by the supporting leg.

FLEXIBILITY EXERCISES

Hip and ankle flexibility are the two most important areas for sport-walkers. You can improve the range and smoothness of your hip action by stretching your hips, quadriceps, and lower-back muscles. Walking more with your hips will help improve flexibility in that area. But you should also do flexibility exercises before and after walking, which will, over time, stretch these muscles even further.

Practice at least one stretch, preferably the lunge stretch before walking and the side hip stretch and bend-over stretch while walking.

Choose one or two stretches from the following lower-back and hip stretches to do before or during rest stops.

Lower Back:
- Bend-over stretches while walking
- Legs over head
- Back arch
- Side stretch
- Squat stretch

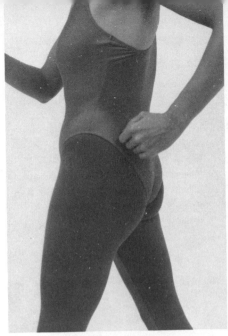

Racewalkers like Ingrid can demonstrate the best hip extension because it is important to their sport.

Give your hip an extra push from behind to stretch out your stride.

Legs over-head stretch helps reduce lower back tension making it easier to work your hips while walking.

Hip Rotations:
- Prone, knees to chest
- Prone, knees to shoulder
- Prone, knee across chest to shoulder
- Legs across shoulder
- Lunge stretch
- Standing hip stretch

The karate lunge kick shows strengthening without weights. From the lunge stretch position, bring your rear leg forward, give a karate kick . . . then return your kicking leg directly to the starting position. Repeat three times on each side.

STRENGTHENING

The wider your stride, the more your hip and abdominal muscles come into play, and the more they are worked and strengthened. The hip flexor muscles are already quite strong but can be strengthened further with the standardized full sit-up, which, ironically, works your hip muscles more than your abdominal muscles.

Also practice the sit-up with a cross-over curl at the end to strengthen your oblique abdominal muscles. The oblique abdominal muscles provide support for your lower back and are important for the hip extension. You use the oblique abdominal muscles in the torso twisting that results from extending your hip and turning the opposite shoulder toward it.

Hip-Strengthening Exercises:
- Karate lunge kick
- Sit-ups (twisting variety is best simulation of walking)
- High steps (skip one or two steps for high leg)

High kick also stretches and strengthens your stepping-out action, and improves your speed.

Curls: Darielle marches in place lifting each leg in turn as high as she can while touching her elbow to her knee.

Abdominal crunches: like a sit-up, except that you pull your knees to your chest as you curl up your abdominal muscles in short quick strokes. Because of the shorter curling distance you can do 25-100 repetitions.

Weight Training:
- Walking action prone with leg weights

Abdominal and Lower-Back Exercises:
- Curls (elbow-knee prone, standing, seated)
- Crunches
- Back extensions (also twisting back extensions)

LEG ACTION

After hip action, leg action is the most important area in sportwalking. You'll want to develop a smoother, longer, and stronger leg action. Striving to take a longer stride with each step will make your walking faster and more efficient. You also reduce fatigue and muscular tension by fully stretching out the leg muscles before they contract and by fully extending, bending, or flexing the various parts of your leg around their hip, knee, and ankle joints.

By planting your foot properly, you keep your body in proper alignment during the leg action. By learning how to contract certain leg muscles while relaxing others, you ensure the proper application of force for minimum loss of energy. For example, you should keep your thigh muscles relaxed as you swing your leg through until your forward leg contacts the ground. Then you should rapidly tense your thighs in order to straighten your leg.

BENEFITS

All leg-action exercises increase walking speed and improve technique, which is particularly important for racewalking. Leg strengthening and hip extension are the two techniques that will help you increase the stride length six to eight inches, maybe more.

With a greater leg reach, you can increase overall walking speed without actually having to move your legs faster. It also provides a wider ranger of strides for adapting to various terrain changes. For long-distance walking, a longer stride not only improves efficiency but also provides a longer leg action, which more fully stretches muscles and therefore keeps them more relaxed and fatigue-free. For volksmarching, longer strides help you vary your walking style enough to refresh without having to break. Increased stride length also helps you accelerate the walking pace whenever you want to pass other walkers and break out of crowded walking conditions.

Prewalking exercises for leg strengthening and flexibility not only improve performance but also cut down training-time preparation for sportwalkers. Stronger quadricep and calf muscles will significantly improve your hill walking and trekking.

Leg-flexibility exercises are important for all sportwalkers to help increase stride length. Full ankle flexibility, for example, not only makes

Double-leg support.   **Left foot forward.**

the leg action go smoothly but also adds inches to your stride. Leg flexibility is very important for improving hiking and climbing; a more fully flexed ankle helps increase walking speed and stride length and reduces fatigue in the lower legs, which can result from climbing or hiking on the balls of the feet and from taking steps that are too short.

BIOMECHANICS

After hip extension, leg extension or straightening is the most important advanced-walking technique. The leg-straightening action occurs as the leg moving forward contacts the ground and begins moving back (it's then the single leg supporting the body). The leg-straightening action ends at the toe-off or when both legs are on the ground briefly in the double-support phase.

Each leg action is divided into three phases: the supporting leg (single and double support), the swinging leg, and the driving leg.

Supporting leg phase. The double-leg support phase is a brief period when both feet are on the ground. It really marks the beginning of the walking action because leg extension or straightening is completed and the toe-off and forward-swing phase is about to begin. The single-leg support phase is really the start of the leg straightening and blends into the double-support phase. The single-leg support is also when your leg moving back pulls under the body and is on its way to becoming your rear driving leg.

The swinging-leg phase: Just skim the surface and . . . raise your leg when the terrain becomes rugged.

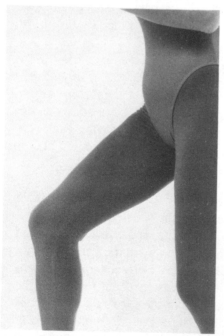

Lead with your knee and use inner thigh and hip flexors.

Pull quadricep muscles back to strengthen your legs. Notice how quadriceps and shins are tense during straightening.

Swinging leg phase.   After you push off with your rear leg, bend it again at the knee so you can pull it under your body and extend it forward. Depending on the terrain, you should raise or lower your leg so that it passes one to three inches above the ground. On smooth, flat ground it should just skim over the surface. On rugged terrain you can adopt a higher swinging style.

The photo on page 118 shows that you lead with your knee and use your inner thigh and hip flexors to swing your leg forward. Keep your lower leg relaxed and in line with the point fixed at your knee, trying not to tense your thigh muscles too much. Use your peripheral vision, to glimpse your kneecap and thigh pushing forward (do not lower your head). Too much tension at this point will actually slow down your leg's forward movement. Instead, you should rely more on your hip muscles to accelerate your leg forward. Your thigh muscles should remain relaxed until your forward-moving leg contacts the ground, whereupon the muscles really go into action, straightening out the leg.

Leg straightening.   You straighten your leg by pulling it back. It is common for many sportwalkers not to extend their legs, avoiding the opportunity to fully stretch the working muscles. The photo on page 120 shows incorrect heel contact with a partially bent leg. Straighten out your leg as soon as your swinging foot contacts the ground. Then, keep it straight as you pull back with your foot. A fully extended leg allows for a longer stride length, not only because it adds inches of leg length, but also by making the leg into a sturdier lever that will help propel the body forward even more.

The photo on page 120 shows how a fully extended leg adds two to three inches to the forward leg action and another three inches to the rear leg action by allowing the rear foot to maintain contact with the ground by rolling up to the toe-off. A straight-leg pull-through also complements the rotation of the opposite hip, allowing it more room to extend forward.

Practice straightening your leg fully the moment your heel touches the ground by locking your knee and tensing up your quadricep muscles, pulling your leg under your body using the front muscles of your upper and lower legs. Keep your leg straight and pull back as it moves from the forward to the rear position. Be sure to hold your leg straight until your rear foot rolls up, onto your toe. The more you prolong this straight leg contact with the ground, the greater the velocity you will achieve.

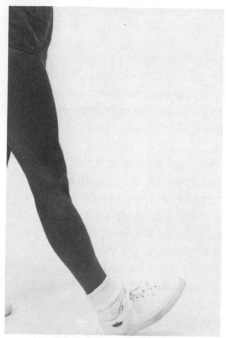 

Incorrect: knee still bent.   **Correct.**

Keep your rear leg straight as you roll all the way up to your toes before pushing forward.

Racewalkers go beyond simple leg straightening to hyperextension. The photo on page 120 shows how the walker's leg bows or bends back, producing even more dynamic tension before the toe-off.

It is a common walking fault not to straighten the leg enough while climbing hills and stairs. The photo on page 126 shows how pressing your heel down will help you stretch out the leg on inclines. And the photo on page 126 shows how you can stretch out on staircases.

Driving leg phase.   The driving leg phase begins when your rear moving and suppporting leg passes under your body and your center of gravity moves ahead of this leg. The leg then begins to accelerate the body forward. Also, at this point the relative position of your leg changes. The leg that was forward is now in the rear, and vice versa.

The rear-leg drive should be forceful (i.e., straight back). The drive should be smooth-flowing, not a kicking or jerking motion. If you push too hard, you'll send your body airborne; if you push too little, you won't make maximum use of the rear driving leg.

STRENGTHENING

Leg strength is an important factor in sportwalking, especially as you propel your body forward when straightening your leg and during the rear-leg drive. While walking many miles contributes to leg strength and muscle development, the following prewalking leg-strengthening exercises accelerate the leg-strengthening process and provide the extra leg power needed for walking up stairs, hills, and mountains, where quadricep and calf muscles are particularly used. There are hundreds of different muscles in your legs; these exercises concentrate on the calf, quadricep, and hamstring muscles.

THE QUADRICEPS

The quadricep muscle group (front of the thigh) is used to straighten and pull the leg back under the body. Various exercises for bending and extending the legs will strengthen the quadricep but not as effectively as half knee bends and the wall seat, where you lean against a wall in a seated position while using your quadricep muscles to raise and lower yourself, as well as hold yourself in the seated position

Exercises with weights.   Exercises using weights accelerate muscle development more effectively than walking does.

Half-knee bends.

Leg extensions.   Using an iron shoe, free weight, or weight-training machine, from the seated position, extend one or both of your legs fully and hold for at least two counts. Slowly lower the leg back down to the count of two. Practice with each leg at least 12 counts per set.

Leg curls with weights.

THE HAMSTRINGS

The hamstring muscles (at the rear of the thigh) are used along with the calf muscles to produce the rear leg drive.

Leg curls with weights.   Leg curls with weights varying from 1 to 10 pounds are the most effective method for strengthening hamstrings. Lying on your stomach (using weights or an exercise apparatus), curl your leg back. It is important to bend it fully back, touching your buttocks with your heel. Do 12 to 20 repetitions for each or both legs.

STRENGTHENING

The foot action is strengthened by bending and flexing the foot and strengthening the calf muscles. The calf muscles are walking's power-house; they are responsible for the final part of the rear-leg drive. Because of their primary use, they need to be stretched out frequently so they will be as long and flexible as possible. However, without ankle flexibility, the calf muscle cannot perform its full function.

Standing heel raises.   Standing on a two-inch block so your ankle is fully flexed, raise your erect body all the way up on your toes and then lower it. Maintain an erect posture during this exercise. Do not let your shoulders advance in front of your body. Do 12 to 20 repetitions per set on each or both legs.

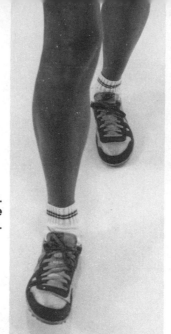

Forefoot landing—incorrect.
Also incorrect to let your knee
pronate inward.

FOOT ACTION

Good foot action is essential for good leg action. The more smoothly your ankles flex during walking, the faster and more energy-efficient your stride will be. You should contact the ground with your heel first, except on steep inclines and stairways with short steps. The photo above shows the incorrect method of landing on the middle or forefoot. When you land on your forefoot, your leg extension and, therefore, your stride length will be shortened. You will also shorten the rolling surface of your feet, impeding the smoothness and fluidity of your walking action.

BIOMECHANICS

Foot placement.   Like posture, foot placement should be adjusted to terrain and changes in walking speed. The advanced walker learns to change the distance between his or her feet depending on the speed and terrain. On a smooth surface, a fast walker can "walk the line" by placing one foot in front of the other. On more rugged and inclined surfaces, a sportwalker can vary foot placement distance to provide maximum stability.

Also, the foot of your forward-moving leg should contact the ground at the back edge of the heel. When setting your heels down, be sure that your toes are pointed straight forward and upward at about a 45-degree angle with the ground. This angle allows your foot to roll forward properly. At this point, it is important to check that your foot is not turned inward or outward so you can't roll needlessly to the left or right. Note also how close the foot passes to the ground. The closer you can swing it to the ground, the more energy you will save and the faster your leg will move forward.

Foot roll.   Your foot should smoothly unroll onto the ground, on the outer edge, not the flat part, and up to the forefront and then the toes. You use the outer edge of your foot because it is the smoothest rolling surface and acts like a rocker. It helps prevent your knee from turning inward while walking. The photo below shows how walking on the flat part of your foot will turn your knee inward. Your rear foot should not leave the ground until you have completely rolled it up to the toes, not just to the forefoot. This will add an average of three inches to your stride length.

When you walk faster, your foot will be almost vertical before you leave the ground. These extra inches also give you extra time to swing your forward foot farther out in front of you. Also be sure that your rear driving foot is pointed in the direction of travel. Some sportwalkers have a tendency to point the foot outward, so look back from time to time to check the position of your foot.

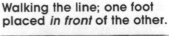

Walking the line; one foot placed *in front* of the other.

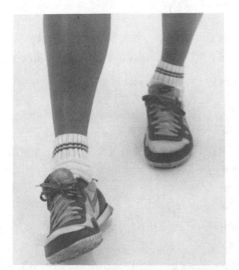

To avoid pronating, set your foot down on its outer edge when taking your forward step.

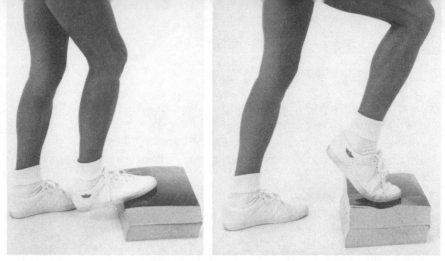

Stair-walking series: Land on forefoot, roll to the heel and back again.

FLEXIBILITY

Try to walk a full ankle flex with every step. The following photos show how you can fully flex your forefeet and ankles in a variety of walking situations. The photo above shows how a heel press-down is easy on a moderate incline, how you must land on your forefoot first before rolling back, and how to complete the heel press down. Toeing-off allows a fuller range off motion.

The series of exercises for leg muscle and ankle stretching and rotation complement the leg-strengthening exercises that follow. The ankle exercises are the most important for improving forward-leg mobility. Practice at least the quadricep/ankle pull and the calf muscle and Achilles tendon stretch as well as knee and ankle rotations during every training session. Then choose one or more of the remaining flexibility exercises as time permits.

Upper-Leg Pull:
- Quadricep and ankle
- Hamstring stretches
- Knee joint rotation

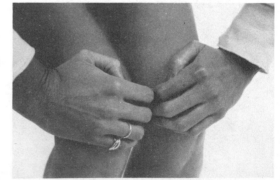

Knee and ankle rotations: Ingrid shows the calf and Achilles tendon stretch you do by leaning forward and bracing yourself on your forward knee. Hold for 6 to 12 seconds and switch leg positions. Be sure to keep your back heel pressed to the ground.

Rotate clockwise and counterclockwise, balancing on the balls of your feet.

Forefoot bend and stretch.

Calf muscle and Achilles tendon stretch.

Lower-Leg Stretches:
- Calf muscle and Achilles tendon stretch
- Ankle rotations for limbering up
- Forefoot bend stretch—Note that you use your hands to help rotate and stretch knee and ankle joints. For example, use your hand to pull back the forefoot against the leg during the quadricep and hamstring stretches.
- Side ankle stretches (left/right)
- Ankle rotations

ARM-SHOULDER ACTION

For exercisewalking, arm pumping and swinging are important to work the upper body while helping propel it forward with the legs. In sportwalking, the arms pump closer to the body, and the shoulders, assisted by the torso muscles involved, initiate and absorb the forward propelling forces of the upper body.

BIOMECHANICS

Arm-shoulder action starts with the rear driving leg, which produces a line of force that goes up through the hip rather than directly through the center of gravity, approximately in the center of the torso behind the belly button. The rear leg drive tends to also rotate the torso rather than just pushing it forward. The swing of the opposite arm and shoulder prevents overrotation and uses less energy. Later, the shoulder rotation is added to the arm swing to help shorten the swing as well as transfer the work away from the arms to the shoulders.

The opposite arm, by swinging against the twisting torso, helps absorb the rotation (so you do not overrotate) and directs the energy in front of the torso. Also, both arms rotating simultaneously in opposite directions of the hips help keep your body stable, reducing the energy requirements needed to correct an overrotation. To prove this to yourself, try walking while keeping your arms anchored by your sides; you'll feel how much more energy you need to move yourself forward while holding back your torso. Each arm is better able to absorb the trunk rotation, rather than the trunk itself, because it is smaller. The arms also keep the hips in check and prevent them from swinging laterally. Thus, the right arm swinging forward helps move the left hip forward (rather than to the right side), and the right arm swinging forward helps move the left hip forward.

The upward swing of the arms, one front and the other back, helps spread the legs farther apart for a longer stride and, therefore, faster walking. Arm swinging also helps keep the body erect. Finally, arm action helps synchronize breathing and leg action for a faster, smoother stride.

There are three basic arm swings, which you should use interchangeably for varying foot placement and walking speed, and for shifting work loads away from muscles.

Straight arm swing:
arms held too far away from the body.

Ingrid's forward hand swing and her back
swings. Note her loosely clenched fist.

Straight forward–straight back arm swing. Swinging the arms
straight forward and back is the most common swing and is particularly
suited to a wide foot placement. It also helps reduce any unnecessary
lateral hip movements. Swing your arms close to your body so that they
lightly brush against it. The photo on page 129 shows an incorrect arm-
swinging position; the arms are held too far from the body. If your arms
are farther away, you will be holding them up as well as swinging them,
thereby causing unnecessary fatigue. In addition, it is difficult to swing
your arms fast when they are too far from your shoulder joints.

It is also important to keep your shoulders relaxed during the arm
swing. Swinging your arms only chest high on the forward swing
(shoulder high on the back swing) and swinging them with a loosely
clenched fist will enable you to keep your shoulder and arm muscles as
relaxed as possible.

Cross-chest arm swing. Faster strides and close foot placement require a tighter arm swing. Bend your arm at an angle of 90 degrees or less and swing it across your chest to midchest.

Shoulder-arm swing. To keep your arms from getting tired, you can shift some of the counter-rotation work to your shoulders, closing your arms even more tightly to your body. Execute the cross-chest arm swing, but slightly rotate your shoulders inward. This method of arm-shoulder swinging also lets you use your oblique abdominal muscles to help move your hips forward. By working your stride in this way, you let your arms relax while you concentrate the body action on your major muscle groups—hips, abdominals, and shoulders—which will not tear as fast. Note in the photo on page 131 how the opposite shoulder and hip come together as they do in a crossover abdominal curl, making that exercise also good for strengthening for the arm-shoulder swing.

During all three swings it is important to keep your shoulders relaxed by not raising or hunching them up as has been incorrectly done in the photo on page 131. Keep shoulders in a steady line as you rotate them forward and back. As you rotate your shoulders with your arm, you will notice that your opposite shoulder rotates slightly backward as the backward arm swing causes the opposite shoulder to rotate forward. This movement is tolerable as long as your shoulders remain relaxed. Also, your shoulders will rise slightly. As your legs pass each other, the shoulder on the side of the swinging leg rises slightly as the opposite shoulder drops. If you are tense, both shoulders will rise.

It is best to use all three of the arm-swinging methods, particularly on long walks where changing the muscles you use will prevent any one group from becoming fatigued too soon. You can also shift to the straight arm swing from time to time. Letting your arms hang down as they are swinging relaxes your arm muscles and reduces the tension in your shoulder muscles.

Remember: Synchronize breathing with your arm swinging. Breathe naturally and rhythmically while you walk, and use the most comfortable combination of lung and diaphragm breathing needed for oxygen consumption. Some sportwalkers have a tendency to hold their breath too long when climbing. Practice breathing while holding your stomach in to learn how to exert force without holding your breath. You should also practice breathing with your belly by pushing your stomach all the way out and all the way in to breathe deeply while walking in a relaxed manner. This method of deep breathing helps you relax your trunk muscles.

Cross chest arm swing: Bend at 90 degrees.

Incorrect: hunching up shoulders while you swing your arms.

Note how I swing my shoulders in toward my chest.

Breathing with stomach held in.

Forward and backward double-arm swing.

FLEXIBILITY

For arm-shoulder swinging, it is important that your shoulder joints be flexible to allow for a full range of arm movement. The following shoulder stretches help improve shoulder mobility, especially on the back swing.

Arm-Shoulder Rotations:
- Single- and double-arm windmills
- Forward and backward double-arm swing
- Cradle swing
- Side and crossover swings
- Shoulder-arm swing

The best single-shoulder flexibility exercise is shoulder shrugs and rotations, which can be done while walking. Choose other flexibility exercises as needed and practice them during rest stops to tighten and relieve muscular tension.

Arm-Shoulder Stretches:
- Extended-arm stretches
- Forward
- Side
- Overhead
- Back

Cradle swing: Clasp your fingers together like this.

STRENGTHENING

The stronger your arm, chest, and shoulder muscles are, the less fatigued you will become from holding up and swinging your arms over many repetitions. Concentrate on strengthening your deltoid muscles. (The deltoid muscles, on top of the shoulder joints, are used to pull your arm backward and forward.) The single most important prewalk shoulder strengthener is the push-up. Arm pumping while holding weights is also very effective for accelerating the muscle development you need for an arm-pumping action. Finally, choose two or three exercises per session from the following:

Without Weights:
- Push-ups
- Arm-ups
- Chin-ups

With Weights:
- Arm-shoulder action with barbells
- Bench press for front shoulder and chest or pectoral muscles
- Dumbbell flyes for chest and shoulders
- Straight-arm pull-overs

BENEFITS

All sportwalkers can benefit from improved arm-shoulder motion as well as flexibility and strengthening exercises. Arm swinging and arm-shoulder strengthening help maintain an erect posture and help walkers hold up and swing arms without tiring too soon. For racewalking, the arm-shoulder technique affords economy of movement—a faster, tighter, and more compact walking style—eliminating lateral movement in favor of forward movement.

For volksmarching and long-distance walking, improved arm-shoulder action provides the ability to shift arm swinging from arms to shoulder and torso and thus spreads out the work so as not to fatigue any muscles too early.

For hiking and mountaineering, short arm-shoulder swinging is an abbreviated upper-body action that complements shorter or faster steps. Shifting from straight-arm to bent-arm to arm-shoulder swings provides

Too much backward leaning.

a variety of upper-body actions to match changes in terrain, speed, and step length.

COMMON WALKING FAULTS

THE WHOLE BODY

Too much forward lean is the most common reaction to overall body fatigue. This not only upsets your posture, but also affects breathing and morale and causes back tension. It also makes it difficult to fully straighten the leading leg. The best solution is to monitor the position of your head and correct it as you walk along so you can walk upright again. A 5- to 15-minute rest stop every walking hour will also help refresh your whole body. Developing stronger stomach and back muscles will help support your body upright.

Backward-leaning trunk. If you lean too far back, you'll shorten your stride length and create a bouncing and jarring effect. Fatigue may be due to weak back muscles and poor back posture. Back-strengthening exercises like the back lift will help improve posture. Tucking the buttocks under the spine will flatten an arched back, thereby straightening the posture.

LEG ACTION

Too much vertical action. Too much vertical action occurs when both the trunk and shoulders rise and fall with each step, causing a bouncing action as well as tension in the upper body. The cause and solutions are as follows:

1. Your rear leg lifts off the ground too soon, from the ball of the foot rather than the toes. Concentrate on heel-toe action and practice ankle-flexibility exercises.
2. Your hips have too much lateral rather than forward swing. Practice pushing your hip forward as your swinging leg passes your supporting leg. Improve your hip flexibility by practicing a series of hip-stretching and rotating exercises. Use a straight forward–straight back arm-swinging style to keep lateral hip swinging in check.
3. Your arm action is too vigorous, or your arm swing is too high (above your chest). Practice shoulder-flexibility exercises and reduce the height of arm swinging.

Difficulty straightening supporting leg. Straightening out your leg requires concentration and muscle power. The causes for not straightening your leg and the solutions are as follows:

1. Your speed is too great for your technical skill. Reduce your speed and concentrate on pulling back your supporting leg when it makes heel contact with the ground. Hold it straight until foot rolls up to the toes.
2. Your leg muscles are weak. Practice fully straightening and bending your legs while walking more slowly. Also practice extension exercises with weights.
3. Your hamstring muscles are too tight to allow for a full stretch. Practice hamstring stretches.
4. You are leaning forward too far. Practice upper-posture exercises.

ARM-SHOULDER ACTION

Shoulders rise and fall. If shoulders rise and fall, this results either from excessive or uncontrolled arm swinging. Concentrate on good technique and slow rhythmic arm swinging. This walking fault may also result from tense shoulder muscles. Windmill exercises and shoulder shrugs help relax your shoulders during arm-shoulder swings.

Dr. Mort Malkin demonstrates: Foot falls, legs look stiff.

Leading foot falls forward. When your stride is too long, your forward-swinging leg looks stiff and thrown forward. It lands with a thud rather than a smooth motion, making you bend your rear leg too soon to keep up with this overextension. Shorten your stride length to smooth out your gait. This phenomenon also occurs when your leading leg swings forward too high off the ground. Direct your forward-moving foot so it just skims across the ground, and use more vertical hip action.

HIP ACTION

Too much lateral hip swaying. Too much lateral hip swaying means you are probably forcing the hip extension rather than trying to achieve it through natural hip action. Slow down your walking speed and concentrate on basic hip extension as well as straight back-and-forth arm swinging.

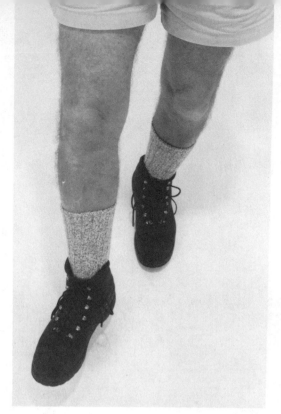

**Splayed
foot action.**

FOOT ACTION

Wobbly foot placement.   When foot placement is wobbly, it is
difficult to keep your balance. Poor balance may really be the cause of
the problem. Straight-line foot placement requires good balance, flexibility, and practice. Try walking a straight line of 25 yards on your toes,
then again on your heels to help improve your balance. Then practice
walking on a straight line with heel-toe action so that your inner soles
just touch the line but do not go over it. Be sure that your arm action and
hip action are correct and are not themselves putting you off balance.

Swinging your arms from your body can put you off balance, as can
much hip swaying from side to side. Your thighs may be too big to allow
close, easy passage of your leg for straight-line foot placement. If this is
the case, place your feet more widely to accommodate your own
walking. Your thighs should only brush lightly against one another.

In complete heel-toe rolls, your feet may be pointed too far outward.
Be sure to point both feet in the direction of travel throughout the heel-
toe roll. A splayed foot action will make it difficult to roll completely off
your outer foot.

7
DISTANCE TRAINING

SPORTWALKING IS PRIMARILY an endurance or distance event. Most walking endurance is achieved by walking increasingly greater distances at higher speeds.

Endurance, both general and specific, is the body's capacity to work (walk) for a prolonged period of time without becoming tired or breaking down. General endurance is the ability to walk long distances with easy to moderate effort. Specific endurance is the capacity to work at greater intensity commensurate with the goals or requirements of the sportwalk event.

Distance training uses *continuous* walking and *interval* walking routines to build up both general and specific endurance. If you are not already at a good fitness level (minimum is Level III), you will build up your general endurance until you reach Level III. From there, while continuing to build up your general endurance, you will add specific endurance training for your specific sportwalking goals. In other words, you will train to distance levels that are related to the distances of your planned sportwalk event(s).

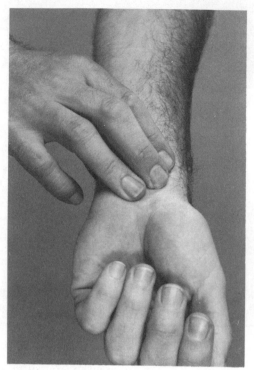

Take training pulse at wrist or neck.

TYPES OF TRAINING AND THE TRAINING EFFORT

The training effort is the distance, frequency, and rate of speed, or intensity level, at which you train. It is measured as a percentage of your maximum effort (a percentage of your best walking speed measured over a specific distance—usually more than a mile). When you are training for a specific sportwalking event, it may be helpful to measure your training effort as a percentage of your best walking speed over the same distance as the event.

There are various types of distance training—continuous, interval, mixed, and extended. They are distinguished not only by the distance walked but also by the training effort put into the walk. The training effort also varies according to the conditioning or "training fitness" of the individual sportwalker.

CONTINUOUS WALKING

Continuous walking means walking an extended distance at a set pace without any breaks for recovery. This type of walking trains your whole body, conditioning it to use food and oxygen to produce energy. Continuous walking training is the equivalent of aerobic walking in exercisewalking.

By gradually building up the number of your continuous walking miles and the pace at which you walk them, you will be able to exert a 100 percent effort for the sportwalk itself and become more physically fit to boot. During the general endurance-training phase, you can also substitute other forms of continuous or aerobic exercise like running, cross-country skiing, skating, biking, swimming, and aerobic dancing. While these will improve your cardiovascular (heart-lung) conditioning, most will not train the same muscles used in walking. So you have to come back to walking training at least when you are developing your specific endurance. This is true for all sports training routines. The best way to train for a sport is to practice the sport itself. Substitute training methods will improve and accelerate sport practice, but they cannot replace it completely.

You can also accelerate both your specific and general endurance training with resistance walking and strength training, which are particularly helpful if you start your training late in the season or if your sportwalk event(s) require more muscle strength, as mountain walking does. Resistance walking includes weight-loaded walking. You can use weight walking as aerobic training, instead of jogging. If you want to learn more about weight walking, read *Gary Yanker's Walking Workouts*, which contains extended weight-walking routines and programs. They are not included here because sportwalk events rarely require attaching weights to your limbs, although occasionally participants carry a weight-loaded backpack.

For general endurance, a sportwalker can train by walking continuously at a lower effort, between 50 and 75 percent of his or her maximum effort. In general, your continuous walking speed will be 75 percent of your maximum walking speed measured for one mile. Of course, for sportwalking you also need specific endurance training. This means you will have to train under the specific conditions of your planned sportwalk(s).

For specific endurance, continuous walking should be 75 percent of the rate you wish to perform for a sportwalk of a specific distance. This

SAMPLE CONTINUOUS WALKING ROUTINES

Type of Walk	Training Effect	Training Period	Purpose
Long-distance hiking or backpacking in the mountains, 6 to 10 hrs.	General endurance	Off-season	Relaxation
75%-effort road or track walk, 1 to 5 hrs. (3 to 20 mi.)	General endurance	Build-up, pre-event participation	Technique, distance training
Hill walking for 2 hrs. (up and down)	General and specific endurance	Build-up	Variety and relaxation
Mixed walking at 75% and 50% effort, 2 to 3 hrs.	General endurance	Build-up and off-season	Variety and relaxation
Mixed walking at 75% and 100% effort, up to 2 hrs.	General and specific endurance	Pre-event participation	Fartlek (speed play) training (see Chapter 8)
Walking at 100% effort, 10% to 25% of sportwalk distance	Specific endurance	Pre-event and event participation	Trial walk for speed
Walking at 75% effort, 50% to 100% of sportwalk event distance	General and specific endurance	Build-up, pre-event participation	Trial walk for distance

SAMPLE CONTINUOUS WALKING ROUTINES (Continued)

Type of Walk	Training Effect	Training Period	Purpose
Walking at 100% to 110% effort over short distance, 200 yd. to 3 mi.	Speed training	Pre-event racewalking	Trial walk for speed
Walking at 100% effort, 75% to 100% of sportwalk event distance	Specific endurance	Pre-event	Trial walk 2 to 4 wks. before event

may be higher or lower than 75 percent of your walking rate. Likewise, if you are hill walking, you'll have to train using a sloped terrain or an equivalent type of resistance walking (i.e., sloped treadmill or stairs).

Any walk of over one mile qualifies for continuous distance training. The table gives some examples of continuous walking routines during the various walking season training periods.

INTERVAL WALKING

Whereas continuous walking helps improve both your general and specific endurance, interval walking works mainly on your specific endurance. It usually involves walking a shorter distance with a series of more intense efforts (90 to 100 percent of maximum effort) interspersed with rest breaks. Interval walking helps you prepare for your specific sportwalk performance. It helps you narrow down your training effort so you can achieve a specific distance at a specific pace. If the distance is long, you can build up to it with a series of interval performances that add up in mileage to the final distance. In the next chapter, you will also use interval walking, but for a faster rate over a shorter distance to help you train for sportwalks that are shorter and more oriented to speed performance. Interval walks for endurance range from 880 yards up to three miles. In speed training, you will also do interval walking at shorter ranges (220 to 880 yards), as described in the next chapter.

You should rest from 5 to 15 minutes on interval walks of under three miles. Allow your pulse rate to return to below 50 percent of your maximum training rate but not higher than 120 beats per minute. For distances above three miles, you should rest as follows: 15 to 60 minutes every 3 to 12 miles, and 1 to 12 hours every 12 to 50 miles. Don't start interval walking until you have established a good foundation with continuous walking and reached Fitness Level III.

The next table gives a sampling of interval walking routines for distance training. Note that you can fashion your own routines by varying the distances and speed of the walk, as well as the frequency and length of the rest periods. Rest time of 5 to 60 minutes between long-distance walking intervals will do the trick when interval training for walks over 50 miles. You should plan on two or more training days using overnights as your rest periods. Your total interval walking mileage should add up to the event distance. No interval should be longer than half the distance of the sportwalk you are training for.

SAMPLE INTERVAL WALKING ROUTINES

Event	Distance/Frequency (Training Intervals)	Training Effort	Rest	Training Effect
1–3 mi.	5 1-mi. walks or 2 2.5-mi. walks	75%	15 min.	General and specific endurance
12 mi.	4 3-mi. walks or 2 6-mi. walks	75%	30 min.	General and specific endurance
20.6–50 mi.	3 9-mi. walks or 2 13.3-mi. walks	50%–75%	1 hr.	General and specific endurance
50–100 mi. (1-day or 24-hr. event)	1st day, 25 mi.; 2nd day, 25 mi., *or*	50%	12 hrs.	Specific endurance
	1st day, 50 mi.; 2nd day, 25 mi.	75%	12 hrs.	Specific endurance

MIXED WALKING

You can combine continuous and interval walking into one-day training sessions, but instead of resting, slow down your walking pace to a stroll. When you are going fast, your effort may vary between 75 percent and 100 percent. When you are going slow, your effort is in the range of 50 to 75 percent.

EXTENDED DISTANCE TRAINING

Extended distance training uses continuous walking to train beyond the distance of the planned sportwalk. Start practicing extended walking at the end of the build-up period. It will give you a greater level of general endurance and, therefore, greater confidence. It also allows you to train ahead for the longer sportwalks on your schedule.

SPORTWALKING FITNESS AND ENDURANCE

Your training effort is related not only to your walking speed, but to your current level of cardiovascular endurance. So, the more conditioned you are, the higher the effort at which you will be able to train. You will be able to raise your walking speed over longer distances by increasing your endurance. Therefore, you should monitor not only your speed but also your heart training rate as you do when exercisewalking.

TRAINING FITNESS

Your training fitness is a combination of several factors: the cumulative and continuous miles you can walk, your continuous walking speed, and your pulse rate. These indicate the progress of the training or conditioning effect. They also help you meet the intermediate goals on your way to your first sportwalk, subsequent walks, and your most challenging walk of the season.

You have to determine and monitor your initial training fitness level to know the mileage and speed levels at which you can start training. Thereafter, you should monitor your progress in terms of training fitness levels. As you increase levels, you can increase the rate at which you add miles and increase your walking speed. The fitter you get, the faster you can accelerate your progress.

There are two methods for measuring and monitoring your training fitness levels—the pulse-rate method and the distance/speed method.

The pulse-rate method. The pulse-rate method monitors your current training effort and enables you to compare walking efforts on flat, sloped, and rugged terrain, because you are measuring not just the speed of the effort but also how hard your muscles and heart-lung system work in combination. Measure your pulse rate from time to time to determine whether you are walking at a heart training rate, which is 70 to 85 percent of your maximum heart training rate. This is the zone where the most efficient conditioning results. It also correlates with the speed zone, i.e., walking at 75 percent of your maximum walking effort for about one mile.

The training effect takes place at all heart rates above the resting rate, but if you train at a lower rate, you have to go a greater distance. Thus, 50 percent heart training effort for 6 continuous miles equals a 75 percent effort for 4 continuous miles.

$$50\% \times 6 \text{ miles} = 3 \text{ miles}$$
$$75\% \times 4 \text{ miles} = 3 \text{ miles}$$

Your maximum heart training rate is determined by subtracting your age from 180. To measure your training pulse rate, count your heart beats for six seconds while training. If you find it difficult to take a measurement while walking, stop walking for the few seconds it takes to count. Now, divide this by your maximum heart training rate to arrive at your current training rate or effort.

Thus, if your heart beats 12 times in 6 seconds, then your beats per minute are 120 (12 × 10). If your age is 30, your maximum training rate is 150 (180 − 30) and your current rate or training effort is 80 percent (120 divided by 150 is ⁴/₅, or 80 percent). You are within the continuous walking training zone (70 to 85 percent). I am often asked if it is necessary to train so that your heart rate is in the 70 to 85 percent training zone to get results. The answer is yes and no. The training effect takes place at all heartbeats above the resting rate, so you can train at a lower rate. It just takes longer because you go a greater distance. Thus, 50 percent heart training effort times six continuous miles equals a 75 percent effort times three continuous miles.

$$50\% \times 6 \text{ miles} = 3 \text{ miles}$$
$$75\% \times 4 \text{ miles} = 3 \text{ miles}$$

The speed/distance method.   A really quick way to monitor your training effort without stopping is to compare your *heart rate* with your *step rate*. You'll find that your step rate is a good estimate of your training rate in the so-called aerobic training zone. This is the middle walking speed zone of 3½ miles per hour (100 steps per minute or spms) to five miles per hour (140 spms) where most sportwalkers train. You can use the six-second count method to make your own more accurate beat-per-minute step-per-minute correlations by comparing the speed of your heart against your step rate. Count your steps for six seconds and multiply by ten for your steps per minute rate. This is the first part of the speed/distance method of measuring your training effort. The other part involves measuring your walking speed over a series of endurance distances (over one mile in length). Determine your specific walking training fitness by comparing your long, intermediate, and short-distance performance levels to the charts on page 148. These have been correlated to levels of fitness needed to complete these distances at a continuous walking training rate.

ORGANIZING YOUR DISTANCE TRAINING PROGRAM

Your distance training should be varied, progressive, and directed. *Variety* is at the heart of sportwalking. You should not only vary your course from track to field but also vary your type of training.

LONG DISTANCE: MILES WALKED IN ONE DAY (10 HOURS)

Fitness Level	Walking Distance (10 Hours)
I	1–9 miles
II	10–19 miles
III	20–29 miles
IV	30–39 miles
V	40–49 miles

INTERMEDIATE DISTANCE: MILES WALKED IN ONE HOUR

Fitness Level	Miles Per Hour
I	1–2
II	2–3
III	3–4
IV	4–5
V	5–10

Or, compare your walking speed over one mile.

SHORT DISTANCE: MINUTE MILE PACE FOR ONE MILE

Level	Minutes Per One Mile
I	30–60 minutes
II	20–30 minutes
III	15–20 minutes
IV	12–15 minutes
V	10–12 minutes

Progress in distance training takes place over weeks or months. Six-week training periods are the normal times when your progress reaches new plateaus. But you can reach new plateaus more quickly throughout the different training periods of the walking season. During the off-season and event-participation period, your training will remain at relatively constant levels. During the build-up period, you will train for longer times and distances and with greater intensity as your conditioning increases.

Directed means that your training should be organized so that you become fit in time to participate in the sportwalk event you have selected. This means matching the progress of the program so that you reach your fitness peaks by the event.

A distance-training session is really a microcosm of the whole sportwalking program. It includes all sections of the other special training sessions, with the primary focus on increasing your mileage and increasing your walking speed. Distance training also incorporates shorter versions of all the other more in-depth types of training: techniques, strength, speed, and flexibility. While walking, you will also concentrate on improving your technique.

Each training session will include a minimum of flexibility exercises for those body areas you work more. You will also do a minimum number of strength exercises, such as push-ups and sit-ups. In the distance-walking portion, concentrate on building up both your walking mileage and your walking pace. But, remember, the primary focus is on walking miles.

BUILDING UP MILEAGE

Building up walking mileage is the most important conditioning factor and takes the greatest part of the training time. In each distance-training session, practice one or more continuous walks at a set distance for a set pace. These walks are short (under three miles) or longer (three to five miles), depending on the type of sportwalk(s) you are training for.

Build the pace as you build the distance. Table 7–1 serves as a guide for building up your mileage. The goal is to increase your total weekly training mileage so that it equals the distance of the sportwalk you are training for.

TABLE 7–1
MILEAGE INCREASES BY TRAINING LEVEL

Level	Mileage Range Per Week	Increase in Mileage Per Week	Frequency of Mileage Increase
I	1½–7	¼	Every 14 miles
II	14–21	1	Every 7 miles
III	22–28	2	Every 7 miles
IV	29–49	3	Every 7 miles
V	50+	4	Every 7 miles

BUILDING UP SPEED/PACE

The pace you set for distance training depends on both your walking speed and your training fitness level. Your continuous walking speed will range from 3 to 5 miles per hour for most long-distance walks of over five miles) but up to 10 miles per hour for short racewalks. Your ability to sustain a faster walking pace over a distance will increase week to week during the build-up and the event-participation periods. Use time trials to keep track of your best walking time over the series of sportwalk distances you plan to do. This will help you monitor your progress in developing endurance.

Note how each fitness level represents a certain number of weeks as well as cumulative hours and miles of walking training.

STEP-BY-STEP METHOD

Use a step-by-step method to build up your walking mileage and pace to reach your sportwalk goals. First, establish your current training fitness level and make a note of your current longest walk at a steady pace. This is your base line from which to add miles and subtract minutes. Match your base line to the miles and pace of a similar training week in Table 7-2.

Build up your pace and miles according to the training schedule or organize your own training program using the training rules in the box nearby.

Once you have established your base line, calculate the number of walking hours it will take you to reach your new speed and distance goal. For example, if you are now walking 6 continuous miles at 3 miles per hour, and you want to walk 20 miles at 4 miles per hour, you can start to raise your walking mileage from 1 to 5 miles a week, depending on your current training fitness. Levels I and II can increase 1 mile for every 3 to 4 hours of continuous walking training per week. Level III can increase 2 to 3 miles for every 4 to 5 hours per week, Level IV can add 3 miles, and Level V can add 4 to 5 miles per week. Increases in walking speed also depend on a number of additional factors such as technique and strength training and are more difficult once you have reached a speed of over 5 miles per hour or 12 minutes a mile.

Most sportwalkers will strive to maintain a steady pace ranging from 3½ to 5½ miles per hour, or 7- to 11-minute miles. With racewalking you'll be able to hold your long-distance pace between 5½ and 7½ miles per hour or 8- to 11-minute miles.

Speed increases in the first range can come in the first 12 to 24 weeks of regular training. Regular training is in the range of 3 to 8 hours a week. Increases thereafter will take months more of regular training or an increase in training hours to 8 to 20 hours per week.

TABLE 7-2
YEAR-ROUND PROGRAM

Fitness Level	Weeks	Miles per Day	Hours per Week	Miles per Week
I	1–6	1–2	1–2	1–9
II	7–13	2–3	2–3	8–13
III	14–20	3–4	3–4	14–27
Maintenance Level	21–27	4–5	4–6	28–32
IV	28–34	6–7	6–7	33–39
V	35–40	8	7–8	40–49
V	41–46	9	9–10	50–59
V	47–51	10	10	60–69

20-WEEK ACCELERATED PROGRAM (LEVEL III TO LEVEL V)

Week No.	Hours per Week (L/M/H)	Miles per Week (L/M/H)
1	4/8/12	14/35/50
2	4/8/12	15/35/54
3	4/8/12	16/36/58
4	4/8/13	17/37/62
5	5/9/13	18/38/66
6	5/9/14	19/39/70
7	5/9/14	20/40/75
8	5/9/15	21/41/79
9	6/10/15	22/41/83
10	6/10/16	23/42/87
11	6/10/16	24/43/92
12	6/10/17	25/44/96
13	7/11/17	26/45/100
14	7/11/18	27/46/104
15	7/11/18	28/47/108
16	7/11/19	29/47/112
17	8/12/19	30/48/116
18	8/12/20	32/49/120
19	8/12/20	33/49/120
20	8/12/20	35/50/125

L = low, M = medium, H = high

TRAINING RULES

1. Choose a sportwalk that will correspond to your training fitness level a week before the event. The sportwalk distance you choose should equal your cumulative training mileage for the week that falls two weeks before the event. In other words, plan your mileage-building program based on how many weeks it will take you to reach the event mileage level.

2. Train to reach the mileage/speed level for your sportwalk event by increasing your distance gradually, based on the rate of increase for your training fitness level. At any time during your training program, you can participate in a sportwalk event whose total distance and average speed for completion equal your total weekly training mileage and your average weekly training pace.

3. If you want to target an event that is above your training level you must add extra training distance and time to each week of walking based on the following formula. In effect you will be accelerating your training schedule by adding more training hours. Depending on your current training fitness level, each distance and speed increment represents additional training hours.

4. You should train at 75 percent effort (the speed defined as .75 times your maximum walking speed over one mile) three times a week and at 100 percent effort two times a week. Your interval walking effort will be 90 to 100 percent. You'll find that your training effort will grow stronger week after week and that your actual maximum walking speed will go up. Test yourself every one to six weeks.

YEAR-ROUND MILEAGE BUILDING ACCORDING TO FITNESS LEVEL

The year-round chart allows you to schedule mileage and training levels week-to-week starting with the beginner's level. An accelerated program is shown starting at Fitness Level III. It is the most likely level at which you will start your sportwalking training, the level to which you will return during the off-season, and the minimum level you will want to build up to and maintain for basic walking fitness.

Note that the weekly mileage should approximate the sportwalk event mileage levels. For example, you must reach the beginning of Level IV

5. Practice a time or distance trial not later than two weeks before the event. Both the speed and distance of the trial should be equal to the distance of the sportwalk if it is under 12 miles and 75 to 100 percent of the distance if the sportwalk is over 12 miles long.

6. Gradually increase your weekly walking pace as you increase your distance. Decrease your average training time per mile by one-quarter minute to one minute, depending on your training fitness level. Each week, Level I decreases time by five minutes per mile (i.e., from 60-minute to 30-minute miles in six weeks). Level II decreases time per mile at the rate of two minutes per mile per week. Level III decreases time at the rate of one minute per mile per week. Level IV decreases time at the rate of half a minute per mile per week. Level V decreases your time at the rate of one-quarter minute per mile per week. Note that although the distance increases as you get fitter, it is more difficult to increase the speed as you approach maximum walking speed.

7. You can use the sportwalks themselves as trial walks by scheduling them two weeks apart and using the "step method" of increasing your speed and distance. Table 7-2 contains the "step increases" in speed according to the hours of walking practice. Choose a distance or speed performance, and reach it by gradually raising your levels of speed and distance.

8. Over the long term it is important to gradually increase to the intermediate distances given in Table 7-2. Practice according to the hours and duration of training recommended for each level. Target a goal expressed in terms of distance and pace. Each distance goal corresponds to the level of training fitness you must reach at least one week before the sportwalk event.

to do a 10-hour, 50-mile hike. You must reach the top of Level V to be in shape for an Olympic racewalking trial. There's really not much more time in the week to train above 125 miles, although you could walk 35 to 50 miles a day for seven days a week to bring the average to 245 to 350 miles per week. But, this is unusual. You wouldn't want to train at this level in preparation for any walk.

EXAMPLE: 50-MILE HIKE

Let's say you wanted to do a 50-mile hike in 10 hours. Here's how you should prepare. Train over the next weeks and months to reach Fitness Level V. Your accumulated training mileage for one week should reach

50 miles. Of course, you could probably manage to walk 50 miles at a lower fitness level, but you will not be able to finish it in 10 hours, and you will undoubtedly be very sore and stiff the next day. To complete the hike in 10 hours, you'll have to walk an average of 5 miles per hour. Your weekly training rate should be at 75 percent of 5 mph or 3.85 mph or a 16-minute mile. Your actual walking speed will increase from 3 to 3.85 mph during the period. If you are unable to walk that fast right away, you are probably not yet fit enough to do the walk and will have to train for a period of weeks, gradually building up your pace at lower speeds.

Don't train at the 50-mile distance, but divide the total mileage among a series of 3 to 5 weekly training periods. If you train 5 times a week, you should eventually be able to walk 10 miles each session day.

If five miles a week is all you are fit to walk, you'll have to make up the mileage during long weekend walks. First, you have to determine what kind of continuous walk you can complete in 1 day by measuring your walking fitness. Let's say you can walk 20 miles in 10 hours. The top chart on page 148 shows you are at Level III. Use 20 miles as your starting point and build up the additional 30 miles at the rate of 3 miles per week. In the current example, 3 additional miles per week would take 10 weeks of walking training.

EXAMPLE: 12-MILE VOLKSMARCH

Let's say you were a beginning walker who wanted to finish a 12-mile volksmarch in a day. Your current level of walking fitness is I, or poor, meaning that you can finish at most a five-mile walk. From Level I you will add one mile per week for seven weeks. You'll also be walking weekly at a base mileage of five plus the additional miles.

Assuming an average of three hour-long sessions of walking per week, you would train for 2 to 2½ miles per session, gradually adding mileage increments and increasing your weekly training time. Of course, at distances under 12 miles, some walkers will progress faster.

EXAMPLE: 20-KILOMETER OR 12-MILE RACEWALK

The 12-mile distance racewalk requires not only mileage building as it does with volksmarching, but also speed building. Say you can now walk a mile in 15 minutes and can sustain this pace over three miles before getting tired. You are between a Level III and IV walker. You want to improve so you can walk 12 miles at the average rate of 12 minutes each.

A 15-minute mile puts you at the high end of Level III, meaning that you can increase your walking speed at the rate of one minute per mile per week, if you train nine hours per week. It would take you three weeks or 27 hours of training to improve your performance. But you also have to increase your mileage. Mileage building at your level can be at the training rate of three miles per week or 2¼ hours extra training time. Each three-mile addition adds approximately 45 minutes to your weekly training schedule. By combining distance and speed increases, you would train an extra 29½ hours. Each speed increase of one minute would also add three hours to your weekly training time.

During the special three-week training period, you would also practice interval walking with shorter walking distances where you could manage a mile in 12 minutes or faster. You would start with 220 yards and gradually increase the distance. By completing interval walking segments that total 12 miles, you should be able to raise your average continuous pace over the whole distance.

Finally, to improve your performance, you must also practice speed, strength, and technique training along with endurance training. And, if your target is faster than a 12-minute mile, it will be difficult to progress as quickly as this example indicates.

Mark Bricklin demonstrates close-in arm-shoulder swinging.

8
SPEED TRAINING

Speed training follows distance training in the sequence of exercises because the two are often done together. Basically, speed training involves walking fast over short distances using faster forms of interval walking. Eventually, you will be integrating your speed work into your distance work by using it to raise your continuous walking speed.

Speed training should be practiced only once or twice every week, as it can be exhausting. In general, you should do your speed training when you are fresh, either at the beginning of a distance-training session, on a separate day from distance training, or several hours before or after other types of training. Don't forget to do warm-up and cool-down exercises at the beginning and end of any speed-training session. Probably the best way to integrate your speed training into your regular walking training is to divide up your training distance for the week into distance and speed segments.

MAXIMUM WALKING SPEED

With timed trials, establish your fastest walking speed for short distances (200 to 300 yards) and long distances (1 to 5 miles). Use an average of these speeds as your maximum short- and long-distance speed upon which to base you speed training rate. From there you can monitor your improvement. Your distance-training speed is 75 percent of your walking speed for one mile. Your speed-training rate is about 90 to 110 percent of your speed for that effort. Speed-training effort is your best training time for any walking distance of 880 yards (three-quarters of a mile) or less. Short distances are between one-eighth and one-half of a mile.

THE SPEED CONTINUUM

You can use short-distance speed training to boost your continuous walking speed. Establish your three base speeds for walking 100 yards, one mile, and three miles. From these baselines, you'll be able to monitor your speed increases.

BENEFITS

Walking faster over short distances helps test your maximum speed, and over time you'll be able to train your legs to move faster even over long distances. For most sportwalkers, speed training provides an important *psychological* advantage by breaking the artificial speed barriers that come from being set in your walking ways. Even self-paced walking requires short bursts of speed to pass fellow walkers or finish the event on time. Speed training up and down hills develops the muscular endurance needed for climbing mountains and strengthens legs.

How often you speed train depends on whether your sportwalk goals are related to speed or long distance. If you are racewalking, every other day would not be out of order during the build-up period. For long-distance walking, once a week is the maximum needed.

METHODS

There are three methods of speed training: (1) interval walking, (2) time trials, and (3) Fartlek (speed play) walking.

It's best to practice your speed training on a flat, smooth surface such as a track, a straightaway, or a smooth trail. You do not want to fall or be interrupted by others while practicing. A quarter-mile track is probably the best course.

Check increases in your walking speed every few weeks. You'll find that better technique, greater mileage, and increased leg strength will all help increase your continuous-distance speed. In addition, every few months, you'll also note some increases in your short-distance walking speed. Use these to raise the speed of your 75 percent training effort.

Interval speed training. Interval speed training is like interval walking, but the effort is greater (at 90 to 110 percent), and the distances are shorter. Do not start speed training until you have built up your general endurance to Level III.

You have two options for practice:

1. Determine your base speeds in steps per minute and minute-miles for several short distances such as 100 yards, 440 yards (one-quarter mile), and one mile. Convert these speeds into miles per hour. Use your 100-yard speed as your fastest walking speed. This maximum rate is really to determine your top steps per minute, or just how fast you can move your legs. You can convert the time it took you to walk 100 yards into a minute-mile figure by multiplying the number of seconds by 14.27 (or 14, rounded off), which is the number of 100-yard segments in a mile. Divide by 60 seconds for the minute miles.

2. Choose a speed-training distance between 25 yards and 880 yards that correlates with your sportwalking distance goals. The longer the sportwalk distance, the longer your short-distance speed training should be. If you are planning to walk long distances (20 to 50 miles), practice 440- to 880-yard segments. If you are planning to walk intermediate distances (12 to 20 miles), practice 220 to 440 yards. And for short-distance sportwalks under 12 miles, 100 to 220 yards. Basically, you should speed train at a distance of 20 yards for every mile in your planned sportwalk event. If the event is 35 miles, your speed-training distance can be 20 times 35 yards, or 700 yards. If it is 12 miles, then it should be 12 times 20, or 240 yards, or one-eighth of a mile.

Establish your fastest speed and the training frequency for your speed-training distance by determining *how many times* you can walk this distance at a speed that is nine-tenths of your fastest time and until you are too tired to continue. This will be your *base frequency* rate. Allow sufficient recovery time between intervals. Your heartbeats should return to 120 beats per minute between trials. Now, take an average of all your speeds within the 90 percent maximum rate zone. This will be your base speed.

During your next speed-training session, either increase your base frequency by one or increase your base speed by 10 percent, but do not do both. Each time you speed train, you can either add more frequency or walk faster during each interval. If you add intervals, you should do the speed walks below your last average. If you go faster with the same frequency, you should increase the speed of each effort, trying to raise your average speed above your base average.

Limit your frequency of intervals to 3 to 20. You can eventually do up to 15 intervals at the selected distance. Or you can start another speed-training series at another distance, say 880 yards, splitting five intervals at 880 yards with 10 at 440.

Time trials.   Time trials are speed walks ranging from one to six miles where you try to translate speed gains made in interval training into a longer distance. A time trial is one effort rather than many.

Practice time trials for distances that relate to the sportwalk(s) you are training for. The longer your planned sportwalk, the longer the trial walk. Here are the correlations:

Time Trial (miles)	Sportwalk Event (miles)
1	1–6
2	7–15
3	16–24
4	25–31
5	32–40
6	41–50

Time trials of over 20 miles should be done only once before the sportwalk event.

Here's how to increase your speed-trial walking speed. Say your one-mile time-trial speed walking as fast as you can was ten minutes, or five miles per hour. You would practice distance training for distances above a mile at 75 percent of that speed rate. Convert your one-mile speed into miles per hour (10 minutes per mile = 6 mph) and multiply by 75 percent: $\frac{3}{4} \times 6 = 4.5$ mph. Convert back to minute-miles: 60 minutes $\div$ 4.5 miles = 13 minutes per mile. You should train at this rate.

Jody Lewis demonstrates fast walking style. Jody teaches modified racewalking called Speedwalking for exercise.

Fartlek walking. *Fartlek* means "speed play" in Swedish, and it is probably the most enjoyable form of speed training for sportwalking. I prefer it over the other two training routines because it best represents the spirit of sportwalking: having fun.

With Fartlek walking, you walk as fast and as far as the spirit moves you. In other words, you walk very fast for brief periods, slowing back down to a steady pace when you can't sustain the effort. As soon as you have recovered your energy, you speed ahead again. The training involves repeating the fast-paced, steady-paced routines until you become too tired to continue.

I show Kelly Kane the lunge stretch. Kelly was the exercise model and technical advisor for both my *Walking Workouts* book and video. Her outstanding flexibility comes partially from the fact that she practices flexibility exercises every morning and partially from her young age: 22. Her primary walking exercise is commuting 2 miles a day on foot.

9
FLEXIBILITY TRAINING

FLEXIBILITY TRAINING INCREASES the range of motion of your joints. Flexibility is a broader training concept than just stretching muscles. You also rotate your limbs around your joints, stretching ligaments and strengthening the muscles that operate the joints. Whole texts have been written on flexibility exercises. This chapter gives you the exercises that concentrate on the joints and muscles you use for walking.

BENEFITS

Flexibility training extends the reach of your arms and especially your legs. This increases your walking stride length and, therefore, your overall walking speed. Flexibility training also makes your walking action smoother and more rhythmic and allows you to go at a faster pace. It also helps you avoid soreness, stiffness, and possible injury to joints and muscles during high-mileage walks and training weeks. Finally, by rotating limbs about the joints, flexibility training also strengthens your muscles.

You should concentrate on training the four joint areas most used in sportwalking: shoulder joints for a fuller arm movement, spine for better posture and hip action, hip joints for greater leg rotation, and ankle joints for a fuller drive.

SHORT- VERSUS LONG-FORM

For *short-form* flexibility training, practice at least one stretching or rotational exercise for each area being used heavily during that particular training session. If you have more time, add exercises for other major joint areas. Practice these exercises at any time after you have completed the warm-up. Do not hesitate to use the stretching and rotational exercises as you need them to reduce tightness in a specific body area.

But, when doing the short form, do not practice any exercise more than once. Choose three to six exercises at most and do them when really needed. You can consume too much energy with too much flexibility training at the expense of the other training forms. Save the exercises for the long-form or specific training sessions.

For *long-form* or specific flexibility training, you can practice each stretching and rotational exercise in sets of ones (beginner), twos (intermediate), or threes (advanced). Depending on how flexible you are, you should stretch and rotate each position farther and longer. Beginners, intermediates, and advanced should all practice their first set comfortably. The second and third sets are developmental and can be held and stretched longer and farther.

One second equals two counts. Unless an exercise gives specific counts, beginners should hold each stretch 3 to 5 seconds and perform 3 to 5 rotations, intermediates should hold stretches 6 to 8 seconds or 12 to 15 counts and do 6 to 9 rotations, and advanced should hold 1 to 3 seconds or 12 to 60 counts or longer and do 10 to 60 rotations. If the exercise has to be performed on both the left and right sides, each side should have a full number of holding counts or rotations. When no specific rotation numbers are given, rotate three times clockwise and three times counterclockwise for each set.

MAKING PROGRESS

As your training progresses, you should be concerned with moving your joints and muscles by moving the limbs connected to them to their extreme position. Unless you are naturally flexible, you will not be able to reach these extreme positions until you have experienced many months of training, if ever. Do not worry; flexibility is very individualized training. Exercise as best you can; do not try to imitate walkers who are more flexible than you are.

To allow for a wider range of flexibility exercises to choose from, descriptions are minimal, with only one photo per exercise whenever possible. If you want more details, go back to my first two books, where fewer exercises are described in fuller detail. I have also given you a range of counts or repetitions, leaving it up to you to determine how many you should perform based on your own degree of flexibility. The choices and combinations of exercises are also yours, depending on what areas of your body need more work or to complement higher levels of strength and walking training.

Quadricep pull.

PRACTICE RULES

1. *Stretch every muscle you work or strengthen.* As you become more involved with exercising, you will discover that certain exercises are better suited to your own body structure. You will find out which ones by experimenting with new exercises.
2. *Avoid bouncing or jerking.* This will make your muscles contract and resist the exercises. Do not overstretch or overrotate.
3. *Maintain proper body alignment when doing flexibility exercises* (see posture exercises in Chapter 6 for guidelines).
   a. Point toes straight ahead and keep feet flat on the ground during leg exercises, unless otherwise indicated.
   b. Do not turn your legs outward.
   c. Do not lock your joints—elbow and knee—but keep them slightly bent.
   d. Keep your back flat (not arched) during most stretching.
   e. Keep your head and chin in a neutral position. Look out in front of you. Don't stretch out your neck or bend your head too far forward.
4. *Initiate the stretch from near the area being stretched.*
   a. Do not use your head, arms, or shoulders to initiate stretches that are far from or do not involve those joints.
   b. If you are not very flexible, use a towel to close the distance.
   c. As you stretch and feel the muscle tension diminish, gently extend the mobility range out a little farther in the second or third set.
5. *Tailor the exercises to fit your own body.* Everybody exercises differently, so don't imitate others who are stronger or more flexible than you are. Do not extend your range arbitrarily. Instead, feel whether the stretch is right.
6. *Beginners should practice easy; intermediates and advanced can be more developmental in their program.* The first exercise set should be done easily and comfortably by all. You should feel some muscle tension, but it will stay the same or diminish as you hold the position.
7. *Increase the amount of time and the number of exercises gradually.* After a while some of the exercises can be held or performed for 60 seconds or more. I have indicated with a higher count range those stretches and rotations which can be practiced longer.
8. *Perform the exercises slowly and deliberately.* Come out of each stretch as slowly as you went into it.

FLEXIBILITY-TRAINING EXERCISES

NECK

Neck extensions.   Bend your head back, forward, and to each side, guiding it with your hand rather than letting it roll. If you look forward while doing the exercise, you will relieve neck tension as you walk. The neck is often where tension and fatigue start. Hold each neck extension 2 to 10 seconds.

SHOULDERS

Shoulder shrugs.   Shrugging is the simplest way to stretch out shoulder muscles even while you are walking. Perform these shoulder shrugs as frequently as needed. Hold the shrugged position 10 to 60 seconds.

Shoulder rotations.   You can perform shoulder rotations with arms stretched out as in the windmill-type exercises or with arms held by your side, concentrating on just the shoulders, as in the photo below. Rotate clockwise and counterclockwise between 20 and 60 rotations per minute.

Shoulder shrugs.

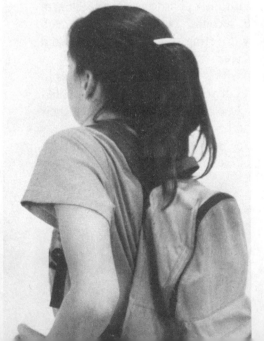

Neck extensions.

Shoulder rotations:
Extend arms out
180 degrees.

Straight-arm stretches. Press your arms back to stretch your arm and shoulder muscles in each of the following four positions for 10 to 15 seconds.

- Position 1: Arms held straight out 45 degrees from the body
- Position 2: Arms raised 90 degrees from the body
- Position 3: Arms raised 135 degrees from the body
- Position 4: Arms raised 180 degrees, i.e., overhead

Bent-arm stretches. With one arm bent at the elbow and raised overhead, push back at the elbow with the opposite hand. Switch arm positions. Hold each side 5 to 10 seconds. **Note:** You can stretch different muscles in your shoulder by directing your arms up, back, and to the side, guiding the stretch with your opposite hand.

Other exercises. The extreme position for the shoulder stretch is to reach behind your back and grab hold of your fingers. Beginners should use a towel behind their backs to close the gap, gently moving their hands up the towel.

There are many additional shoulder mobility exercises and exercise variations to choose from. I have illustrated them in the series of photos that follow:

- Hanging from bar
- Towel stretches (three positions)
- Reach-out stretches

Straight-arm variation.

Bent-arm stretch: overhead.

Bent-arm stretch: sideways.

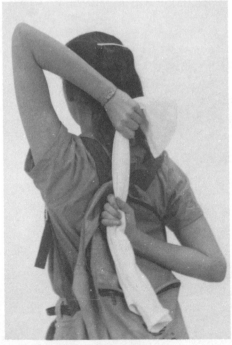

A towel closes the gap.

Chin tucks: head up.

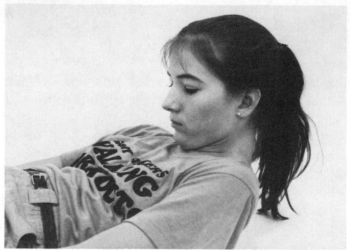

Chin tucks: shoulder blades up.

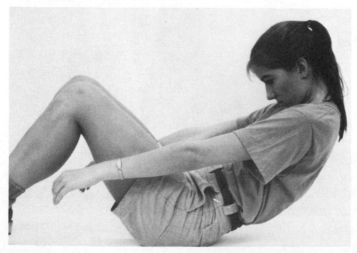

Head to knees.

Prone twist.

Prone twist
crab.

SPINE: BEGINNERS

Prone twist forward. Lying on your back, gently lift your head, tucking your chin into your chest. Hold position 3 to 5 seconds. Slowly lower your head back down to the ground. Next, repeat the procedure but lift up your shoulder blades, too. Continue the exercise, curling up more of your spine each time, trying to bring your head to your knees.

Prone twist side. Lying on your back, bend your torso to each side, trying to touch your right foot with your right hand while keeping your back and shoulders flat against the ground. Hold the position 3 to 5 seconds. Repeat three times on left and right sides.

Prone twist crab. Lying on your back, raise your buttocks off the ground as you slowly walk your feet up toward your shoulders so you arch backward in the crab position. Hold this position 3 to 12 seconds. Repeat 1 to 3 times. From the crab position, walk your body around to the left and right side while holding your buttocks high.

Torso bends:
back arch.

Reach-throughs.

SPINE: ADVANCED

Torso rotations.   With your arms extended above your head, rotate your torso gently making a complete circle over your body, back, side, and front positions as in the photos. Repeat the clockwise and counter-clockwise rotations three times each.

Torso bends.   With your hands on your hips, bend your upper body over so it becomes parallel to the ground:

- Back arch
- Side bend, left and right
- Front
- Reach-throughs—Reach with both hands between your legs for an extra stretch. Hold your position 12 to 20 counts.

Spinal twist. This is sometimes called the pretzel. Sit on the ground, placing your left back hand on the outside and under your left knee. Twist your torso around as far as you can to the right and grab hold of your left arm with your right hand. Hold this position 15 to 30 seconds. Repeat the exercise, twisting in the other direction and reversing your respective hand positions.

Standing twist. With your feet spread 3 to 5 feet apart, touch your right hand (arms extended) to your *opposite* (left) foot. Look up at your raised arm as you bend over. Repeat the exercise left hand to right foot. Hold each position 1 to 3 seconds. Repeat each side 8 to 12 times.

Standing twist.

The spinal twist, also called the pretzel, is shown here.

Hip raises.

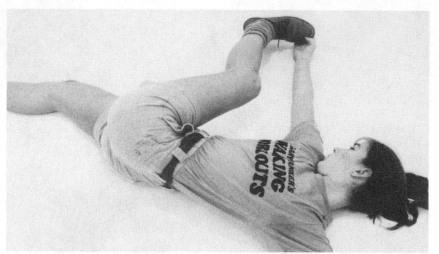

Prone hip crossovers across chest . . .   . . . and across shoulders.

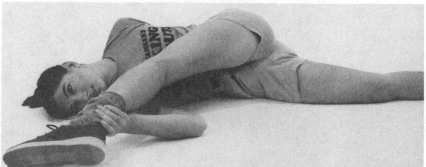

Dropping knees.

HIPS AND LOWER BACK: BEGINNERS

Hip raises.   Raise your legs together or separately, pressing your bent knees against your chest. Hold the position 5 to 15 seconds. This exercise stretches the lower back.

Prone hip crossovers.   Lying on your back, legs 60 degrees apart and arms stretched out 90 degrees to your torso, cross your right leg over your body and try to touch your left hand with your right foot. Hold the stretch three to five seconds. Repeat three times to each side.

Dropping knees.   With your knees raised to your chest and your shoulders flat on the floor, move your legs sideways to the right, touching your knees to the floor. Hold position 10 seconds. Repeat to the other side.

Standing hip rotation.

HIPS AND LOWER BACK: ADVANCED

Head over heels. Raise your legs and bring them over your head, touching both feet to the floor. Hold position 15 to 30 seconds without letting your back curve. Use a pillow or blanket to protect your neck and shoulders. From this position, keeping your legs together and shoulders on the ground, walk your legs around to the right and then to the left of your shoulders as far as they will go. You can use your arms to help you keep your balance, moving them to the side opposite your feet.

Hip rotation. From the standing position, and holding on to something to keep your balance, raise and bend your left leg so your thigh is parallel to the floor. Rotate your right leg around your right hip joint in as large a circle as you can, while keeping your lower leg bent at a 90-degree angle to your thigh. Repeat the rotation exercise with your left leg and hip joint. Practice 3 to 15 rotations on each side.

Other hip and back exercises.

- Seated, soles pressed together
- Legs crossed—side-to-side roll
- Squat stretch

The butterfly stretch (seated with soles pressed together).

Side-to-side roll with legs crossed.

Squat stretch.

Standing legs crossed.

Squat raises.

LEGS: HAMSTRING STRETCHES FOR BEGINNERS

Standing, legs crossed.   With one leg crossed in front of the other, bend over and press your hands against your legs, pressing them backward.

Squat raises.   Squat, putting your hands under your feet. Slowly rise, trying to straighten your legs while holding on to your feet.

ADVANCED: HAMSTRING STRETCHES

Seated hurdler stretch.   Start by sitting on the floor with your torso erect and the soles of your feet pressed together with your knees bent outward. Extend one leg straight out at a 60-degree angle to the other. Lift leg out in front of the thigh of your right leg at a 90-degree angle to the left. Bend the lower part of your right leg to a 90-degree

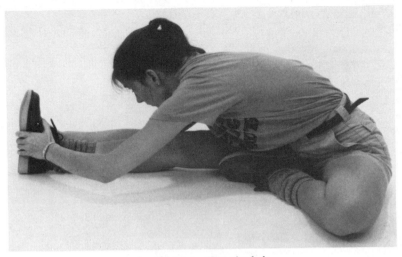

Seated hurdler stretch.

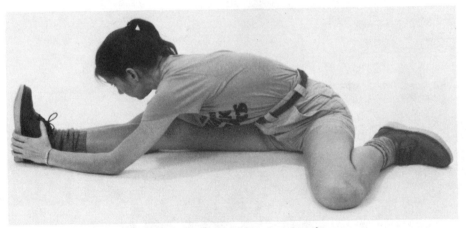

Hurdler stretch with leg back.

angle with the upper part. To stretch farther, advanced walkers can place the bent leg back behind themselves.

Grasp the forefoot or ankle of the extended leg with one or both of your hands, and bend forward, pulling your head to your knee. If you cannot easily reach your feet, use a towel to help pull yourself forward. Hold the stretch 5 to 15 seconds and repeat on the other side.

Other hamstring-stretching variations.

- Raised-leg hurdler's stretch
- Seated split leg
- Side splits
- Leg-wall splits
- Inverted-V stretch

Richard Goldman demonstrates the hurdler stretch from the squat position.

The raised-leg hurdler stretch can be done by propping your foot on anything knee to waist high.

Seated leg split.

Side splits.

Wall leg splits.

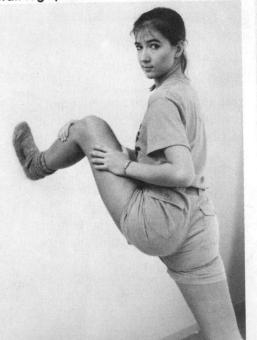

Inverted "V" stretch.

**Ankles/
calves stretches.**

**Hand-assisted
pull back.**

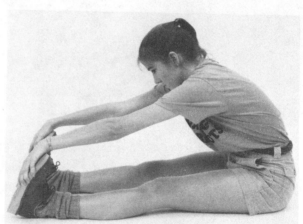

ANKLES AND CALVES

Ankle stretch.   Sit on the floor with your legs straight out in front
of you. With your feet pressed together at the heels and big toes, push
your feet forward and down, trying to press your forefeet and soles to the
floor. Then point your toes toward your body, using your hands to help
pull them back. Next, press your soles together so your little toes touch
each other.

Hand-assisted ankle stretches.   In a seated, prone, or standing
position use your hand to pull your forefoot back (see photos).

Ankle presses.   Stretch your ankle by pressing first the bottom,
then the top of your forefoot against the ground or against a raised
surface. Repeat with the other foot.

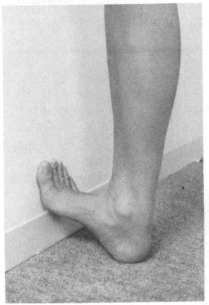

Ankle press against a raised surface.

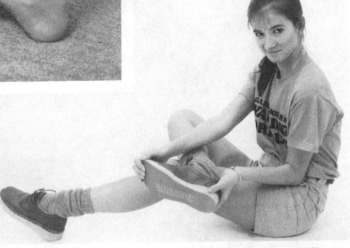

Hand-assisted ankle rotations.

Ankle rotation.   While seated with your feet six inches apart, cross your left leg over your right so your left foot is dangling. From this position rotate your left foot and ankle in a full circle clockwise and then counterclockwise 15 to 30 rotations in each direction. Switch feet and repeat.

Hand-assisted rotations.   From the seated position, rotate your ankles using your hands to guide them as well as provide resistance against the rotation movement. Note how you can safely test the range of ankle rotations by gently pressing to the outer ranges with your hands. Practice 3 to 15 rotations in each direction.

Calf stretch.   Leaning forward with your heels pressed to the ground, stretch the calf muscles, Achilles tendons, and the forefoot. Then roll your feet back and flex your ankles.

Other ankle-exercise variations.

- Heel-toe rolls
- Heel walk—walk a few steps forward and backward while staying on your heels only
- Heel raises
- Toe raises

Roll back.

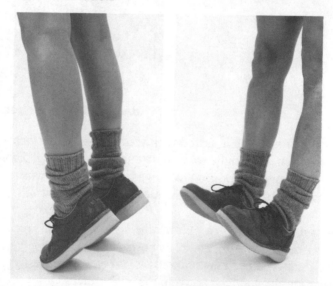

Heel-toe roll: Roll both feet simultaneously forward . . . and back.

10
STRENGTH TRAINING

Strength training includes both calisthenics and weight-training exercises. Start with calisthenics for the first six weeks or until you have reached a strength Level III, and then switch to or combine calisthenics with a weight-training routine.

Train by body part and concentrate on the dynamic training method (lower resistance with greater repetition). Start with the largest muscle groups and work your way down to the smallest. Concentrate on developing muscular endurance rather than strength. This means that for particular arm and leg exercises you should do 25 to 30 repetitions of each. Train with a weight load that is one-half to one-third of the maximum weight you can do with one repetition of the exercise.

Practice one, two, or three sets using the number of repetitions indicated at the end of the exercise description. Each additional set represents an additional level of strength corresponding to Levels I, II, or III at the low-repetition ranges and Levels III, IV, and V at the high-repetition ranges. (For further details, see the chart at the end of this chapter.)

Wheelbarrow walk: Walking on your hands with a partner will strengthen your arms and shoulders, thus making your arm swing more powerful when walking upright.

CALISTHENICS

TORSO

Full sit-ups.   Beginners may have to anchor their feet (as in the photo on page 193), but try to keep free, as this will work the stomach muscles more than the hip flexors. Practice sit-ups with 15 to 25 repetitions.

Crossover sit-ups.   With hands across your chest or with fingers clasped at the back of your head, raise your torso about 45 degrees from the ground and twist to the left. Return torso to the ground. On the second sit-up, twist to the right. *Variation:* Twist right and then left on every sit-up before returning your torso to the ground. Practice this exercise with 25 to 50 repetitions.

Abdominal curls.   Concentrate on a shorter curling and twisting motion. This does not bring the hip flexors into play at all. Practice this exercise with 25 to 50 repetitions.

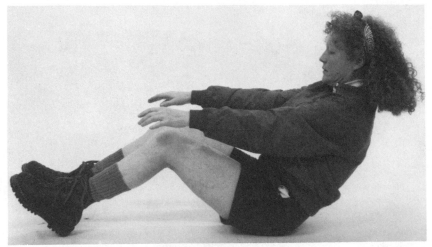

Full sit-up.

Crossover sit-ups.

Crab lift.

Back extension with twist.

BACK

Crab lifts. Lying on your back, lift your torso high using your lower back and buttocks (as in the photo above). Hold the position 2 to 4 counts. Repeat this exercise 8 to 12 times.

Back extensions. Lying on your stomach with your legs and arms stretched out forward and back, simultaneously lift both legs off the ground as you arch your back. Hold the position for 2 to 4 counts. Repeat this exercise 6 to 12 times.

Back extension (with twist). Lying on your back with your feet anchored, lift your back off the ground, twisting to the right and then to the left.

STRENGTH-TRAINING RULES

1. Don't forget to practice warm-up and stretching exercises before and after your strength-training routine. Rotational exercises are not absolutely necessary. If you have to skip anything, don't skip warm-ups,

and remember to do stretching exercises at least after you train. It is important to stretch muscles that have been used in strength training.

2. Maintain proper body alignment for standing, prone, and seated calisthenics. Keep your buttocks and stomach tucked in, your shoulders and hips square, feet placed apart, toes pointed.

3. Breathe in during the relaxed portion of the exercise and out during the exertion portion.

4. Stick to the gradual progression of repetition in Table 10-1, dropping back whenever your strength training falls off.

5. For muscular endurance in arms, legs, and torso, do 25 to 30 repetitions each of one (beginners), two (intermediate), or three (advanced) sets. The first set can be heaviest, with each succeeding set containing a lighter weight, or each set can be equally weighted.

6. When weight training, train the largest muscle first, thereafter training by size in descending order.

7. For maximum strength do one set right after another. But for muscular endurance do a greater number of repetitions. The lighter method is preferred for sportwalking. To reach higher repetitions, practice your sets in intervals interspersed with a rest interval or different type of exercise.

8. Practicing *heavy sets* is good for strengthening muscles that are particularly weak from lack of use. For walkers, these may be quadriceps, calves, hamstrings, shoulders, and arms. You should use more weight but limit your repetitions to 3 to 12 per set.

9. *Light sets* are good for building muscular endurance (a combination of cardiovascular endurance and muscle strength). Sportwalkers should favor these. Use light weights and practice in the range of 25 to 100 repetitions per set. For light sets you can also exercise using muscle combination. For example, the walking arm's pump and curl exercise combines work for bicep, tricep, forearm, and shoulder muscles.

10. Use a weight load that is two-thirds of your maximum weight repetition for heavy sets and one-tenth to one-third for light sets. The maximum weight repetition (MWR) is the heaviest weight you can exercise in one repetition. Each exercise has its own MWR. Take care not to strain yourself; have a coach or trainer supervise your MWR testing, and add weight cautiously to determine your maximum. When combining heavy and light sets, practice the heavy ones in between the light ones.

11. Practice weight and calisthenic training every other day or split daily sessions among different muscle groups to allow muscles 48 hours to recover.

12. For short-term strength training, practice 3 to 6 exercises, one set each. For long-form training, practice 6 to 12 exercises, up to three sets of each.

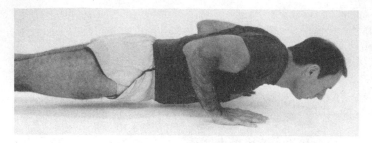

Advanced push-ups.

Beginner push-ups.

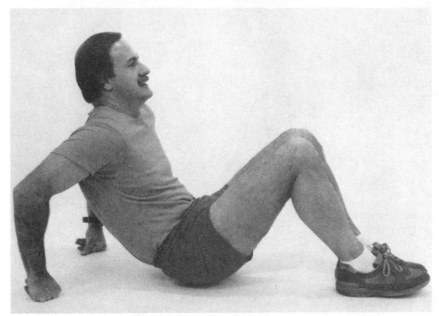

Arm dips.

ARMS/SHOULDERS

Push-ups.   Push-ups can be done with varying degress of difficulty by raising your feet higher to shift more of the work load to your arms and shoulders. Ultimately, you should be able to press from a reverse squat into a handstand. Repeat push-ups 6 to 25 times. This exercise strengthens arms, chest, shoulders, and triceps.

Arm dips.   Arm dips strengthen the triceps and chest. Lower yourself between parallel bars or from a sturdy table or chair edge, then raise your body up again as you straighten your arms. You can make this exercise more difficult by suspending your legs from the ground as in the photo here. Practice with 2 to 15 repetitions.

Pull-ups.   Pull up and lower your body slowly using an overhand or underhand grasp. Practice with 2 to 15 repetitions.

Other arm-shoulder combinations.

- Wheelbarrow
- Rope climbing

Back wall seat.

LEGS

Back wall seats.   With your back against the wall, slide slowly until you are in a seated position. Hold three to six seconds. Repeat three times.

Half squats.   Raise and lower yourself with half knee bends.

Squat jumps.   Sink into a half knee bend. Jump up three to six inches while straightening your legs.

Jump tucks.   Jump up, tucking your knees up to your chest.

COMBINATION EXERCISES

The following strength-training calisthenics combine a number of movements that strengthen arm, shoulder, leg, and torso muscles:

- Squat thrust push-ups
- Sit-up twists
- Arm-supported leg raises
- Side-supported leg raises
- Crab position press and walk

From this position . . .

. . . squat jump.

Sit-up twists with stick . . .

. . . and without.

TABLE 10-1. WEIGHT AND CALISTHENIC TRAINING

	Beginner (1 set)	Intermediate (2 sets)	Advanced (3 sets)
Sit-Ups			
Calisthenic	5–15	16–25	26–50
Light weights	N/A	N/A	N/A
Heavy weights	N/A	5–15	16–25
Short curls	15–25	26–50	50–100
Back Lifts (extension)			
Calisthenic	3–5	6–12	13–20
Light weights	N/A	6–12	16–25
Heavy weights	N/A	3–5	6–12
Short curls	6–12	13–20	21–30
Torso Twists			
Calisthenic (stick)	12–20	21–30	31–50
Light weights (bar)	N/A	12–20	21–25
Heavy weights (bar)	N/A	N/A	N/A
Arms/Shoulders			
Push-ups	5–20	21–30	31–50
Arm dips	2–4	5–12	13–25
Pull-ups	1–3 sec.	4–5 sec.	6–20 sec.
Arm Pullovers			
Light weights	5–12	13–20	21–30
Heavy weights	3–5	6–12	13–20
Bench Press			
Light weights	5–12	13–15	16–20
Heavy weights	2–5	6–12	13–20
Walking Arms			
Light weights	5–12	13–20	21–30
Heavy weights	2–5	6–12	13–20
Legs			
Back wall sets (hold)	3–5 sec.	6–12 sec.	13–60 sec.
Half squats	3–5	6–12	13–60
Squat jumps	N/A	3–5	6–12
Leg Raises (extensions)			
Calisthenic	5–12	13–20	21–50
Light weights	3–5	6–12	13–20
Heavy weights	N/A	3–5	6–12

Leg Curls			
Light weights	3–5	6–12	13–20
Heavy weights	N/A	3–5	6–12
Walking Legs			
Light weights	3–5	6–12	13–20
Heavy weights	N/A	3–5	6–12
Head Raises			
Calisthenic	5–12	13–20	21–50
Light weights	3–8	9–12	13–25
Heavy weights	N/A	5–12	13–25

Standing torso side bends.

WEIGHT-TRAINING EXERCISES

TORSO

Torso twist with weight bar. Seated, with legs anchored, bend over backward, shifting the exercise work from your back to your abdominal muscles.

Variation: Do these twists from a standing position as side bends. By bending over so your upper body is parallel to the ground, you shift the exercise from your side muscles to your back as in the photos. Practice the torso twist on a Roman chair, so you can raise and lower yourself, adding more resistance to the twisting action.

Practice 20 to 100 twists for each of these exercises, doing 2 to 3 sets of 20 to 30 rotations each.

Resistance sit-ups.   Add resistance to your stomach curls and sit-ups by holding a weight against your chest as in the photo. You can use a board or seat. Practice a high number of sit-ups (up to 100 per strength-training session), distributing them among one, two, or three sets of 12 to 50 repetitions each. One set can be practiced as full sit-ups or with the shorter range abdominal curls.

The Nautilus sit-up machine depicted here allows you to do short- and full-range exercising. If you are strength training indoors, you can intersperse your sit-up sets with other weight and calisthenic sets to make your exercising more interesting.

Sit-up twists.   Sit-up twists provide the best exercise for strengthening muscles used in walking. Start crossing over either as you begin raising your body in a wide arc or after you are in a sitting position (in a quick twisting motion doing shorter curls). The quick twist comes closest to what you do with your arm, shoulder, and hip rotations when you walk. Practice the twist as fast as you can, trying to duplicate your steps per minute. The sit-up twist works the frontal and side (oblique) abdominal muscles.

Straight-arm pull-over.   Grip one barbell and move it from the chest to the back of your head, keeping your shoulder and back flat against the bench and your arms straight, bending them only when you move them over and behind your head. This exercise works the pectoral, latissimus dorsi (side torso), and triceps muscles.

Dumbbell flyes.   You can do dumbbell flyes standing or prone. The straighter you keep your arms, the more you shift the work from your chest to your shoulders.

Bench press.   Keep your back flat and press the barbells up from your chest. Place your feet on top of the bench to concentrate the work on your arms and chest and to help keep your back flat.

Walking arms.   While standing, work your deltoid, pectoral, and tricep muscles by simultaneously curling and pumping your arms while holding the barbells in your hand. You can also practice these exercises while lying on your stomach as follows: Lie down on the edge of a bench so you are hanging over from the belly button up while your partner holds your feet down. This version of the exercise will also strengthen your back muscles. Finally, practice walking arms in the sit-up position to combine arm-shoulder with abdominal strengthening.

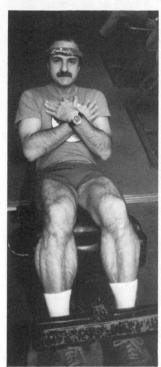

Straight-arm pullover with barbell.

Resistance sit-ups by holding a weight.

Dumbbell flyes.

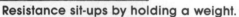

Bench press.

Walking arms: prone.

Walking arms: seated.

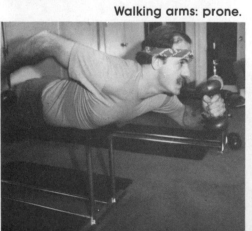

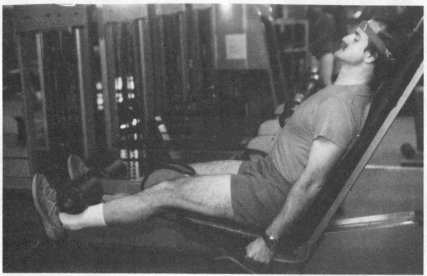

Leg extensions.

LEGS

Leg extensions. Using a weight machine or weight shoes, slowly raise your lower legs while counting until they are fully straightened. Hold your legs in this position for two more counts, and then bend and lower your legs back for two final counts. This exercise strengthens the quadriceps and is particularly beneficial to backpacking and mountain climbing. Using both legs, you can load up to half your body weight.

Leg curls. With a weight machine or iron shoes, slowly bend, hold, and lower your legs. Take two counts for each movement. In the hold position, your heels should touch your buttocks, your knees should be just over the bench. This is the best strengthening exercise for your hamstring muscles.

Walking legs. Lying on your back, exercise your weighted leg, keeping it straight and moving it through a full range of motion. Repeat with the other leg. This exercise works your hip flexors.

Heel raises. Rest the bar on your shoulders, using a towel for padding. Raise and lower your entire body, standing with your forefoot on a two-inch-high block. This exercises your calf muscles for a stronger rear leg drive, while fully flexing your ankles.

Leg extensions with leg weights, in a chair.

Walking legs with raised bent legs.

Heel raises with
bar and padding.

PART THREE
PREPARING

ALL SPORTWALK PREPARATIONS are really strategies and tactics. They involve how you participate in and prepare for competitive and noncompetitive events. Thus, this part of the book describes what you can do before and during the sportwalk to give it your best. It is really a strategy and tactics manual for preparing you mentally and nutritionally and for assembling the needed equipment for the sportwalk event.

Strategy is your overall plan. There are two basic types of strategy, the noncompetitive and the competitive. The noncompetitive strategy is to complete the sportwalk distance within a reasonable time, for example, not more than 10 hours per day of walking. In any case, good sportwalk form means you will have enough time and energy left over so you can walk the next day. You do not want to stress your body from one walk so much that it will take you days and weeks to recover from muscle soreness, blisters, and general exhaustion. That's bad form.

The *tactics* for both competitive and noncompetitive sportwalks events are similar; only the end is different. Tactics are the individual actions and savvy tricks involving yourself, your equipment, the environment, and other walkers that you use before and during the walk to implement your strategy. Tactics include tips on proper eating, foot preparation, clothing, and pre-event warm-up as well as stretching exercises en route.

The strategy is either winning, placing among the top, or making the best possible performance. The strategy you choose will influence the tactics you adopt.

Chapter 11, "Timing and Pacing," discusses preparing and executing a plan for how fast you will walk and when you will rest. Chapter 12, "Walk Tech," presents equipment selection for the various strategies. Chapter 13, "Sportwalk Diet and Nutrition," not only discusses good nutrition for training but also shows you how and when to eat and drink. The last two chapters of this part are not a product evaluation and dieting program, as you will find in many other sport and exercise books. Instead, strategy and tactics make products and diet more relevant to sportwalking itself.

11
TIMING AND PACING

YOUR STRATEGY IS to adopt a pace that will ensure that you go the distance in good form. If you are long-distance walking or participating in multiple-day walks like those in the two- and four-day marches, it is especially important to complete your day's distance in under 10 hours. You will need the remaining time to recuperate for the next day's walking. If you walk more than 10 hours, recovery will be difficult. Coming in under 10 hours does not mean that you have to race to finish, it just means that you have to maintain a brisk, steady pace throughout the walk and time your rest periods properly.

THE START

How fast should you go at the beginning of the walk? When should you pass? When should you rest? You have to answer these important tactical questions in order to complete the sportwalk event in good form. From walking many miles and doing trial walks, you will learn for yourself the answer to these questions. But you may not be aware of some of the subtle factors involved in your choice.

Whether you are an early-morning person or an evening person will

Deena Karabell and David Balboa show training is easier when done with a friend.

affect your form. If you are an early-morning person, you will probably fade at the end of the walk, particularly if it lasts all day. In that case, make a fast start. A fast start is also important in international walking events like Nijmegen where there are many walkers. It helps you work your way to the front of the pack, where there will be more room and faster walkers to help set a fast, steady pace.

If you are a slow starter, probably an evening person, you can look forward to higher energy levels later in the day. Start slow; the line of walkers will thin out about a quarter of the way into the walk, when you can start picking up your pace. Slow starters can improve their pick-up with a pre-event warm-up walk. It may wake you up and increase your energy levels earlier in the day.

If you are racewalking, a fast start is probably less preferred. It is psychologically more important to start slow and build up your pace so you will pass walkers and not have them passing you. In competition walking, psychological factors generally play a greater role than in participation walking. On the other hand, if you are a fast racewalker and can maintain your pace, you'll want to start off fast and continue at that pace all the way to the finish line. Or you might start off very fast in hopes of "killing off" your competition early on so you can settle into a steady pace in the latter half of the race.

It is important to realize that quick final bursts of speed are less effective in racewalking than they are in running, because a walker has limited acceleration potential. Racewalking is more of an endurance event than running. The steady pace with good form is what wins or places in racewalks.

In long-distance and hill walking, a fast start plays even less of a role. With daily long walks and multiple-day acceleration, a fast start is less important than "gradualism." You walk an even pace to conserve your energy and make your walking output as efficient as possible. Start slow, and as you warm up, gradually increase your speed. Fast starts tend to rob you of unnecessary energy. In hill walking and hiking, it is more important to use the energy saved from avoiding fast starts to pick up the pace and pass other walkers on the trail so you will not be unnecessarily slowed down.

PASSING MOVES

Knowing when and how to pass is an important tactic for both competitive and noncompetitive sportwalks, because you need to keep your walking field as clear as possible. It is frustrating and energy-draining to have to hold back your walking pace behind a slower walker. You not only lose time but also become tense.

The best time to pass is when you sense the walker in front of you is growing tired and slowing down. I find that the element of surprise is important in passing. Accelerate your pace when the walker in front is least aware that you are coming up. A "surprise pass" is less likely to invite energy-draining head-to-head competition. Some walkers, knowing in advance that you want to pass, will become competitive and turn your effort into a sprinting race.

It also helps to be polite; say "excuse me" when passing in a tight situation to avoid making the passed walkers feel challenged by your move. Unless you are racewalking, I find it a good tactic not to race the walker in front of you if he or she speeds up while you are trying to pass. Instead, let the walker go; he or she will clear the walking field for you. Stay with him or her, keep up your pace, and maintain a steady distance between you. When the walker knows you are not trying to race, he or she will either keep up the increased pace or let you pass.

The best places to pass are uphill, downhill, or at a bend in the course. Slow walkers tend to slow down going up and down a slope. This is the time you should speed up. On the uphill, you'll meet the least resistance. Increasing your leg speed is not as difficult as you imagine. On the downhill, you should practice increasing your speed with a longer stride than usual rather than increasing leg speed. When passing on a curve, the inside track is best, but often the outside is less crowded and other walkers will be less aware of you passing.

VARIABLE PACE

While conventional wisdom holds that the "steady pace" is the best pace because it is most efficient and least tiring, the type of pace depends on the distance and purpose of the sportwalk as well as the fitness and energy level of the sportwalker. If you are walking long distances and not racewalking, a strategy of fast, slow, and moderate-paced sections will use the ebb and flow of your energy levels to the best advantage throughout the event day.

My favorite strategy for long-distance walks is to start slowly and build up speed as I warm up to the idea of walking. Once warmed up, I accelerate to a fast steady pace for the first couple of hours until the lunchtime stop. After lunch I start slowly again until I'm warmed up. My pace is usually slower than it was in the morning. During the afternoon I get bursts of energy, allowing me to hold a fast steady pace for 20 to 60 minutes at a time.

LONG-DISTANCE WALKS

In long-distance and in multiday walking, it is important to walk wisely and comfortably, preserving your energy and committing to an increased effort when it makes good sense. In other words, if you have 10 hours to walk in a day, pace yourself in terms of the hours. After a few months of sportwalking you'll learn more about your energy cycles and how to put them to best use.

The speed of walkers around you will also influence your pace. It's good to find a group of walkers to pace yourself with. This usually means working your way to the front of the pack to the fast-walking group. In large group walks I alternate between setting my own pace for sections and letting faster walkers set the pace for me, particularly when I'm feeling low and slow.

Plan your variable-speed sections with reference to your average event pace. Compute your average event pace by dividing the walking event distance by the time for completion (or the time limit you set for yourself). Except for racewalks, the speed range for the average sportwalk is 3 to 5 miles per hour. If your average event pace is 3½ miles per hour, your variable-speed sections should also average out to that number. Monitor your average event pace by keeping "cumulative" totals of the time actually spent walking and the distance you walked. Compare these totals to the time and distance that remain.

First set your goal for completing the distance of the event in terms of actual walking hours. Divide your walking event day into halves or thirds and monitor your pace or distance, so you can adjust your pace to stay within your average.

EXAMPLE

Event Goal = 35-mile event in 10 hours
Average Pace = 3.5 miles per hour
Plan for First Six Hours:
    First 4 hours × 4 mph = 16 miles
    Next 2 hours × 3 mph = 6 miles
Cumulative Totals: 6 hours = 22 miles
Average Pace: 3.66 mph

Plan for Final Four Hours:
Distance Remaining: 35 miles − 22 miles = 13 miles
Time: 4 hours
Average Pace: 3.25 mph (13 miles ÷ 4 hours)
This can be accomplished with:
    1 hour × 4 mph = 4 miles
    1 hour × 2 mph = 2 miles
    2 hours × 3.5 mph = 7 miles

SHORTER WALKS

When racewalking or distance walking for less than 12 miles, pacing rules change. Because of the shorter distance and the quicker speed, you will have a greater advantage if you can maintain your highest training pace throughout the event. Your pace should be equal to or better than the best one you timed during trial walks. You may be able to go faster than this pace by picking up speed during various sections of the event. Or you can keep up with a fast-paced walker whose time average is faster than yours.

Make a practice of learning about the time records of other racewalkers before the event. Ask them, if you have to, in the minutes before the event. You can start the walk with walkers whose pace is the same as yours, and use slightly faster walkers to pick up your pace during sections of the walk.

FINISHING

You shouldn't plan on making too much progress by saving bursts of speed for the final 1,000 yards of the event. By then the results of the race will probably have already been set. Racewalking is a technically judged endurance event. Bursts of speed in the final quarter can disqualify you because judges are watching to determine whether you are violating rules.

It is important to win or place in an event in the first three-quarters of the event distance. Here you can use increases in speed to keep up with faster paced walkers or shake others loose. It is important to know your own special endurance limits, i.e., how well you can resume and hold a steady pace after you have finished a burst of speed.

RULES

The rules on the following pages are interesting in how they define *walking* in paragraph 1 as unbroken contact with the ground (really not running or allowing your body to go airborne) and straightening the supporting leg "at least one moment" in the vertical position. Because it is difficult to observe walkers closely and at all times, judges must look for indicators of bad form. These are the bobbing of heads or lifting of the body associated with running and the look of creeping associated with walking with bent knees.

REST STOPS

The best overall strategy for rest stops is to rest or, if you are not sure, to skip rest stops in favor of maintaining the 12-hour recuperation period. This is the period of time you should allow your whole body to recuperate between walking days. If you shorten this period with sloppy, slow, and extended-period walking, every subsequent walking day will become more difficult to do, so you'll have to stop completely for a day or two.

Rest for five minutes every hour when you really need it. If you feel tired or your pace is below average, it is a good practice to keep your feet elevated while resting.

From time to time you may also want to make a quick rest, where you don't actually sit down but just stop walking and catch your breath. You can also practice one or two muscle stretches. Quick standing rest stops are often better than sitting or lying down to rest. You don't cool down the temperature of your body (specifically the temperature of your muscles), so you can continue walking at a steady pace without the delay of a warm-up walk.

Since you will be doing so much of them, it is best to combine resting with eating and drinking. Eating is more important during sportwalks than other sporting events because the time and distance are longer. You also burn a lot of calories. On a 50-mile hike, you burn the equivalent of two days' calories. See Chapter 13 for more on eating and drinking during the sportwalk event.

FOOD STOPS

On a sportwalk day, drink the equivalent of eight glasses of water (or more if it's hot). A glass to start and a glass to finish the day leave six during the walking day or about one every hour and three-quarters. Your body will need more fluid than it lets on with its thirst signals, so get in the habit of sipping water from a cup or canteen every fifteen minutes or so.

RULE 150—TAC GENERAL RULES OF RACEWALKING

1. DEFINITION OF RACEWALKING. Racewalking is a progression of steps so taken that unbroken contact with the ground is maintained.

a. During the period of each step, the advancing feet of the walker must make contact with the ground before the rear foot leaves the ground.

b. The supporting leg must be straightened (i.e., not bent at the knee) for at least one moment when in the vertical upright position.

c. Failure to adhere to the above definition of racewalking will result in disqualification. (See Rule 39.)

2. RACE CONDUCT. For all racewalking events, the following code of conduct must be adhered to, else disqualification will ensue:

a. In track races a competitor who is disqualified must immediately leave the track, and in road races the disqualified competitor must, immediately after being disqualified, remove the distinguishing numbers which he or she is wearing, and leave the course.

b. In road races, a competitor may leave the road with the permission and under the control of a judge, provided that by going off the course the walker does not lessen the distance to be covered.

3. SPONGING AND REFRESHMENT STATIONS.

a. Sponging and Drinking Water Stations: At all walking events of 10 kilometers or more, sponging and drinking water stations may be provided by the Meet Director, Sponsor or Organizers at suitable intervals, corresponding to weather conditions.

b. Refreshment/Feeding Stations: In all races of more than 20 kilometers, refreshments shall be provided by the Meet Director, Sponsor or Organizers, and refreshment stations shall be arranged at approximately 5 kilometers and thereafter at every 5 kilometers. Refreshments, which may either be provided by the organizer or the athlete, shall be available at the station assigned to the competitor. The refreshments shall be placed in such a manner that they are easily accessible for the competitors or so that they may be put into the hands of the competitors. A competitor taking refreshments at a place other than the assigned refreshment station may be disqualified.

4. COURSES AND CONDITIONS FOR WALKING EVENTS.

a. In Championships, the circuit for the 20-kilometer walk should be, if possible, a maximum of 2,500 meters, and the circuit for the 50-kilometer walk should be, if possible, 2,500 meters, with a maximum of 5,000 meters.

b. The organizers of walking events held on the roads must take care to ensure the safety of the competitors. In the case of Championships, the organizers must, where possible, give assurance that the roads used for the competitions will be closed in both directions; that is not open to motorized traffic.

c. The road walking events shall be so arranged as to ensure that the walkers finish in daylight.

d. The course for all Championship events and qualifying races must be certified according to Rule 133.

RULE 39—JUDGES OF RACEWALKING

1. JUDGING.

a. The Judges of Racewalking shall have the sole authority to determine the fairness or unfairness of walking, and their rulings thereon shall be final and without appeal. Judging decisions are made as seen by the human eye.

b. The appointed Judges of Racewalking shall elect a Chief Judge.

c. The Chief Judge shall assign the judges to the respective judging areas and explain the judging procedures to be used during the race.

d. All the Judges shall act in an individual capacity.

2. WARNING.

Competitors must be warned by any judge when, by their mode of progression, they are in danger of ceasing to comply with the definition of racewalking (see Rule 150); but they are not entitled to a second warning from the same judge for the same offense. Having warned a competitor, the judge must inform the Chief Judge of his or her action.

3. DISQUALIFICATION.

a. When, in the opinion of three Judges, a competitor's mode of progression fails to comply with the definition of racewalking (see Rule 150) during any part of the competition, the competitor shall be disqualified and informed of the disqualification by the Chief Judge.

b. Disqualification may be given immediately after the competitor has finished, if it is impractical to inform the competitor of the disqualifications during the race.

c. It is recommended that a system of signalling "warning" by a white flag and "disqualification" by a red flag be used as far as possible during a walking race for the information of the officials, competitors and spectators. Each Judge may also use a paddle or disc with the symbol ∿ indicating "Loss of Contact" and the symbol ❯ indicating "Bent Knee" on reverse sides to show the reason for the warning or disqualification call.

SAMPLE SPORTWALK DAY

Here is a sample schedule summarizing and applying pacing and resting tactics to a 10-hour walking day that starts early (6:00 A.M.) and therefore ends early.

5:00 A.M.: Wake up, pack, dress, have breakfast.

6:00 A.M.: After breakfast, start out walking slowly (e.g., at 1 to 3 miles per hour) to warm up. Take your time. After 15 minutes of walking, stop for 5 to 10 minutes for some flexibility exercises. Start walking again, this time at a faster pace (2 to 4 miles per hour). Try to reach a high steady pace to take advantage of your greater energy in the morning. If it's not working, as is sometimes the case with day-in and day-out walking, reduce your pace to one that is comfortable. The more fit you are, the faster your steady speed will be. At this point, I usually maintain a pace between 4¼ and 4¾ miles per hour.

7:00–10:00 A.M.: By now you should be warmed up and ready to rip. The first three or four hours of walking in a day can be the best, so I do not stop and rest until the midmorning coffee break. Often I will even skip this break and shoot for lunch as my first stop. If I'm not feeling tired, I take fewer rest stops in the morning to avoid having to repeatedly warm up and cool down. But, if I'm feeling tight or my feet are sore, I stop immediately to adjust equipment and stretch muscles or rotate joints. I never put off dealing with discomfort. As day breaks, I start to sightsee and watch the world wake up with the smug feeling that I have gotten a head start.

10:00 A.M.–Noon: Now I'm beginning to think about lunch and resting. If I'm only tired and not sore, I'll stretch out the walking time before stopping by varying my pace up and down. I will also shift my arm-swinging technique every 20 or 30 minutes to give arm and shoulder muscles a chance to rest. I also consciously stretch out my stride with each step. The sportwalking day can be more fun and will go faster if you vary

To wake up your body, coffee, tea, and soft drinks with caffeine can be consumed at low-energy periods like breakfast and after lunch. Decaf tea, coffee, or soda can also provide a psychological boost for those who have to restrict their caffeine intake. Fruit juices, fruit, and candy can also be consumed for energy boosts. Sugar in natural form in fruit rather it; walk faster, practice technique, talk to fellow walkers, do some sightseeing, and reflect.

Noon–1:00 P.M.: If you start your day early, you may be ready for lunch earlier, too. This lunch, rest, and equipment checkstop can take from 15 to 60 minutes. If you are trying to make time or don't feel like stopping, take the lunch break later. You might need it more then than you do now. Or make this break a short one and save some of the time for later rest stops. It's a good idea to do some stretching exercises before you sit down for lunch. After lunch (or after any longer rest stop), start out walking slowly. This will warm up muscles and joints and reduce later muscle soreness and stiffness.

1:00–2:00 P.M.: With lunch in your stomach, you will feel a little tired and sluggish, so these next two hours are walked at a slow to moderate pace until you feel the energy level rising for a "second wind." On any walk day it may come sooner or later; don't try to force it.

2:00–4:00 P.M.: If no second wind hits, you can pick up the pace on your own. If you can't hold it steady, you might do 20-minute intervals of fast- and slower-paced walking. You are probably trying to complete your mileage goal of the day, so you don't want to drag out your walking beyond the 10-hour limit. During this time frame, I find that five-minute rest stops every hour help make the walking effort in the remaining 55 minutes more energetic.

4:00–5:00 P.M.: Depending on how many rest stops you took during the day, you'll finish on the earlier or later side of this time period. The 10-hour time limit applies to walking time. You have to add an additional one to two hours rest time to this.

Some days I have a "fast finish"; other days, I'm glad to finish at all. But even a fast finish does not mean sprinting the final 200 yards. Sportwalking is not like that. Finish at your highest steady walking pace; this is the pace you can sustain for a mile or more.

Don't forget to cool down. It's a *must* after a long walking day. The stretching and rotation exercises you do now will help reduce the muscle soreness and tightness you feel tomorrow morning.

than in processed form will probably extend the energy boost longer.

You should eat a balanced diet through the sportwalking day, but you should consume food and drink in small amounts, eating more frequently if you have to. Fight the temptation to overeat because you are doing more activity.

Even after I stop walking, I keep my legs and body covered against the wind to keep my muscles from cramping.

12
WALK TECH

THIS CHAPTER IS about "walking technology"; it will help you be on the lookout for technical details in footwear and clothing design that most people never even notice. Product development for walkers is just in the beginning stages, and the tests that follow are far ahead of many product designs. Some products may have one or two but not all of the ideal specifications.

By expressing your wants and desires to retailers and manufacturers, you will be accelerating the process of improving products for walkers. Some manufacturers have tried to graft onto walking the methods used in lab testing of competitive sports products. While some lab testing is needed to improve materials, it should not be done at the expense of practical experience. The best laboratory for developing products for walkers is still the open road. The tests provided here are based on my experience and the experiences of other sportwalkers. They are intended to serve as guidelines for both walkers and manufacturers.

EQUIPMENT DESIGN
SELECTION

The general criteria for good walking-product design are not only how it feels and looks in the store but how it performs for you on the road in long or fast walks and on high-mileage training. Each item has two tests: a store test and a road test. You'll give it a preliminary test in the store and a more extensive one in training. This is a testing process rather than a one-time exam. In search of what's best for you, you'll be trying out many items of walk equipment while you are training.

USE

The test for proper equipment is not only extended use of a particular item in training but also the use of more than one set of items. This allows you to give each item time to "bounce back." The use test should determine whether walk equipment makes your walking more comfortable, provides full range of motion, protects you from weather, and cushions and supports your feet to reduce fatigue, stiffness, and soreness.

CARE

Care includes not only how you care for the equipment but also how you care for the particular part of your body using the item. You need to know when equipment is used up or how to rejuvenate it before it hurts your performance.

FOOTWARE

Footware is the word I have coined to help break the barriers of traditional thought about what you should wear on your feet. With sportwalking you need to go further away from fashion to function, and you should not look at shoes alone, but consider how they work with socks, orthotics, and other foot aids. Shoes are the most important equipment in sportwalking as well as exercisewalking, but socks and orthotics (shoe inserts, for example) are very important, too, and are included with shoes under the footware heading.

Custom biomechanical orthotic devices will stop excessive motion that the foot and leg go through. They are made for people with specific leg problems. It is advisable to be examined by a trained sports medicine podiatrist if you are experiencing foot or leg problems during your walks.

The best way to select a perfect walking shoe is to combine the hands-

THE SPORTWALK EVENT
AND TRAINING PACK

Here's a summary of what you should wear or pack along in your day pack:

Footware
moleskin
Band-Aids
Vaseline (for feet or inner legs)
2 to 4 pair thin socks
1 to 2 pair thick socks
1 pair light shoes
1 pair sturdy shoes

Bodyware
sun or wool cap
wristwatch
sunglasses with strap
long johns or tights
shirt

T-shirt or halter top
extra T-shirt
turtleneck sweater
sweat/headband
rain/wind suit
plastic bag (for wet clothes)

Other Supplies
canteen of water
chocolate
fruit
lunch sandwich
toilet paper
loose change for phone calls

on testing method (introduced in *Exercisewalking*) with a "road test" method for sportwalking. While hands-on testing is a good start, sportwalking training will give you an opportunity to "road test" an assortment of footwear so you can put the right combinations together for the sportwalk itself. Because you will do many more miles of walking (about 1,000 miles per shoe), you'll have the opportunity to road test more than one pair. Over a year, you will probably go through two to four pairs of shoes, so you should use the training period to try out different kinds to determine the ones that are right for you.

MULTIPLE PAIRS

You should have at least two kinds of walking shoes for sportwalking: one *sturdy* and one *light* pair. You should have multiple sets of each kind for training and testing. The sturdy pair should be thicker, firmer, and stiffer. It will probably be made of leather or a combination of leather and synthetic materials. It's the pair you'll walk your most mileage in, and it's the pair you'll put on when it's wet. The light pair will probably be a jogging-style shoe, lightweight, with thick cushioning, and very flexible. You'll switch to the light pair to give your feet a change and a rest. Carry the light pair with you in your day pack.

THE BASIC CRITERIA

Walking footwear should:

1. *Flex* with, not resist, your foot in the heel-toe action. Your foot should flex at the ball of your foot, just behind the toes. Your shoe should bend along the same area, in the same direction of your foot's flex.

2. *Breathe*, allowing air to cool and keep your feet dry.

3. *Cushion* your feet, particularly the forefoot, heel, ankle, and upper foot surface. As you walk, you put your foot down and flex your ankle 1,400 to 1,500 times per mile. You need a well-cushioned shoe to avoid the formation of hot spots and tender areas on the skin's surface which can later become raw or form blisters.

4. *Hold your feet in position* so they do not sway from side to side over your sole.

5. *Keep your feet dry and warm* on long walks and in cold-weather walking.

In-store (and closet) test.   In the shoe store or when testing shoes from your closet, you can use a hands-on and feet-in test to check for flexibility. The uppers and sole of the shoe should bend or flex easily at the forefoot as in the photo on page 219. The more difficult it is to flex the shoe, the harder on your feet the shoe will be. The type of materials and the thickness will affect the degree of flex.

Forward-flex test.   Grab the shoe by the forefoot and heel, and bend it forward and back. Note where the foot bends (see the photo on page 219); the shoe should bend at the forefoot.

Lateral-flex test.   Twist the shoe and flex it laterally to test the firmness of the sole construction. Your sturdy pair should be firm, to give you lateral support; your light pair need not be as firm. Grab the back of the heel and twist and squeeze it to see how firm it is. Examine

The forward flex is a hands-on flex test.

Lateral flex.

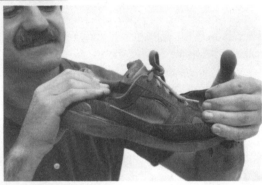

Sole grip.

whether it is reinforced. If not, the heel "counter" will soften and collapse, giving you no lateral support and protection from moving side-to-side on your shoe. The photo above shows a worn-out heel counter.

Sole grip.   For dry, smooth surfaces, a smooth outer sole will do, but for ice, snow, and other rugged terrain, you need a shoe bottom that grips the ground surface, or you will slip and fall. Consider having your sturdy shoes with a grip sole and your light shoes with a smooth sole.

Hands-in and feet-in tests.   Reach inside the shoes with your fingers and feel for a smooth inner surface. There should be no seams that protrude and will likely cause blisters. Reach forward and feel inside the toe box area. It is important to make this examination with your fingers, as your toes are less discriminating. Of course, your toes and feet will later feel it painfully well if your fingers did not make an honest evaluation.

Cushion pad test.   Bring along an orthopedic device to see whether it fits comfortably inside the shoe, even on top of the existing support. You will want to add cushioning devices for long-distance walking. Added cushions will not necessarily require you to increase your shoe size. However, you should choose walking shoes with laces so you can adjust the space in the shoe from above to allow for the additions.

Shoe size test.   Measuring the length and width of your feet is only the beginning. Next, you have to see whether your feet can flex inside the shoe. Is the toe box area sufficiently rounded and wide or high to allow your toes to spread out? Spread out your toes to see if there is sufficient room. Feel for arch support—a curved, cup-like ridge. Push down with your fingers into the bed of the shoe to see how much you can depress and, therefore, how much cushioning you have. If there's a question about fit, lean toward the side of a half-size larger. Your feet will probably grow by a half-size just from walking more miles. You may also need room for extra socks and cushioning in your shoes.

Shoe cut test.   Your walking shoes, including walking boots, should be cut below the ankle bone to allow for maximum foot flexing. This advice may seem counter to the "hiker's wisdom" that the ankle should be covered and protected, but most mountain walking, except technical climbing, is done on trails, where a stiff heel counter is really all the support you need. Some hiking boots have padding (as in the photo on page 221) along the tips of the ankle cut to help keep the dirt and pebbles from getting inside the shoe.

Weatherproofing test.   Waterproof shoes are more important for walking sports than other sports, because you not only walk in almost any weather and spend more time on your feet, but you also spend more time walking during wet and snowy seasons and over a variety of terrain. It is important to keep your feet dry because water will soften your skin, and soft skin hastens blisters, the bane of sportwalkers.

Leather (treated with waterproofing wax) is still the best proofing. Unfortunately, synthetic materials resist only moisture and light rain at

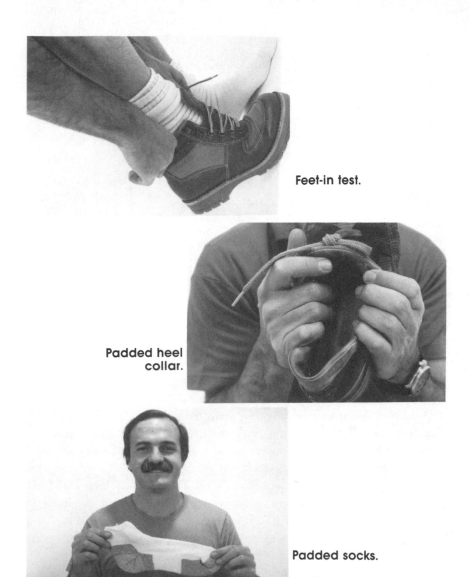

Feet-in test.

Padded heel collar.

Padded socks.

best. As soon as it rains moderately to heavily, puddles form, so you need more than water resistance. This is when you switch back to your sturdy shoes.

SWITCHING SHOES AND SOCKS

During a long walking day, you should change socks and shoes at least once, usually after lunch. This gives you an opportunity to start with fresh dry feet and also gives the shoes and socks a chance to dry and air out.

During switch-offs you can use your light shoes. You'll be amazed at how much lighter they feel on your feet. Moving from the sturdy to lightweight shoes is somewhat like a foot massage. The light shoes reduce the pressure on top of your feet, giving your foot muscles a chance to relax.

FOOT AIDS

Foot aids include medicants and massage to protect your feet from fatigue, soreness, and blistering. Tense foot muscles are the result of fatigue and can make you even more tired. Rubbing against shoes and socks causes skin abrasion and soreness.

Remember to:

1. *Toughen your feet* with gradual build-up of mileage, stopping right away when you feel tenderness and soreness.

2. *Not procrastinate* when treating feet, because immediate attention can head off blistering.

3. *Massage bare feet often* while walk training and during event participation. This relaxes muscles and stimulates blood circulation to sore and tender areas. The photos on page 223 show how to massage the toes, balls of the feet, and the heels and ankles.

4. *Expose your feet to sun and air often.* This will help keep your feet dry and give them the chance to recuperate from the constant pounding and sweating. During 5- to 15-minute rest stops, make a practice of removing your shoes and socks and giving yourself a quick foot massage.

SOCK TEST

Design construction and thickness are probably more important in socks than the type of material. Your walking socks can have extra padding under the forefoot, around the heels and across the top of your foot just contiguous to the line where your toes end. But they should not be so thick that they promote sweating.

Wool has been the traditional favorite for hiking because of warmth and moisture absorption. Combinations of wool, cotton, and synthetic

As soon as you feel discomfort, take your shoes off, check your feet for hot spots, and massage them.

materials offer walkers a lightweight, thinner sock that allows the foot to breathe and also provides cushioning. Both approaches to materials are valid.

If you want your socks to cushion your feet, wear two pairs, a regular pair outside of a thin pair. To keep your foot drier, the thin pair can be replaced as it gets wet. I find that layering two pairs of socks feels more comfortable than one thick pair.

Pack extra pairs for training and event participation. Fresh socks will not only help you keep your feet drier and blister-free, they will also give you a psychological boost. The feel of fresh dry socks on your feet goes to your head. You feel less tired.

BLISTERS

Blisters are probably the number one injury for sportwalkers. You *can* avoid them; they usually occur because of improperly fitted shoes or socks and wet feet, in that order. Never take your feet for granted. Tend to them right away when you feel the slightest irritation.

Hot-spot test. If your feet feel hot or tender, take off your shoes and socks and inspect the area immediately. Massage the area and feel how tender it is. If it looks or feels tender, apply tape or moleskin to protect it from getting worse.

Blister protection. If a blister or raw area has formed, treat it carefully. Only if the blister is painful should you use a sterilized needle to open a small hole to drain out the fluid. It is most important *not* to remove the dead skin from a blister because it acts as the best protection for the area. Put some antibiotics on it and cover the area with gauze or padding. Perhaps the most advanced method of blister protection was the one I saw used by the Dutch medics at Nijmegen. It's called *dachbau* and means roof shingling. Narrow strips of special tape are applied tightly over the raw or blistered area (once the blister has been popped and cleaned). Narrow tape is better than wide because you are able to fit it more to the contours of your foot surface. This will keep the tape from wrinkling when you walk on it and prevent further blistering.

BODYWARE AND BODY AIDS

Bodyware is all the inner and outer clothing you take with you when training and during the sportwalk itself. The selection, use, and care of bodyware and body aids relate to the high frequency of their use in the walking action.

Bodyware and body aids should:

1. Be *designed for a full range of motion* during all phases of the walking action.

2. *Protect muscles against rapid cooling* from wind, rain, and cold.

3. *Shield your head and neck from sun and light glare* to prevent headaches.

4. *Allow for air passage* to and from your skin to cool and evaporate sweat.

5. *Provide layering* to stabilize body temperature in hot and cold weather.

6. *Absorb excess moisture* on the inner or "sweat" layer.

7. *Keep your muscles relaxed*, avoiding contraction from excessive use, cold, or heat.

Dachbau.

MOTION TEST

Wearing the apparel, move through the full range of walking action. Check whether parts and clothing bind or pull against you during the arm and leg swing.

LAYERING TEST

Bodyware should consist of three layers: (1) inner, or sweat, (2) outer garment, and (3) weather-protection garments or wind and rain gear. Each layer traps air, which is warmed up by your body heat. Each layer of clothing should be thin and flexible, so you can wear one layer over the other. When you are sportwalking or training, add or remove layers as you feel hot or cold, either from exertion or a change in the air temperature. Remove the inner layer when it gets wet and replace it with extra layers from your day pack.

When you're selecting items for purchase, try on all three layers at once and test for range of motion. The thickness and type of material will affect the flexibility of the items.

Inner layer. The inner layer provides for sweat absorption in the summer walk events. It is often wet so your body stays cool. In the winter walk events, you should change or remove your inner layer if it gets too wet to avoid cooling down. The inner layer (underwear) is usually made of a cotton blend so it is light and absorbs moisture.

Some walkers choose an inner layer that passes moisture through to the next layer. The inner layer for the lower body is long underwear or

Three layers for peeling off and putting on.

tights in the winter and undershorts or pants in the summer. The inner layer for the upper body is a long-sleeved T-shirt in the winter and a short-sleeved T-shirt or halter in the summer.

Middle layer.   The middle layer provides warmth and some protection from cold air and wind. You will be wearing this and the inner layer throughout most of the walk. The middle layer for the upper body is a long-sleeved shirt (perhaps a turtleneck shirt) in cool weather or a long- or short-sleeved shirt or sweatshirt in the warm months.

The middle layer for the lower body is long pants or sweat pants or shorts when there is no wind or cold. Great care must be exercised in the use of short pants for long walks. If there is any wind blowing, you should cover up your legs because prolonged (more than one hour) exposure to wind will cool down your leg muscles and cause them to contract or cramp. Always cover up your legs with long pants when it's cold or when a wind is blowing.

The middle layer also includes a cap with a brim to shield your eyes from the sun.

Outer layer.   The outer layer should be resistant to wind and rain. It also traps enough air so that it will suffice along with the first two layers to keep you warm in the coldest weather. The outer layer for the upper body usually includes a zip-up or button-up jacket with a hood. Your outer layer suit for very cold weather should also have a hood.

226

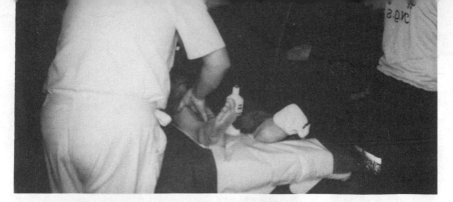

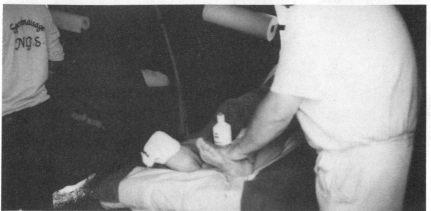

Sport massage: Apply constant pressure directly to muscles and tendons. Although it may hurt, your muscles will feel better afterward.

BODY CARE

SPORT MASSAGE

Massaging leg muscles during the event or a long training period will help relax them and reduce soreness. Although regular massage is best done by a skilled physical therapist, it doesn't hurt to try to do it to yourself. It can help recovery by removing waste products that build up in muscles. Many international walk events have medical stations along the route where you can get a sport massage. This involves manipulation primarily of the leg muscles—quadriceps, hamstrings, calves—by kneading the muscle and also pressing against it to relax it and stimulate blood flow (as in the photo above).

ELEVATING LEGS

Elevating your legs and lying flat on your back will help make your rest stops more refreshing.

13
SPORTWALK DIET AND NUTRITION

IN THE SPORTWALKING context, nutrition means not only what you eat but how and when you eat. These considerations are all equally important. Food is a source of long-term and short-term energy, as well as a source of pleasure. Balance of food calories and training calories will help you control your weight. More so than participants in other sports, except perhaps cross-country skiing, sportwalkers eat while they train and as they are participating in walking events.

SPORTWALKING AND WEIGHT CONTROL

Sportwalk events are high calorie burners. The four-day Nijmegen walk, for example, burns over 12,000 calories, or the equivalent of a week's worth of extra eating. A two-mile volksmarch or racewalk, completed in a couple of hours, is worth 1,200 calories. You can manage this distance every other weekend. A 50-mile hike over rugged terrain is worth 6,000 calories. The terrain burns 25 to 35 additional calories per mile because it is more work. A 24-hour, 100-mile walk adds 5,000 extra calories because you skip sleeping time. By staying on your feet so many hours, you add 12 hours of awake and standing time to your walking calories.

A trekking or touring vacation of a week or two burns 1,200 to 3,500 calories a day. A 15- to 45-day road walk of 300 to 1,000 miles burns 30,000 to 100,000 calories. Hill walking and mountain climbing are worth 200 to 300 calories per mile. A walk up and down Ben Nevis, Britain's highest mountain at 3,000 feet, burns 3,000 calories in 3½ hours. Calories burned climbing up and down are two to three times the level of walking calories.

Thus, dedicating yourself to walking as a sport will mean that you will increase the rate at which you burn calories 7 to 30 times, or about 100 to 1,000 calories more per day. This assumes about 100 calories on the average for every mile you walk. A Level III sportwalker will burn an average of 2,800 to 3,200 calories a week, which amounts to an extra day or two of eating, or about a pound of calorie burning a week. This amounts to 1,400 to 2,100 calories more than the number needed to maintain your weight, or about a half of a pound of potential weight loss per week. (One pound equals 3,500 calories.) In a week, sportwalkers at Levels IV and V will burn 3,200 to 6,000 calories (one-half to one pound of potential weight loss) and 6,000 to 10,000 calories (one to two pounds of weight loss), respectively.

To stay in equilibrium, you need to burn between 200 and 300 exercise calories a day, or 10,000 exercise calories a year. In a year, walkers at Level III burn 42,000 to 87,000 (4 to 8 times the minimum), those at Level IV burn 87,000 to 175,000 (8 to 15 times the minimum), and those at Level V burn 175,000 to 350,000 calories (15 to 30 times the minimum). If you are new to sportwalking, you will lose a lot of weight unless you change your eating habits. Based on 3,500 calories burned per pound of body fat, the potential weight loss is:

Level	Potential Weight Loss
III	20–25 pounds per year
IV	25–50 pounds per year
V	50–100 pounds per year

Of course, to some degree you'll offset the high mileage and calorie burn with increased appetite and, therefore, calorie consumption, but not completely. You'll be increasing your muscle mass as you burn away fat. The net result will be weight loss. How much you lose depends on how much you control your eating while you train and sportwalk.

Here's a simple prescription for sportwalker's weight control and weight loss: If you are overweight, hold the line on your calorie consumption at the early stages of your training, i.e., up to and including Level III. The first 6 to 16 weeks of training (Levels I to III) will be done at a moderate level. This means that your appetite will not increase dramatically during this period. Research has shown that moderate exercise does not raise appetite as rapidly as high-intensity exercise. You will lose 5 to 15 pounds in this four-month period without feeling much pain.

You can accelerate your weight loss by restricting your calories to a minimum of 1,200 to 1,600 a day. This means you will lose 200 to 500 calories a day of fat by dieting in addition to your walking calories. The dieting calories add up to an additional one-quarter to one-half pound of weight loss, or 4 to 8 pounds during the four-month period, for a total of 9 to 23 pounds. If there ever was an exercise program you could combine with dieting, it is sportwalking. Sportwalking, at moderate or early levels, tends to suppress your appetite and distract you from wanting to eat.

By the time you reach the upper regions of Level III and head to Levels IV and V, you should be much trimmer and more muscular. But beware: If you do not watch your eating and drinking, you can gain weight even at Levels IV and V. It is possible to gain weight during high activity by eating and drinking to excess. Think of your training levels as providing you with one-half, one, and two pounds or one, two, and three days of extra eating capacity, respectively. This means about one (for Level III), two (for Level IV), or three (for Level V) extra big meals with dessert or drinking bouts per week. Do not exceed this margin, or you will gain despite the walking mileage.

WHAT TO EAT AND DRINK: THE NUTRITION TRADITION UPDATED

Sportwalk nutrition is really derived more from the outdoor living habits of hikers and alpinists than it is from the training tables of track

GUIDELINES TO NUTRITIOUS DINING

1. Avoid foods and seasonings with unsaturated fat. (Choose lean red meats, for example.)
2. Improve the quality of any increased calories consumed. It's a more "savvy" way of eating.
3. Derive sugar from sucrose in fruit rather than processed sugar.
4. Avoid processed foods, which break down the whole food value. (For example, eat whole grain rather than enriched breads.)
5. Eat rich, namely, high-calorie foods in moderation (one per week extra per training Level III and above).
6. Eat and drink the following favorite foods in moderation:
   a. *Chocolate*—Walkers and climbers consider chocolate to be food for nourishment rather than indulgence. They are so active they need the calories and energy boost it gives on the trail. Eat chocolate only on sportwalk or high-mileage training days above 12 miles, then limit yourself to one bar for every five miles.
   b. *Bread and Cheese*—Limit your consumption to weekends and

and field athletes. Sportwalkers have favorite foods: fresh fruit, chocolate, raisins and nuts, milk, wine and beer, bread and cheese. This is basically the typical picnic basket of Europeans. Being able to eat more of these favorite foods is one of the "noble goals" of sportwalkers. They look forward to walking vacations because they know they will keep their activity level high and be able to sample the local cuisine at will.

Sportwalkers also look forward unabashedly to the end-of-the-day meal or glass of beer or wine, because they feel they have *earned* it. I'd say there is a greater joie de vivre among sportwalk enthusiasts than other athletes. They know that sport participation makes life more enjoyable.

Nevertheless, modern sportwalkers should apply new information about nutrition and weight control; they can eat "skillfully," without spoiling the fun of the sportwalking picnic or victory dinner.

TRAINING DIET

During training, you should start with breakfast and eat at least three regular meals per day or five smaller meals spaced throughout the day.

sportwalk events, choosing whole-grain breads and low-fat cheeses.

c. *Alcohol*—Avoid consuming any alcohol until your walking day is over. It will slow you down and make it hard to walk farther. Limit yourself to one glass a day of wine or beer during the week and two to three glasses of either at the end of a sportwalk day. Beer and wine are preferred over other alcoholic beverages because of their higher water content.

d. *Meats and Fish*—Order your favorite meats lean (either select a lean cut or ask that the fat be cut off) and your fish white. This allows you to feast with lower-calorie meals. Order sauces and seasonings separately so you can apply them sparingly yourself.

e. *Dessert*—Fruit and cheese make a lower-calorie dessert than cake and ice cream. An extra glass of wine or cup of coffee can often top off a gourmet feast just as well but with fewer calories than a rich dessert. Limit yourself to one creamy dessert per week.

f. *Fruit, Vegetables, and Water*—Fill yourself up on fruit, vegetables, and water before you start eating and drinking the high-calorie portions of your meal. This way, you will eat and drink for taste and not to fill yourself up.

Breakfast is the most important meal for the training diet. Studies show that skipping it will physically, if not psychologically, affect your performance. Try to eat two hours before intense training such as speed training. You can continue to train moderately right after eating, so long as you do not experience stomach upset. If you train too hard while digesting a meal, your muscles will be competing with your stomach for the available blood supply.

Throughout the training year and particularly on weekends, you should maintain a well-balanced diet, eating a variety of foods from the four basic food groups and selecting items that are low in fat and sugar and high in fiber content, and staying within the limits of servings per group.

DAILY SERVING LIMITS

The sample menu shown in Chart 13-1 illustrates limits on foods selected from the following groups. Be sure to include something from each group:

- *Fruits and Vegetables* (high water and fiber content)—Yellow and green vegetables, tomatoes, grapefruit, oranges, apples, and pears.
- *Bread and Cereals* (roughage, lower calories, better if not presweetened)—Whole-grain breads and wheat and bran cereals.
- *Meat and Fish*—Avoid large quantities of red meat, choosing instead white fish and poultry.
- *Milk Group*—Skim or low-fat milk, low-fat cheese (mozzarella, cottage, farmer's), yogurt.

CHART 13-1
SAMPLE TRAINING MENU

Breakfast
1 glass skim milk
cereal or bran muffin or 1 or 2 eggs (poached)
bacon (only 3 times a week)
toast
coffee
1 glass water

Lunch
fruits
chocolate
bread
lean meats (2 oz.)
vegetables
1 glass skim milk or diet soda

Dinner
fish or meat (broiled, poached, or baked)
salad
vegetables
skim milk or beer or wine (limit 1 glass)

Snacks
midmorning: small sandwich or piece of fruit
midday: cottage cheese, salad, or soup

STRIKING A NUTRITIONAL BALANCE

Sportwalkers do not eat to win; they eat to nourish and enjoy. They are a different breed who practice the philosophy of moderation, even in their training diets. Above all, the sportwalk training diet should be well-balanced in two respects:

1. The energy balance
2. The nutrient, or food group, balance.

The *energy balance* refers to the quantity of food consumed and stored, measured against the quantity of calories burned in daily training. Energy calories are derived from carbohydrates and fats. The *nutrient balance* refers to the quality of food consumed, namely sufficient protein and vitamins to protect bodily processes and basic health. Nutrients help to maintain and nourish your bodily systems for daily living and growing.

You can derive the special energy you need for muscular exercise in sport from two main food ingredients, carbohydrates and fats. *Carbohydrates*, which consist of sugars and starches, are found primarily in fruits, vegetables, breads, cereals, and pasta, but also in the meat food group. Carbohydrates are processed by the body into glucose, which is stored in your muscles and liver as glycogen, a real powerhouse for walking! *Fats* are also a source of energy, including a stored form of energy. Pound for pound, fats contain more stored energy than carbohydrates. Fats are contained primarily in meat and milk products but also in vegetable oils.

ENERGY BALANCE

Practicing an endurance sport, walkers derive most of their energy from carbohydrates, but these should be used in combination with fats. Relying on one form of energy will not produce optimal results for endurance activities. Studies have shown that athletes are able to work longer on a high-carbohydrate diet than a high-fat diet, particularly if the activity performed lasts for more than one hour.

Moderate-intensity exercise draws most of its energy from fat, while high-intensity exercise draws most of its energy from carbohydrates. The longer distances you walk, the more you will draw on carbohydrates, but you also draw on fats in your day-to-day shorter-distance, more moderate walking training. This suggests loading up more on carbohydrates before and during sportwalks, so you'll have more long-term endurance energy, then reverting to more balanced sources of energy during training. It is important not to rely strictly on carbohydrates for moderate exercise, because you will condition your body to rely on them or wear down the glycogen levels in your muscles even during moderate exercise.

Carbohydrate loading is necessary only before sportwalks of 12 or more miles. You can start eating more carbohydrate (starchy) foods like pasta, cereal, and bread two or three days before the event. At that time, cut back on fats and proteins, such as red meats.

NUTRIENT BALANCE

The nutrient or quality balance affects how you maintain and build up your body. This is therefore related to strength and speed training more than endurance training. Basic nutrients are proteins and vitamins.

Proteins build up tissues and organs in the body. They are found primarily in the meat group but also in the milk group. They are secondarily derived from fruits and vegetables. Protein should especially be consumed during the build-up period to help with muscular growth and strengthening.

Vitamins are important to basic health and resistance to infections. Generally, a balanced diet with daily servings from all food groups will produce a sufficient number of vitamins. Of special note is vitamin C, which many sportwalkers believe helps them resist colds when walking in cold and wet weather or when exercise fatigue may have lowered their resistance. Vitamin C can be derived from eating fresh fruit. Vitamins play only a secondary role in sportwalking to ensure that rugged training and participation conditions do not wear down the body's resistance to disease.

NUTRITION DURING THE EVENT

On the morning of your sportwalk, you should have breakfast—a hearty one if the walk is longer than 12 miles. Eat a breakfast that is high in carbohydrates (plenty of cereal, bread, and jam). You can also have milk, coffee, eggs, and fruit. If you are nervous about the event, try to eat two to three hours before, to avoid nerves affecting your digestion.

On sportwalk days you should eat and drink frequently but in small amounts throughout the day. Table 13-1 shows a sample menu for an event day. You should snack or have a small meal at the 10- to 12-mile mark and at every three to five miles (about one hour of walking) thereafter.

TABLE 13-1
SAMPLE EVENT DAY MENU

Breakfast
fruit juice/fresh fruit
bread/cereal (hot or cold)
meat (bacon, ham, or sausage) and eggs
coffee or tea

Midmorning Snack
sandwich, fruit, or chocolate bar

Lunch
sandwiches or hot meal
salad
vegetables

Hourly Snacks
fruit, soda, or small sandwich

Dinner
hot meal
vegetables
salad
dessert
beer or wine (limit 2 glasses)

Evening Snack
fruit, dessert, or sandwich

Drinking water is perhaps most important. You should sip one-half to one glass of water every hour—even more often if you are walking in hot weather. Your thirst may not be an adequate guide to your needs. Your body does not signal dehydration or heat exhaustion fast enough, so sip water even if you are not thirsty and err on the side of more rather than less.

SPECIAL EATING DURING RACEWALKING

During racewalks of under 20 kilometers, there will be no need to eat, nor will it be allowed. However, water stations should be placed every 3 to 5 kilometers and clearly marked. In events longer than 20 kilometers, and especially in 50-kilometer events, eating is important. Many racewalkers prepare special drinks, mixing water and glucose. The high-intensity work requires that you replace fluid and maintain the sugar level in your blood.

PART FOUR
ORGANIZING

WHAT MAKES SPORTWALKING different from spur-of-the-moment walking is the degree to which it is better planned and organized. Part IV presents a wide range of organizational possibilities, from organizing the one-person walk, to getting together with one additional walker, to bringing together thousands of walkers at one walk. The choice of how organized you want to get is really yours. Regardless of size, all sportwalks and walking clubs should share the same organizational and management functions.

Organizing leads to better socializing. The benefits of being better organized are expanded opportunities to take interesting walks and meet more and experienced walkers with whom to walk and talk. For instance, at international events you will meet interesting people from different cultures. Walking clubs are current, up-to-date clearinghouses for information about walks and walking. They can provide you with better training from walking instructors and coaches.

Walking is truly a democratic sport. For example, if you are a businessperson, you'll probably find yourself walking with top management. The CEO of any major corporation is probably by this time a walker; he or she has become wise and self-confident enough to enjoy life on the "slow" track. On a typical sportwalk, everybody walks together at the same level, head-to-head and shoulder-to-shoulder. Sportwalking fosters equality more than many other social functions, work situations, even other sport events. Since there are no winners and losers in most sportwalk events, you don't have to worry about passing a friend or your boss; you can simply walk along with him or her and enjoy the conversation and scenery.

Although annually there are probably 250,000 organized walks worldwide, the walking revolution is still in its beginning stage. The current level of 6,000 American and 25,000 worldwide clubs and chapters of clubs spreads very thinly over the 300,000-plus communities in the United States and 750,000 communities throughout the world. There's a lot of room for the development of more organizations. So, if you can't find a walk or walking group, don't wait; organize one yourself. Or join or organize a chapter of one of the national and international walking club systems listed in the Appendices.

14
EVENT WALKS, RACEWALKS, CHALLENGE WALKS

THIS CHAPTER IS a general guide to planning and organizing your own sportwalk events, including personal challenge walks. There are three basic types of sportwalks:

1. Event Walks—Noncompetitive group walks usually following a circular route
2. Racewalks—Competitive walking races on a track or road
3. Challenge Walks—24-hour or multiday long-distance walks.

Special organizational preparations for racewalks and challenge walks are given at the end of the chapter. Otherwise, the guidelines for planning, budgeting, staffing, and operations apply to all three kinds of events.

PLANNING THE EVENT

An idea for a sportwalk is inspired by the lack of similar events in the area and the desire to promote walking. For instance, the purpose of an event is often to raise funds for a charity or community organization.

Once you have some ideas, you should research the possibilities for holding an event in your community.

ESTABLISHING THE PURPOSE

What is the purpose of your sportwalk? Your purpose will probably be to promote walking in your community and perhaps also to raise funds for a good cause, publicize a sponsor's name and product among walkers, find and associate yourself with other walkers, or a combination of all of these.

Carefully choose a name for your walk event that will clearly publicize its purpose. This will help you attract the right number and right kind of participants. If your walk is scenic or challenging, name the event after the distance and walking site. You should also incorporate your sponsor's or organization's name into the title, trading on the sponsor's name recognition and goodwill.

DETERMINING THE SIZE

Types of sportwalk events are based primarily on the number of the participants and secondarily on the style of walking that will be practiced at the event. With the exception of racewalking, race or competitive walks do not need special handling.

The amount of planning and organizing work is commensurate with the size of the event. The size of your first event will be limited by your experience, budget, and the amount of lead time. It's best to start small and gradually build up the size over a 3- to 5-year period.

Event walks can be divided into three basic sizes: small (5 to 50 people), medium (50 to 1,000 people), and big (1,000 to 6,000 people). These three sizes are not arbitrary; they are based on the degree of difficulty for organizing and managing large groups of people and reflect 75 years of experience in organizing walking events.

If you are planning your first event and do not have an experienced partner who has organized and directed events, you should definitely start small and set your participation target below 100. But if the purpose of your event is to raise funds or publicize a sponsor, you will probably have to deliver a greater number of walkers, ranging from 100 to 1,000. You will also have to increase the lead time for organization and will probably have to hire professionals. Events with large numbers of participants are built up over many years with a intensive grassroots organization; you cannot, except in rare cases, build up a big event overnight.

The small event walk.   In its simplest form, a walk event starts with an announcement on a bulletin board. The essential elements of the announcement are:

- *A Headline:* Meet Us for a Spring Walk.
- *The Time and Starting Place:* At 9:00 A.M., Saturday, March 28 at the corner of Bank and Hudson.
- *The Route:* Around the Old Mill Pond.
- *The Walking Time and Distance:* For five miles, or about three hours.
- *The Finishing Time and Place:* Ending at the Mill at noon, where we'll have a picnic lunch.
- *Special Instructions:* Wear comfortable walking shoes. Bring along a sweater, because it will be chilly. Pack a lunch and drinks.
- *Contact and Walk Leaders:* R.S.V.P. or information, call Joan at 837-9090.

Your most important consideration is picking an interesting walk.

You can post your sportwalk bulletin on a hospital, social club, community, or corporate bulletin board. This call for walkers is the beginning of your association with other walkers. An announcement like this one may attract 5 to 50 walkers, qualifying it as a small sportwalk. The planning and organizational requirements are minimal. If you do not receive a response, you can post your announcement on more bulletin boards or place it in a help-wanted column of a newspaper. Ultimately, you will find walkers.

Your sportwalk organization is streamlined; it concentrates on simple walks, reducing the need for an elaborate organizational structure. When you think about it, all a sportwalk organization ever has to do is announce a time, place, route, and walk leader. Walkabout International uses this simple walk-announcement system to publicize its events in its own newsletters and local newspaper.

The medium-sized walk event.   A medium-sized sportwalk has 50 to 1,000 participants. A preplanning period is necessary to select and clear a site with local authorities in order to accommodate a larger or faster group of walkers. The larger the number of participants, the greater the amount of lead time you will need for planning the event.

A larger group of walkers can no longer be led by just one person who knows the route; you will need to manage and plan the route, marking it with intermediate-distance checkpoints. You will need to design, print, and distribute registration materials. You will also need a staff of specialists to assist you in directing the event, publicizing it, and managing a budget.

The key to success is the number of experienced, paid staff people who manage reliable, well-motivated volunteers. It is precarious to run an event of this size with just part-time volunteers; they cannot commit the continuous time and effort necessary to organize and manage it.

The big event.   After entries surpass 1,000 walkers, a walk event takes on a different character, that of a big event. To succeed, big events must be run like a business or military organization, with a core staff of paid professionals who manage a network of volunteers grouped into committees. The bigger the event, the more staff, volunteers, and lead time needed.

Big- and medium-sized events present a logistical challenge for the sportwalk organizer, including special governmental permissions, traffic control, sponsors, long lead times, materials and registration, and publicity and advertising. If the walk event becomes really popular, sportwalkers will want to return to it the following year to relive the experience and meet up again with old walking friends.

The big event draws a range of 1,000 to 6,000 walkers but can grow over the years to 10,000, 15,000, 25,000, and even 50,000 participants, becoming a national or international event that attracts one-fourth to one-half of its participants from out of town. So the event will probably build up its own constituency represented by a computerized mailing list. But big events like Nijmegen take five or more years to build up their participation from 6,000 to 20,000. By holding an event every year on the same weekend and by inviting past participants, you will gradually build up a large constituency of satisfied walkers who tell their friends about the event. Word-of-mouth referrals constitute the good reputation that you earn. After a few years, the size of your event will be determined by how well-run it is and how happy the walkers were with the event.

San Francisco
Hill Stride.

CHOOSING THE SITE

The walking site is often created from an area that you feel has potential
to inspire other walkers besides yourself. It is often a natural area near
to the city from which most sportwalkers come. To determine its
availability for a sporting event, check with local officials and pick a
weekend when other sports events are not being held. Will other events
like running races compete for space, or will they be completed before
your walk has to be set up? You have to match the type of event to a
place where it can be held. The most likely candidates are a park, a field,
a track, city streets, and country roads and trails.

Perhaps you might find the best location for a small- or medium-sized
walk along an established route selected as one of America's greatest
city or country walks in my book (see *America's Greatest Walks*
[Addison-Wesley, 1986]).

DESIGNING THE ROUTE

Once you have determined your walk site, trace a route that takes best
advantage of the scenery and is safe for the number of walkers you
expect. If your sportwalk is on dirt trails rather than paved roads, you
will probably have to limit the number of participants. Trails are narrow
and easily trampled by many feet, so you should make some preliminary

sketches of possible routes and walk them to determine their safety, scenic qualities, and ability to support the number of walkers for your planned event.

The route will most likely be circular, so walkers will find variety. There should be a clearing for the start and finish, with nearby parking or access to public transportation. Circular routes with the start and finish in the same area are easier to set up and manage.

SETTING THE DATE AND TIME

You will have to reserve not only a place but also a time slot. Especially in large cities, you will have to reserve parks early for the choice times to hold outdoor events, because most public areas today are used for other sports activities. The demand is usually highest in the spring, fall, and summer, respectively.

Walk events usually start at 9:00 or 10:00 A.M.; the local press won't come any earlier to cover events. Estimate three miles for every hour. If the distances are greater than 12 miles, the events can start as early as 4:00 A.M. In any case, they should finish before sunset. Here's a table of recommended starting times based on event distances:

Distance	Starting Time	Finishing Time
1–12 miles	9:00–10:00 A.M.	1:00–2:00 P.M.
12–20 miles	8:00–9:00 A.M.	2:00–4:00 P.M.
20–30 miles	7:00–8:00 A.M.	3:00–5:00 P.M.
30–50 miles	4:00–6:00 A.M.	4:00–7:00 P.M.

OBTAINING PERMITS

You can be certain that if your walk is held in a public place—as 99 percent of sportwalks are—you will have to obtain permits from one or more of the following governmental agencies: the parks and recreation department; city, state, or national police department; and the traffic department or city hall for using parks or special facilities, crossing intersections, selling food, registering for the event, hanging banners, and setting up sound systems.

Permits take weeks, even months, for approval, so submit them well in advance. Many localities prohibit the publicizing of events using their facilities before permits are approved. Large events also have to post bonds for police and clean-up.

COVERING LIABILITY

While you should certainly obtain signed releases or waivers in favor of organizers and sponsors, they will probably be insufficient in the case of medium-sized and large events. Many governmental authorities require that events be insured for third-party liability. Because insurance for sports is becoming increasingly costly and difficult to obtain, new events are more difficult to insure. Establish the availability of insurance early on. You may wish to insure your event in a rider attached to the established policy of your sponsor.

FINDING RESOURCES FOR FUNDING

Medium-sized and big events should be run like a business organization. This means that you should start with a budget to cover staff and out-of-pocket expenses for printing, mailing, and other logistics. If you are working with an established organization, you may be able to save money by having it assign staff personnel to your event and by drawing on the organization's printing, mailing, and telephone capacities. You can also use its office space as event headquarters.

Medium-sized and large events require funding, so you will have to raise money in advance from sponsors to acquire an event budget. Later, some of your registration fees can be used to cover budget items, but your initial budget should come from sponsor or personal sources.

Once you have planned your event, write up a proposal to send to potential sponsors. The proposal should cover:

- Purpose
- Benefits
- Description
- Cost/Budget
- Staff and Operations

Sponsors plan their marketing budgets 6 to 12 months before execution, so you must solicit early. Allow 2 to 12 months' lead time. Sponsors seek to fund established sports events that offer high visibility and a large number of participants. They may take a chance on you with a new walking event if you can show a unique event theme and have associated yourself with experienced organizations.

STAFFING

Staff functions are areas of responsibility that can be performed by one person in the case of small events but must be split among a staff of people in large events. Three key staff functions—event management, event direction, and public relations—are required to adequately budget, control, and execute the event. The bigger the event, the larger the number of paid and full-time coordinators and workers you will need, and the longer the lead time before the event.

These functions will probably be performed by different specialists, because many functions happen simultaneously. In many small and some medium-sized events, all these functions can be performed by a part-time staff person (often you). But in most medium-sized and large events, these functions become the work of a full-time staff member. Event personnel often work overtime to make an event a success.

EVENT MANAGEMENT

Control of business management and event management should rest in the hands of the event manager, also called chairperson or executive director. In charge of the whole event, he or she delegates responsibilities to different professionals and committee managers. Business management can also be delegated to and exercised by a business management committee, with members of other specialized committees reporting to it, but the chairperson of the committee should be ultimately responsible. All other functions are subordinate to management and subject to budget control.

PUBLIC RELATIONS

Public relations has become a professional skill, just like event direction, but many public relations firms may be too expensive to justify hiring them for a single event. You will probably have to find a freelance publicist. Publicizing your event in advance is both a necessary and an economical way of soliciting participants. Newspapers, magazines, radio, and television will provide announcements of the time, place, and nature of your event, if you can persuade them that it is "newsworthy," that is, an event with a unique purpose, route, theme, or celebrity guest.

Professional publicists can help you write a press release with a news angle. It is important that the release be well-written, one to three pages in length, double-spaced, and accompanied by black-and-white photos, maps, and registration materials. If you can't get a feature news story, try to submit a list of your events for publication in newspapers and walking club newsletters.

In any case, the public relations effort can be used the week before the event if it is small or local, but should be started one or two months in advance of a large event to help stimulate registration efforts.

EVENT DIRECTION

Skills in directing and managing sports events have been developed from events for running and bicycling clubs. The events are usually handled by an event or race director and usually concentrate on managing event activities of the day, including setting up and clearing the event site.

COMMITTEE SYSTEM

The large, well-organized event works best with a committee system. Committees implement the three main staff functions, using volunteers and experts. Volunteers are necessary and must be used wisely and efficiently; focus their efforts on specific assignments. The event organizer must rely on volunteers who will happily contribute their time and effort to promoting the cause of walking, because a sportwalk event cannot support a budget to cover paying all the people needed to handle thousands of walkers.

Staff and volunteers are best organized into a series of four or five committees covering the logistical and operational functions of the event. A workable structure is:

- Business Management Committee
- Start/Finish Committee
- Route Planning and Management Committee
- Logistics Committee
- Walk Leaders Committee

Business Management Committee.   The Business Management Committee is the board of directors. All other committees report to this committee, which should be chaired by the event manager. Chairpersons from the other committees also sit on this committee, as well as the publicist and representatives from sponsors and affiliated organizations. The committee should meet every two to four weeks until two months before the event, at which time it should meet every week until the second week before the event. At that time, meetings daily or every two days are appropriate.

Assignments for the Business Management Committee are:

1. Establish guidelines for event planning
2. Design and approve budget
3. Prepare sponsor proposal
4. Solicit sponsors
5. Negotiate with sponsors
6. Appoint committee chairpersons
7. Distribute written committee assignments
8. Set up schedule of meetings
9. Meet daily the two weeks before the event
10. Prepare a post-event evaluation

Start/Finish Committee.   The job of the Start/Finish Committee is to recruit and register walkers for the event and manage the start/ finish area. The committee also helps design, print, and distribute all event materials—registration forms, route cards, awards, T-shirts—and monitors and tabulates returns and bank registration fees a week before the event. This committee is present on event day to register and check in walkers. It is chaired by the event treasurer, event manager, or event director. The event publicist should sit in on meetings concerning the design and distribution of materials.

Publicity and advertising will help draw new people, but a direct-mail campaign of *registration forms* to previous participants and a large new target group of potential participants will draw the largest response. The registration form should be a direct-mail piece that can be folded and marked. One side contains sales copy announcing prizes and other benefits; the other side contains the form itself.

Registration fees vary from $1 to $20. Even if you do not charge a registration fee, you should register and obtain a signed release (including a parent's release for minors) for all your sportwalk participants.

To encourage walkers to preregister by mail, give them a discount (say, $1 less) from the standard fee. This will reduce the workload for the day-of-event registration and give you advance funds and information on your projected number of participants. Registration forms should be checked for signature and organized alphabetically, so they can be checked quickly on the day of the event. Later, the information on the forms should be compiled into mailing lists and fact sheets for future events.

Each sportwalker should carry a *route card* or bib number that can be stamped, punched, or pulled at each checkpoint. The card is distributed as part of registration and turned in fully certified at the end of the event at the finish line. The card should have the walker's name and club on it before he or she begins the walk. Completed cards are proof the walker has completed the event.

The Start/Finish Committee can also plan and design special *awards* for the walkers, as well as an awards ceremony immediately following the event or on the final day of a multiday event. In competitive events, awards can be given for the first three to ten finishers; these can be medals, trophies, or certificates. You can create awards for the oldest and youngest participants and for other categories such as parents wheeling baby carriages, best costume, or whatever.

In the United States, a T-shirt can be given to every finisher or every paid registrant. The cost of the T-shirt should be charged separately or included as part of the registration fee. All finishers in competitive and noncompetitive events should receive an award or certificate of completion.

While the event is going on, the Start/Finish Committee should begin to tabulate registration forms, route cards, and event results in preparation for the award ceremony immediately following. For example, the committee should determine which are the youngest and oldest participants or which club or group team has the largest number of finishers.

After the event, the Start/Finish Committee will prepare a report including the number and type of participants and other statistics, such as how far walkers came to attend the event. This report will be relevant for the press as well as for future sponsors.

To summarize, the Start/Finish Committee has the following assignments:

1. Receive and process mail registration
   a. Keep alphabetized list of registrants
   b. Supply Business Management Committee with updated registration list
   c. Keep forms in alphabetical order
   d. Keep checks in alphabetical order
   e. Mail out a sponsorship form for each walker in the walker's self-addressed, stamped envelope
   f. Fill out and alphabetize walk cards
   g. Distribute walk packets at office on a designated date before the event
2. Day-of-event activities
   a. Distribute packets and T-shirts
   b. Handle day-of-event registration: 20 to 50 miles, 5:15–5:45 A.M.; 20 to 30 miles, 6:45–7:15 A.M., 2 to 16 miles, 8:30–9:45 A.M.
   c. Validate walk cards at completion of walk
   d. Sign and validate sponsor sheets for walkers
3. Coordinate distribution of registration forms and posters with assistance from all other committees.
4. Determine awards—oldest, youngest, largest group, etc.

Route Planning and Management Committee.   The Route Planning and Management Committee scouts walk sites, designs maps, and marks the routes. A route should be marked and remarked a week before the event, and checked the day before and morning of the event. Committee volunteers are responsible for putting up and keeping up route markers, and will establish and staff checkpoints along the route on the day of the event.

When planning your walk route, consider running it past as many points of interest as possible, including historical, scenic, architectural, and natural sites. Avoid heavy-traffic areas and dangerous intersections, and arrange for traffic control if these are unavoidable. Participants should be provided with a *map* so that they don't get lost. Be sure to give walkers a written and, if necessary for clarity and convenience, oral explanation of how the route is marked.

When marking your route, set up *markers* along the route as well as directional signs showing turns or branch-offs from the main route. You can never have too many signs. Use codes of red, yellow, white, and other bright colors to mark different sections or branch-offs from the route. Volunteers from the route committee should take down all markers and signs and clean up garbage along the route immediately after the event. Leave it cleaner than before the event.

Checkpoints are set up at intermediate intervals (about every one to three miles) along the route. Here walkers have a route card checked or stamped. By collecting intermediate checks in this manner, walkers certify that they have completed the whole sportwalk distance. You can have a checkpoint table marked clearly or have control personnel standing across the trail so walkers will be sure to get their route cards or bibs stamped or punched. At least two volunteers should work each control point. The checkpoints should be placed where they will prevent walkers from taking shortcuts.

The Route Planning and Management Committee's assignments are:

1. Determine walk routes and draw maps
2. Mark route with markers (color-coded ribbons) and pointers (color-coded arrows where some confusion may exist as to where to turn)
3. Determine the site of checkpoints—each route should have at least one unique checkpoint that cannot be reached by a route of lesser distance
4. Establish a schedule for staffing checkpoints that is based on start/finish times and provides for reliefs on longer routes
5. Staff route 30 to 60 minutes before start of the event

Logistics Committee. The Logistics Committee is responsible for securing all materials needed to prepare and execute the event. One person can handle this function up to the week before the event, but afterward volunteers will be needed to help set up stations and tables for food, first aid, massage, and medical evacuation. This committee is also responsible for provisions for the volunteers and participants, including refreshments for committee meetings and water cups and containers at the event. The committee should be responsible for having a doctor available or on call, as well as for assisting the clean-up after the event.

The Logistics Committee is also in charge of painting a banner at the start/finish line and obtaining and setting up chairs and tables for the information and registration staff at the start and at checkpoints along the route.

To summarize, the Logistics Committee has the following assignments:

1. Medical contact, local Red Cross staff, and first-aid station at start/finish
   a. Provide first-aid kit for each checkpoint
   b. Formulate and arrange emergency medical and ambulance service
2. Portable toilets for start/finish area
3. Tables and chairs for start/finish area
4. Coordinate with local police and park officials

Walk Leaders Committee.   In some events, it is important to have event volunteers lead or accompany sportwalkers along the route. These are usually representatives of local walking clubs who know the route and can also act as tour guides for the sportwalkers. The Walk Leaders Committee is responsible for arranging for these people.

More specifically, the Walk Leaders Committee is responsible for the following assignments:

1. Assign at least one leader per route
2. At the start, line up groups in accordance with the length of the routes—longest route first—make signs for each length route
3. Start walks at appointed times
4. Lead walkers along prescribed routes at a moderate pace
   a. Walkers can either stay with leaders or go at their own pace
   b. Leaders may take breaks and lunch stop
5. Coordinate with Route Planning Committee

WORKING WITHIN TIME FRAMES

Each of the basic functions and myriad of individual tasks should be initiated or carried out in a specific time period before the event. Planning and operations should be accomplished within a time frame that gets longer with a larger number of anticipated participants. Big events require 6 to 12 months' lead time, medium-sized events need four to six months, and small events two weeks to four months. You are really counting backward 2 to 12 months before the event to set in motion important directions and activities.

Although the following items are given in detail, they are only samples. You must design a specific plan for your particular event, tailored to its special requirements. Note that the week numbers in this schedule refer to the number of weeks before the event.

Planning Phase
Week 52 to Week 44

- Research walk site and route
- Establish availability
- Do preliminary budgeting
- Write sponsor proposal, including operational plan and checklist
- Send out query letters to sponsors

Soliciting Phase
Week 44 to Week 36

- Send out proposals and meet with interested sponsors
- Negotiate sponsor agreements
- Set final plan and budget
- Obtain preliminary design of materials
- Coordinate meetings with sponsor representatives and other affiliated organizations

Staffing Phase
Week 36 to Week 16

- Recruit professional staff: public relations, event director, business management

Operations Phase
Week 16 to Week 13

- Organize committee of walk and community representatives
- Choose walk headquarters
- Hire event director
- Assign tasks to staff and volunteers
- Plan monthly budgets
- Contact local sponsors
- Identify walk sites and approximate routes
- Begin public relations and distribute press releases for event nationally and internationally

Week 12 to Week 9

- Select awards, equipment
- Open up booths and offices in walk centers
- Recruit volunteers for event administration and routes
- Design and print registration forms
- Distribute entry forms locally to visitors and convention centers, clubs, supermarkets, shopping malls, schools, etc.
- Finalize routes and route maps (measure and lay out course)
- Obtain permits from police and park officials where necessary

Week 8 to Week 5

- Process entries
- Start local ads for the event
- Obtain walk day, weekend, month proclamations from city, county, state
- Distribute posters, registration forms, etc.
- Hold pre-event publicity rallies
- Verify availability of facilities and equipment and delivery time of donated, rented, or purchased equipment so that they will be in your hands at the end of the month

Week 4 to Week 1

- Begin your final public relations push
- Distribute registrants' packets from walk headquarters
- Hold the walk and walk weekend activities
- Look ahead to next walk event and start thinking

The following paragraphs describe in chronological order the items you need to conduct a sportwalk event.

Select a walk site and sketch a route that will accommodate your type of sportwalk and will make it interesting and enjoyable for participants. Site candidates include parks, shopping centers, schools, and city, suburban, and country streets and roads.

Select a date that won't conflict with other sports events at the site and in the area. Also avoid conflicts with other walking events, so you will have a chance for maximum participation. Obtain all the necessary permits from local authorities: city hall, parks department, police department, athletic-conditioning organizations, highway departments, school authorities. Find out about other permits and requirements for insurance and sales.

Prepare a written plan for your event, describing the route, logistics,

CHECKLIST FOR THE DAY OF THE WALK EVENT

Be overprepared. A lot of last-minute "emergencies" can occur on the day of the walk, so be ready for anything. The best way to stay on top is to have enough paid staff on hand to act as a "safety net" for volunteers. Analyze potential problems and have solutions ready when they come up. Ask for double the number of volunteers you think you will need.

This checklist will come in handy at the event walk site:

☐ Routes clearly marked, color codes double-checked
☐ Buses and pick-up vehicles running
☐ Restrooms open, portable toilets near various routes
☐ All equipment in place and working (including checkpoint tables)
☐ Any barriers set up
☐ Start and finish lines clearly marked
☐ Signs and banners in place
☐ Parking areas clearly marked, personnel on hand to direct drivers
☐ Registration and checkpoint tables set up
☐ Aid stations stocked with plenty of water and first-aid supplies
☐ Public address system in place and working
☐ Special shirts distributed to first-aid crew
☐ Officials have shoes, shirts, stampers
☐ Traffic directors in place
☐ Photographers and television film crews on hand
☐ Areas available for reporters and TV/radio crews to interview walkers
☐ Reporters and official guests present if they want to take part, in order to promote the event
☐ Post-walk refreshments and festivities ready
☐ Awards on hand
☐ Interviews arranged
☐ Facilities cleaned and closed up, markers removed
☐ Course cleaned up
☐ Rented equipment returned

and time frame for developing the event. Solicit sponsors and negotiate with them.

Select a start/finish area that will accommodate all your projected walkers, as well as toilet facilities, award ceremonies, registration tables, resting areas, and—for a race—dressing and shower facilities.

Design the materials and forms you will need: posters, registration forms, route cards, logos, award certificates. Design and compose publicity materials: advance press releases and photos, start/finish banners.

Mail the advance registration forms as soon as you have mailing lists.

SPECIAL PREPARATION FOR RACEWALKS

Planning a racewalk involves some additional preparation. You will have to obtain bib numbers and assign these to competitors as they register. Also obtain a starter gun and decide who will fire it. (Usually you will want to ask a celebrity or politician, so that he or she will get a picture in the paper.)

Measure the course, and obtain the following items:

- Timers
- Competition numbers
- Safety pins
- Colored tape
- Finish-line string or tape
- Pencils, pens, clipboards
- Finish-line ribbon for chute
- Bullhorn
- Stopwatches
- Flags for chief judge (one white, one red)
- Refreshments: water stations, post-race fruit and bottled sodas, beer (if allowed)
- Medical services
- Doctor (or hospital) on hand or on call
- Massage and foot-care specialists
- First-aid kits
- Ambulance
- Volunteers and back-up volunteers

DAY OF EVENT

Meet two hours before the event to double-check supplies and volunteers' assignments. Recheck the course or route. Post maps of the course, set up registration and checkpoint tables, sort T-shirts by sizes, and have registration forms on hand.

Meet with the Logistics Committee and have them set up medical people, concessions, and water stations. Meet with the Route Planning Committee and send them to checkpoint stations and traffic-control points.

SPECIAL RACE INSTRUCTIONS

Competitors will want their lap times recorded, and judges will need room to judge walkers. Meet with police officers in charge, judges, timers, number readers, and the person who will give out place tickets. Send them to the starting line. Arrange for intermediate times. Have official cars cruise in front of and behind the walkers to keep the course clear.

Start the race after the finish-line people are in position and the tapes, timers, recorders, and number readers are in place. Line up the walkers, alerting them to the impending start. Shoot off the starting gun in front of and at the right of the race group by saying, "On your marks, get ready, get set! [shoot]." While the race is going on, set up the refreshments and awards table.

When the first-place walkers finish, stop the first-place watches. Stop the second- and third-place watches when the next walkers cross the finish line. Race officials must have an area and tables where they can tabulate results.

Hold the awards ceremony immediately after the race. Be sure to thank the sponsors, officials, volunteers, police, and participants for coming. Clean up the area within 30 to 60 minutes after the ceremony. Send the results and day-of-event press release to local newspapers, and follow up with photos. Send out thank-you letters to all who helped with the event.

CHARTING RACEWALKS

For walks held on tracks (400 meters/440 yards), record on a poster board the times and records of each competitor. Record the time for each participant every quarter mile or once around the track.

SPECIAL PREPARATION FOR CHALLENGE WALKS

Challenge walks can be organized like event walks, involving a group of walkers who walk a circular or linear (point-to-point) route, or like an outing or adventure involving fewer individuals along a route that often cannot be scouted in advance and requires special organization in route planning and logistical support. Challenge walks rarely involve more than 100 participants, so they are small to medium-sized events with the appropriate amount of lead time and number of personnel needed to manage the effort.

ROUTE PLANNING

A challenging walk usually means that the daily walking distance exceeds 20 miles or the number of consecutive walking days exceeds two. In an individual challenge walk, you will seldom have an opportunity to survey your route ahead of time and will choose it according to its reputation and from maps and brochures. So this sportwalk challenges the unknown and creates adventure in the excitement of discovery.

When planning a challenge walk route, organize around distance and terrain features. Finding a walk site and route often takes more research than an event walk does, because special distances and terrain features occur less often than parks and roads. In distance, the challenging category's special features include walks that are longer than 50 miles and that take more than a day. The special features for terrain include geographic features like mountains, deserts, and perimeters of bodies of water such as seas, lakes, and rivers.

Maps are useful and often necessary because challenge walks are too long and far away from organizers to allow for route marking. Challenge walkers should therefore acquire map-reading skills or accompany map-reading walk leaders to guide the walking party. Organizers should distribute marked copies of maps covering the route, including the places of and distances between rest stops. Be sure to indicate any difficult or confusing turns in the route or any extraordinary features of the terrain.

SUPPORT SYSTEMS

Challenge walks involve not only distance, like event walks, but also terrain, weather, survival, and psychological challenges. Modern challenge walkers stress survival skills less than increased walking mileage; walkers therefore must have prearranged support systems, including nighttime accommodations arranged with the assistance of tour operators, lodging chains, or walking clubs, and public transportation. Because the challenge walk often follows a linear rather than a circular route, unlike the typical sportwalk, the start and finish are separated, and a support transportation system must be supplied in order to pick up sportwalkers from the finish.

On multiday challenge walks, a support team is needed to carry provisions for walkers. There are three basic types of support systems: backpack, travel pack, and the station stop.

The backpack system.   The simplest support system is the one the walker carries along on his or her back: the backpack. Colin Fletcher calls it a "house on your back." The backpack contains clothing, and sleeping, feeding, and cooking supplies and equipment. In challenge sportwalks, the size of this pack is reduced substantially, so that it is more like a picnic basket with a change of clothes. Some sportwalkers head out without a support system, to test whether or not they can survive living off the land.

The travel pack system.   The traveling support system is perhaps the easiest to arrange and set up along any challenge walk route. It's the system most often used for trekking and long-distance road walking, but it can be costly and over the budget of individual sportwalkers.

The travel pack system, using a car, vehicle, or pack animal, travels with you or meets you at stops along the route and at nighttime destinations. The support vehicle cruises along the route, servicing walkers along the way or traveling ahead to set up and take down tables and stations as the group advances. A range of 3 to 10 stations or vehicular stops should be planned for each walk day, because more walkers either go as fast as they do in the 300-mile from Paris-to-

Strassbourg racewalk or less if they volksmarch at a moderate to brisk pace, as they do in the Denmark 300 from Vibourg to the German border.

The station stop system.   A station stop system is a network of rest stops and overnight stops. It is often easy to work through a franchise chain or find an organization that has set up a similar network. Otherwise, this kind of support system requires the greatest amount of advance planning, particularly for the establishment of new routes.

Inn-to-inn networks have been established for overnight challenge walks, connecting cooperating restaurants, hotels, and inns along the walk route. The proliferation of motels and fast-food restaurants in the United States, and bed-and-breakfast inns in Europe, allows a relatively easy set-up of a station stop network. In other areas of the world, such as Africa, the Far East, and any wilderness or less populated areas, this system will generally be difficult to organize.

15
WALKING CLUBS AND CLINICS

ONE OF THE by-products of organizing a sportwalk is a walking club. A walking club, in its simplest form, comprises a small group of walkers who regularly get together for walks and also acts as a social club that revolves around staying active and seeing the world.

Keeping the walking club small and intimate permits less emphasis on organization and management and more on the walking itself. Take a page from Walkabout International's book, and concentrate on walking rather than clubmaking. Clubs do not have to have formal memberships, just people desiring to participate.

JOIN, AFFILIATE, ORGANIZE

Before you decide to organize your own club, consider the easier course of joining an established club or organizing a chapter of one of the existing walking clubs. First, try out walks and attend meetings of other walking clubs. This way, you will meet the walkers and can better decide what kind of club you want to affiliate with. You may want to join more than one and give up the idea of organizing a club altogether. The addresses for established clubs are listed in the Appendixes.

Event Walks often include walking clinics to acquaint walkers with helpful exercises and techniques.

If no walking club serves your area, you might want to establish a walking club in a corporation or a community-based organization affiliated with a special-interest group. The advantage is that you can utilize established facilities and recruit membership from that of the affiliated organization: members, employees, or customers on a mailing list. If you can, develop your club to meet your specific purposes. To make life easier, you can pattern your club on one of the existing clubs; the trail and volksmarching clubs have the most elaborate organization, and the walkabout clubs the simplest.

HOW TO ORGANIZE

The best way to establish a walking club is to start small with a walking group that meets for regular sportwalks or exercisewalks.

Here are the basic steps:

1. Develop a club concept
2. Choose a name
3. Announce a walk and first meeting
4. Appoint a charter committee
5. Plan next walk and meeting as charter meeting
6. Post another announcement
7. In the meantime, write a charter. Consider establishing your club as a not-for-profit orgainzation, registering it with the local government. Fees and membership dues may be exempt from taxation.
8. At the charter meeting, present and vote on the charter. Vote in officers (president, secretary, treasurer). Approve club name. Set a calendar of walks. Before the close of the meeting, announce the next walk.

ORGANIZATIONAL EXAMPLES

A walking club can be organized in your neighborhood, workplace, sport club, or as part of another private or public organization. Following are some examples of different types of specialized walking clubs. These should give you some ideas for organizing your own club.

CORPORATE WALKING CLUBS

There are really two basic approaches to organizing a company walking club: asking your employer to sponsor one or organizing a group of your co-workers into a walking group.

Employer approach.   Present your case to the chief executive, the director of personnel, or the special officer in charge of recreational or health activities in your company. Explain that walking offers the greatest possibility for keeping your work force fit. It reduces absenteeism, boosts morale, and raises productivity levels. A corporate walking club is probably the cheapest way to achieve these elements, and the walking club is the cheapest fitness program you can introduce into the workplace.

Also suggest corporate-related activities for this club. Plan interesting walking activities, such as using company facilities as an indoor or outdoor walking course, e.g., factory, parking lot, and office corridors, or "aisle miles," or identify nearby parks for walking. For example, the Traveler's Insurance Company sponsored a walking course for employees in a park near its headquarters. The company can offer a walking fitness test through its medical facility, and the company club can help field a corporate walking team at walking events. Or it can sponsor an employee/customer walk or one with a local community charity.

Corporate walking clubs already exist at a number of major companies, including General Dynamics, Rockwell International, and Xerox Corporation. I was involved in the Xerox walking program, which is organized as an exercisewalking club and based at their training fitness center in Leesburg, Virginia. A summer internist organized a walking club and clinic based on my *Complete Book of Exercisewalking* to serve as a substitute for similar exercise clubs in running and calisthenics.

When asking for help in establishing a formal corporate walking club or sportwalk team (or one that participates in events under the corporate banner), you can send the head of the company a letter that describes the benefits of such an organization.

Employee approach.   If you don't want or need formal corporate endorsement, you can organize a club among co-workers for activities during work breaks and after work. You need not necessarily use company facilities. Sometimes obtaining permission to use a parking area involves clearance only with local security guards; explain to them that you only want to walk around the company grounds to get some exercise.

Word of mouth is an effective method of publicity; the news will usually get you all the walking companions you need. Remember the bulletin board notice for small sportwalk events in the previous chapter? You'll get quick results by posting such a notice on the factory or lunchroom bulletin board. Other, more informal approaches include organizing your work group—account area, secretarial pool, factory cell—into a walk group. You can walk together during coffee and lunch breaks or on weekend walking outings. Seek out employees who want to lose weight or get more exercise. Meet them for lunchtime walks around the company parking lot or use aisles and corridors, especially when it rains.

CUSTOMER CLUBS

Many organizations have the opportunity to use walking clubs to appeal to and solidify their customer base. The American Automobile Association, Weight Watchers, Nutri-Diet Centers, Blue Cross and Blue Shield Plans, and other organizations have formed walking groups for their customers as part of advertising and selling their products and services.

SCHOOL AND GOVERNMENT CLUBS

Like corporate employees, governments and schools have large employee groups desiring exercise in a large facility during work hours. A high school or college walking club should not be much more novel than a ski club; in the warmer months it will probably prove a popular off-season activity for skiers. Involve teachers, coaches, and administrators.

HEALTH ASSOCIATION WALKING CLUBS

Walking is a natural adjunct to health service organizations such as hospitals, health insurance plans, or weight control centers. These organizations probably already have sports or exercise programs in progress; they can expand their menu to include walking. This kind of growth adds credence to walking groups and induces spinoffs into separate, freestanding walking clubs.

You'll find many supporters among health care and medical professionals. In hospitals, for example, walking is already used for cardiac and sport injury rehabilitation. It makes sense to build on this natural constituency by recruiting hospital workers and patients; they too need exercise.

I was involved in the establishment of two hospital-based walking clubs at St. Luke's Hospital in Jacksonville, Florida, and St. John's Medical Center in Steubenville, Ohio. St. John's held a 25th Anniversary Health Walk to celebrate the foundation of the hospital and to publicize the formation of a hospital walking club. Organized by the assistant personnel director, John Mantica, St. Luke started its wellness program through publicity during a "Health Night Out" lecture on walking. The lecture drew 750 people to a local shopping mall, and the hospital signed 100 of those present that night as the charter members of a new Wellness Walking Club. Try tying in with a similar event or lecture to start up a walking club. Pages 269–271 show a sample of the material used in these promotions.

SENIOR CENTER WALKING CLUBS

Older Americans are really the vanguard of the new walking boom; they have the time, courage, and motivation to take up and promote walking. Many of the thousands of senior centers can be converted into walking centers locally or through national organizations like the American Association of Retired Persons (AARP). I have worked with a number of these groups, giving walking clinics and organizing mini-event walks of 100 or fewer participants.

Center-sponsored mini-events can give older members the opportunity to involve friends and family members of all age groups. In this approach, senior centers would host communitywide walk events that start and finish at the center.

SPECIAL-INTEREST CLUBS

Walking clubs can also be established in any number of special-interest organizations, such as sports clubs, women's clubs, singles' clubs, travel clubs, and even political clubs. A walking club that affiliates with a local charity or organizes a walkathon not only helps the charity but also helps itself to add new members. Charities such as the American Lung Association, the American Heart Association, the March of Dimes, and the Muscular Dystrophy Association have used walkathons as fund raisers for many years.

A walkathon is probably the most successful fund-raising vehicle. However, it must be well-organized and established over a number of years before it will become really successful. Travel clubs such as the American Automobile Association and the American Youth Hostels Association, and social clubs like the Lions Club and Kiwanis Club, can

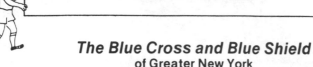

CERTIFICATE
OF
ACCOMPLISHMENT
THE 1983 AMERICAN EVENT
WALK ™ SERIES

The Blue Cross and Blue Shield
of Greater New York

EVENT WALK
May 21 - 27

This is to certify that walker,_____has successfully

completed the_____ walking

_____ miles in_____ day(s) and completed the event in the following walking time:

_____hours _____minutes _____seconds.

EVENT WALKS INTERNATIONAL, INC.   Certified By:

_____   _____
Series Official   New York Event Walk Official
Signature   Signature

Co-Sponsored by American Health Magazine, Grand Hyatt, Kreeger & Sons,
Pan Am, Wilderness Footgear/GEOtech ™

Sanctioned By: The Metropolitan Athletic Congress with the support and participation of: The President's Council on Physical Fitness and Sports, The NY NJ Trail Conference, The NY Road Runners Club, The Brooklyn Lung Association, The Metropolitan Racewalkers Club, The Footwear Council, The Warren Street Social & Athletic Club, Metro North, L.I.R.R., and Outward Bound.

Certificate of accomplishment.

Walking routes for fun and sport 2 to 75 miles in length. Go as you please any walking style: strolling, hiking, backpacking, orienteering, walk climbing, racewalking, briskwalking, long distance walking.

THE 1983 AMERICAN EVENT WALK™ SERIES

Co-Sponsored by American Health Magazine

Sanctioned By: The Metropolitan Athletic Congress with the support and participation of: The President's Council on Physical Fitness and Sports, The NY Road Runners Club, The NY/NJ Trail Conference, The Brooklyn Lung Association, The Metropolitan Racewalkers Club, The Footwear Council, The Warren Street Social & Athletic Club, and Outward Bound, among others.

Grand Hyatt Official Hotel	Blue Cross and Blue Shield Education Center 3 Park Ave. (at 34th St.) N.Y., N.Y.	Pan Am Official Airline

Walker's Hotline: (212) 481-2323, 2354

The Blue Cross Blue Shield of Greater New York

EVENT WALK

May 21 - 27

GEOtech Official Shoe Wilderness Footgear	Kreeger & Sons Official Outfitter

MILEAGE CARD

Front of mileage card.

Walker's Name: _____ Tel. No. _____

Address: _____

EVENT WALK ROUTES:

_____A. **Manhattan Island Perimeter Walks.** Choice of 10, 20, 36 or 50 mile walks around the periphery of Manhattan Island. (3 Park Ave. Start-Finish will stay open for the 36 and 50 mile distance walkers.)

_____B. **Brooklyn Lung Brooklyn Bridge Centennial Walks.** Choice of 2, 6, or 10 mile routes traversing America's most famous bridge and meandering through the scenic sections of Brooklyn Heights. (The 2 mile route begins and ends at Boro Hall, Brooklyn, while the 6 mile route begins at Boro Hall and ends at 3 Park Ave.)

_____C. **The Manhattan Volkswalks.** Walks of 2, 3, 6, 10 and 12 miles through midtown shopping areas and Central Park.

_____D. **Hudson River Walks.** 12 and 26.2 mile routes along the Hudson River and across the George Washington Bridge.

_____E. **Outward Bound Backpacking Event.** 75 mile overnight backpacking route across the George Washington Bridge onto the Long or Shore Paths up to Bear Mountain Inn and the Appalachian trail. (2-5 day overnight event).

_____F. **Fastwalk-Racewalk.** 1 mile and 3.1 miles (5K) races on Sunday May 22. Start at Central Park and 90th Street at 10:00 AM sharp.

_____G. **Special Theme and Historical Walks.** Variety of 2-6 mile special interest group-led walks conducted throughout the Event Walk Week of May 21-27. Call Event Walk Hotline or send stamped self addressed envelope to EWI P.O. Box 888, FDR Station, NY, NY 10022 UNLESS OTHERWISED INDICATED, ALL ROUTES BEGIN AND END AT 3 PARK AVE. (34th St.) AND ALL WALKERS MUST FINISH BY 7:00 PM EXCEPT WHERE INDICATED.

Walk Hotline: 481-2323, 2354
All walkers must start by noon.
All walkers must finish by 7:00 p.m. unless otherwise indicated.

The following information must be filled in or checked by San Diego Event Walk Officials:

Date:_____

	Start:	Finish:
First Route #_____	Check-in Time_____	Out_____
	Officials initials_____	Initials_____
Second Route #_____.	Check-in Time_____	Out_____
	Officials initials_____	Initials_____
Miles walked (total)	Route #_____	Route #_____

Other:

Backpack weight #_____ Backpack weight #_____

Fast Walk time:_____ converted minutes per mile_____

Route #_____ Checkpoints A___ B___ C___ Finish___

Route #_____ Checkpoints A___ B___ C___ Finish___

Walk Leaders Certification Signature_____

If walkathoner, list Sponsor Company Name_____

_____ Address_____

Telephone_____who will pledge $_____/per mile to the

following charity: Name_____

Address_____

Telephone_____

Back of mileage card.

MAKE NEW YORK AMERICA'S WALKING CAPITAL!
Come walk, get a T-shirt, win prizes and go at your own pace in America's 1st National Walking Sports Event.

THE BLUE CROSS BLUE SHIELD

OF GREATER NEW YORK

NEW YORK EVENT WALK™ & WALKATHON
SATURDAY MAY 21, 1983   3 PARK AVENUE (34th St.)
7:00 AM - 7:00 PM
You must start walk before noon.

The New York Event Walk Week May 21-27 during which you can walk routes going
at your own pace, ranging from 2-75 miles in length.

This event is part of The 1983 American Event Walks Series
Co-sponsored by American Health Magazine and Event Walks International
Sanctioned By: The Metropolitan Athletic Congress with the support and participation of: The President's Council on Physical Fitness
and Sports, The NY Road Runners Club, The NY/NJ Trail Conference, The Brooklyn Lung Association, The Metro Racewalkers Club,
The Footwear Council, The Warren Street Social &Athletic Club, and Outward Bound, among others.
Spokesperson for The Event: Gary D. Yanker   Event Director: Tracy Sundlun Series Director: Neil C. Finn

START & FINISH: The main events all start and finish by the Blue Cross and Blue Shield Education Center in the plaza area at 3 Park Ave. (34th St.), Manhattan. The Brooklyn Bridge 2 and 6 mile walks start at Boro Hall, Brooklyn.

STARTING TIMES: For Walks 2-12 miles in length, start at any time between 9:00 AM and 12:00 PM. For Walks 15-75 miles in length start between 7:00 AM - 9:00 AM. Brooklyn Bridge 2 and 6 mile walks start at Boro Hall between 9:00 AM and 12:00 PM only.

ENTREE FEES: $5.00-Pre-entry (postmarked by May 13); $6.00-Late Entry Fee and on day of Event. Make check payable to Event Walks International, Inc. and mail with signed registration form to P.O. Box 888, FDR Station, NY, NY 10022.

EVENT WALK ROUTES:
_____A. **Manhattan Island Perimeter Walks.** Choice of 10, 20, 36 or 50 mile walks around the periphery of Manhattan Island. (3 Park Ave. Start-Finish will stay open for the 36 and 50 mile distance walkers.)

_____B. **Brooklyn Lung Brooklyn Bridge Centennial Walks.** Choice of 2, 6, or 10 mile routes traversing America's most famous bridge and meandering through the scenic sections of Brooklyn Heights. (The 2 mile route begins and ends at Boro Hall, Brooklyn, while the 6 mile route begins at Boro Hall and ends at 3 Park Ave.)

_____C. **The Manhattan Volkswalks.** Walks of 2, 3, 6, 10 and 12 miles through midtown shopping areas and Central Park.

_____D. **Hudson River Walks.** 12 and 26.2 mile routes along the Hudson River and across the George Washington Bridge.

_____E. **Outward Bound Backpacking Event.** 75 mile overnight backpacking route across the George Washington Bridge onto the Long or Shore Paths up to Bear Mountain Inn and the Appalachian trail. (2-5 day overnight event).

_____F. **Fastwalk-Racewalk.** 1 mile and 3.1 miles (5K) races on Sunday May 22. Start at Central Park and 90th Street at 10:00 AM sharp.

_____G. **Special Theme and Historical Walks.** Variety of 2-6 mile special interest group-led walks conducted throughout the Event Walk Week of May 21-27. Call Event Walk Hotline or send stamped self addressed envelope to EWI P.O. Box 888, FDR Station, NY, NY 10022 UNLESS OTHERWISED INDICATED, ALL ROUTES BEGIN AND END AT 3 PARK AVE. (34th St.) AND ALL WALKERS MUST FINISH BY 7:00 PM EXCEPT WHERE INDICATED.

AWARDS: Walkers who complete their routes receive Certificates of Accomplishments for distance walked. Other special prizes include for youngest, oldest, largest family and walking groups. New York as a whole is competing for the "America's Walking Capital Trophy" awarded to the city with the largest turnout. PRIZES INCLUDE CARIBBEAN CRUISE, WALKING SHOES, BACKPACKS, HATS AND CLOTHING.

T-SHIRTS & WALK PACKETS: All registrants will receive walk packets containing T-shirts, mileage card, route maps and schedules. Packets and late registration are available during business hours, May 16-20 at Event Walk Headquarters: 3 Park Ave. (at 34th St.) and on Event days May 21 and May 22.

WALKER'S HOTLINE NUMBER: (212) 481-2323, 2354

WALK—A—THON: Under the auspices of the Blue Cross Blue Shield New York Event Walk, you can raise money for your favorite cause, charity or athletic club. Sponsor sheets are available at Event Walk Headquarters 3 Park Ave. or by sending a self addressed stamped envelope to Event Walks International, Inc. P.O. BOX 88, FDR Station, NY, NY 10022.

OFFICIAL OUTFITTER: Kreeger & Sons 16 W. 46th Street.

SPECIAL ACCOMODATIONS & AIR FARES: THE OFFICIAL HOST HOTEL/The Grand Hyatt Hotel, Park Ave. at 42nd St. offers Event Walkers special discounts (212) 883-1234 or (800) 432-2533.

OFFICIAL HOST HOTEL: Park Ave. and 42nd Street
GRAND HYATT ● NEW YORK
THE OFFICIAL NY EVENT WALK AIRLINE:
● PAN AM.
Offers Event Walkers special discount fares from points in the U.S. (800) 327-8670; Florida (800) 432-2533.

271

also establish walking clubs. Sports and health clubs such as the YMCA, YWCA, and YMHA, or Road Runners clubs, outdoor, and ski clubs are all organizations whose chapters can establish or tie in with a new walking club. Many road-running clubs have race- and fun-walking divisions.

These clubs can all use walking divisions to broaden their range of activities. As the number of participants grows, the division spins off into a separate, freestanding walking club. You can recruit club members from the membership rosters or from bulletin boards at these clubs, which are seen by many people, and work with the organizations themselves to develop fund-raising walks. The walking club or walking team would thus bear the name of the group and be managed under its auspices. These organizations have many connections with members in the community and act as social clubs for their most active members.

MALL WALKING

Mall-walking clubs are good examples of how walking clubs can be based at the walk sites, namely at shopping centers. Although mall walking started with cardiac patients, it has expanded to include young and old exercisewalkers, even mothers pushing strollers. Mall-walking clubs are also a good example of neighborhood walking clubs. The covered shopping mall, like the Chestnut Hill Mall in Newton, Massachusetts, protects walkers from the rain, heat, and cold. It is climate-controlled and provides a smooth walking surface.

The club's priority should be to establish regular walking hours at the mall, which are usually between 6:00 and 10:00 A.M., when the mall opens, and perhaps evenings and weekends after the mall is closed. It is important to ask the mall's management for permission to walk. Anticipate the complaints of shopkeepers who will argue that walkers do not shop while they are walking; walkers are also shoppers, the regular customers of the mall.

Mall-walking clubs are proliferating; they may soon form a national network and hold their own indoor events. Many already have their own T-shirts and patches. Although the primary appeal is exercisewalking, malls are good places to walk and meet with friends. I have walked with many mall walkers during my travels. In Kansas City, I saw hundreds of mall walkers at the Ward Parkway Mall: women walking and discussing wedding arrangements for their children, a mother and son on a weight control walking program, and two buddies after heart bypass operations.

FUNCTIONS OF CLUBS

Walking clubs can serve a number of functions:

- Hold walks and walking clinics
- Teach walking techniques
- Promote walking
- Sponsor walking trips
- Build and maintain trails and walkways
- Bring walkers together
- Provide exercise
- Sponsor walking teams

Once a club is in place, it can also provide various services to its members:

- Plan and organize a series of sportwalks
- Publish newsletters and calendars of walks
- Provide medical insurance and third-party insurance
- Answer questions about walking
- Form liaisons with other clubs regionally, nationally, and internationally
- Provide special walking guides, leaders, or coaches
- Maintain library of maps and guidebooks
- Publicize walks

Of all these functions, three are probably central to all walking clubs: organizing walks, publicizing walks, and holding walking clinics.

ORGANIZE WALKS

Probably the best organizer and manager of a sportwalk or sportwalk series is a walking club. The best way to organize a walking club is to hold regular walks and walking clinics. Like individual sportwalks, you can publicize these on a bulletin board and even more effectively in a club newsletter in which you reconfirm the walk, update information, and recruit walkers. Your newsletter can serve as a press release excerpt that can appear in the calendar section of local newspapers.

PUBLICIZE WALKS

The newsletter or calendar of events is the best publicity vehicle. Of course, publicizing walks assumes previous planning. If your club can't organize enough walks to fill a calendar, then it can serve as a clearinghouse for other walks.

HOLD WALKING CLINICS

Next to holding walks, teaching good walking techniques is probably the most useful function a walking club can serve. Walking clinics have been organized by racewalking clubs, but even if yours isn't there's no reason not to recruit a racewalking coach to teach walking techniques. (A list of these coaches' addresses is in the Appendixes.) You could recruit exercise instructors to teach clinics based on this book and the sequence on how to follow the training program in my two exercise-walking books. Hold one clinic on weekends (Saturday is probably the best day), and one during the evening after work hours.

GROWTH OF CLUBS

A single walking club can grow to include as many as 50,000 members, covering a state or a nation with local chapters. Examples are the Ramblers Association of Great Britain, the Appalachian Mountain Club, and the Deutsche Gebirg and Wanderverein (The German Mountain and Wander Club Federation). The last group is a federation of individual walking clubs, each started on its own. The Appalachian Mountain Club is a regional club that originated in one place and has branched out with chapters. Other clubs, such as Walkabout International and the International Volkssport Association, use a franchise system of expansion. Still others, such as the Walkers Club of America, organize their walking clubs as athletic clubs that train and stage athletic meets and hold walking clinics for fitness walkers.

The American Volkssport Association (with 1,000 chapters nation-wide) and Walkabout International (900 walks in a city) lead in organizing the greatest number of sportwalk events. They also bring out the most walkers by cutting down the organizational structure and using volunteers effectively. The Walkers Club of America probably does the best job of training exercisewalkers, because they now hold regular weekend and weekday clinics in about 36 cities nationwide. For creating and maintaining walking trails, the British Ramblers Association, the NY/NJ Trail Conference, and the Appalachian Trail Conference and Appalachian Mountain Club do the best jobs. The leadership position for the widest variety of walking trips away from home is probably the Sierra Club.

APPENDICES

APPENDICES A THROUGH C will help you plan your sportwalking season based not only on where you are located but also where you might be headed for business or vacation. Appendix D provides training charts for all-season sportwalking conditioning.

Because I could not list all 25,000 events and clubs in the United States, I have included the addresses of statewide, regional, national, and international organizations that act as a referral service to more walks. In addition, information about the nearest events, clubs, clinics, or tours (ECCT) may be received by sending a self-addressed, outsized, and stamped envelope (specifying your question on the outside of the envelope, also) to:

> ECCT
> c/o *Walking World*
> Box K
> Gracie Station
> New York, NY 10022

Attention Walking Clubs: Please keep *Walking World* address posted with your news, clubs, or addresses.

Listing Errors: The addresses, phone numbers (where given), and

personnel of walking organizations are subject to change. I apologize for
any out-of-date information in the following lists and would appreciate
your help in keeping this directory up to date. Send information to:

Walking World Update
P.O. Box K
Gracie Station
New York, NY 10028

If you have any comments or questions about this book please send
them to:

Gary Yanker's Sportwalking
P.O. Box 888
FDR Station
New York, NY 10022

I hope I will be able to join you on a sportwalk in my travels.

APPENDIX A
EVENTS AND
ORGANIZERS

Here's a calendar of the best-established international walking events listed by month, then week or weekend. The organizer's address and telephone number are listed at the end according to country.

INTERNATIONAL WALK EVENTS CALENDAR

See country listing for address and registration information.

April (or June):   The Dune March in Den Haag, THE NETHERLANDS. The Rose March in Nijmegen, THE NETHERLANDS. (Second week): Athens Olympic Marathon Walk, GREECE. St. George Mountain Marathon, South Tirol, ITALY.

May (Beginning):   "Jan Pastoors" flower bulb tour, Haarlem, THE NETHERLANDS. (Third weekend): The 25th Berner Two-Day Volksmarch, Berne, SWITZERLAND (14,000 participants). (Last weekend): Comax Vancouver Island Walk, CANADA.

June (Third week):   Paris–Tubize, BELGIUM. (Fourth weekend):   Dublin International Two-Days Walk, IRELAND. (Fifth week): The Castlebar's Four-Days Walks, County Mayo, IRELAND (24 to 27 miles—38 to 43 km, 12 to 17 miles—19 to 27 km, or 8 miles—13 km).

July (First through second weekend):   The Denmark 300-Kilometer Walk, Vibourg, DENMARK (15,000 participants). (Second week): NWB's Annual Four-Day Walk, Apeldoorn, DENMARK. (Third week): KNBLO's Annual Four-Days March, Nijmegen, THE NETHERLANDS (the world's largest walking event, 25,000 participants). (Fourth weekend): Mount Fuji Walk Climb, JAPAN. (Second half of the month): 6-Day Beach Hike, THE NETHERLANDS (the entire coastline) 140 km (from Hock van Holland to Dan Helder), camping limit 800 people (Strand 6 Daagse).

August (Second week): German Walk Day (Deutscher Wandertag) (the world's largest gathering of wanderers and ramblers, 38,000 participants). (Second weekend): The Bornem (100 km) Walk, 24-hour Death March, BELGIUM JH Kadee Bornem (3,200 participants). (Third week): The Vienna Three-Day Walk, AUSTRIA. (Fourth week): The Belgian Four-Day International Walk, Nieuwpoort, BELGIUM.

September (First weekend): Ninth Annual Marcia Internazionale Mare e Monti di Arenzano, ITALY. (During the month): KNBLO's Airborne Walk, Oosterbeek, THE NETHERLANDS (25,000 participants). Innsbruck Karwaendel Marsch (High Alpine Way Marathon). (Third week): The Welsh International Four-Day Walk, Llanwrtyd, Wells, Powys, WALES. Three Country 100 km Romanshorn Walk, SWITZERLAND (start), AUSTRIA, and GERMANY.

October (Third week): The Jerusalem Two-Day Walk, ISRAEL. The North Cape Walk, NORWAY (32 km).

U.S. WALK EVENTS CALENDAR

January (First week): New Year's Day Hike, 10 miles through South New Jersey. (609) 468-4849.

February (First weekend): The Northwest Trek, Washington State. (Fourth weekend): Wanderers 1,000 Trails, 10 km hike or X-C ski, Hershey, PA. (717) 866-4383.

March (Second weekend): Volkssport Reunion Walk, Austin, TX. (512) 441-0748.

April (Third weekend): Potomac Appalachian Trail Club Dogwood Half-Hundred 50 km, northern Virginia. (202) 638-5306. (Fourth weekend): C&O Canal Justice Douglas Walk, MD. (212) 383-2865. (Fourth weekend): WalkAmerica 1986, March of Dimes, nationwide. (914) 428-7100.

May (Second weekend): U.S. National Race Walk Championship, 5 km, Denver, CO. (303) 355-8000.

June (Fourth week): Los Ninos Marathon, 250-Mile Walk, Santa Barbara to Tijuana. (619) 690-1473.

July (Beginning): Los Angeles Hill Stride (City Sports).

August (Second weekend): San Francisco Hill Stride, CA. (415) 546-6150. (All month): Walkabout International 56-mile One-Day Endurance Walk, San Diego, CA. (619) 231-WALK. San Francisco Hill Stride (City Sports).

September (First weekend):   Stride Boston (Sportscape), 7 miles. (617) 485-2090. Labor Day Walk, St. Ignace, MI, 4½ miles (50,000 participants). (906) 643-7600. (During month): New York Hill Stride (City Sports).

October (Second weekend):   Appalachian Long Distance Association Fifth Annual Gathering, Pipestem, WV. (703) 830-9252. (Third weekend): American Hiking Society, Hike-In/Annual Meeting, Front Royal, VA. (202) 234-4609.

APPENDIX B
INTERNATIONAL
TOURING AND
TREKKING

SYMBOLS OF DIFFICULTY

E	(easy)	= I
M	(moderate)	= II
B	(backpacking)	= III to IV
S	(strenuous)	= IV to V

SYMBOLS OF AREAS

SAM = South America
NAM = North America
NAF = North Africa
SAF = South Africa
NZ = New Zealand
IND = India & nearby countries

EU = Europe (East and West)
IS = Israel
AT = Antarctica
CH = China
AA = Asia and Australia

Above the Clouds Trekking
P.O. Box 398
Worcester, MA 01602
(617) 799-4499
Dest: IND, EU, AA, SAM
MB

Adventure Travel Center
28 Market St., 1st Fl.
Sydney 2000, Australia
Dest: AA
MBS

African Holidays
P.O. Box 36959
Tucson, AZ 85740
800 528-0168
Dest: NAF, SAF
M

Alfred Gregory Photo and Trekking
25–31 Wicker
Sheffield S38HW, England
0742-29428
Dest: IND
S

Alpine Adventure Trails Tours
783 Cliffside Dr.
Akron, OH 44313
(216) 867-3771
Dest: EU
M

Bowland Treks
Lowgill
Lancaster LA2 8RA, England
0468-61277
Dest: EU
M

British Coastal Tours
79 Country Club Rd.
Stamford, CT 06903
(203) 329-1612
Dest: EU
M

Canada North Outfitting, Inc.
254 Dundas St., E.
P.O. Box 1230
Waterdown
Ontario LOR 2HO, Canada
(416) 689-7925
Dest: NAM
BS

Chappaqua Travel
Fred Jacobson Alpine Trails
24 S. Greeley Ave.
Chappaqua, NY 10514
(914) 238-5151
Dest: EU
MS

Country Walking Holidays
6195 Santa Clara Pl.
Rohnert Park, CA 94928
(707) 584-0411
Dest: EU
EM

Dales Center
Grassington, Skipton
North Yorkshire BD23 5AU, England
0756-752757
Dest: EU
EMS

English Wanderer
13 Wellington Ct.
Spencers Wood
Reading RG7 1BN, England
0734-882515
Dest: EU
EMS

Exo Tours
Tours 33 Tej.
80, Boulevard St. Germain
75005 Paris, France
329-36-50
Dest: EU, NAF, IND
EMBS

Folkways International Trekking
14903 S.E. Linden Ln.
Oak Grove, OR 97222
800 547-7400
Dest: IND, EU, AA, NZ, SAM, AF
MS

Footpath Holidays
4 Holly Walk
Andover
Hampshire SP10 3PJ, England
0264-52689
Dest: EU
EM

Glencoe Mountain Ventures
R. J. Hall
Ballachulish
Argyll PA39 4JY, Scotland
08552-239
Dest: EU
EMBS

Highland Mountains Services
22 Attadale Rd.
Inverness IV3 5QH, Scotland
0463-236095
Dest: EU
M

Hiking International
7 Blue Boar St.
Oxford OX1 4EN, England
0865-251195/6
Dest: EU
EMS

Himalaya Trekking and Wilderness
1802 Cedar St.
Berkeley, CA 94703
(415) 540-8031
Dest: IND, CH, AA
MS

Intimate Glimpses
P.O. Box 6091
San Diego, CA 92106
(619) 222-2224
Dest: CH, EU, AA
EM

Mountain Travel
1398 Solano Ave.
Albany, CA 94706
800 227-2384
Dest: AA, EU, IND, SAM, NAM,
   CH, AF
EMS

Mountain Ventures Limited
Brecon House
Greenhill Rd.
Mossley Hill
Liverpool L18 7HQ, England
051-724-2732
Dest: EU
MS

Orion Tour
Halaskargazi Cad Halaskar
Apt. 287
Osmanbey
Istanbul, Turkey
148-84-37-148-80-14-141-46-94
Dest: EU
BS

Ramblers Holidays
13 Longcroft House
Fretherne Rd.
Welwyn Garden City
Herts AL8 6PQ, England
07073-31133
Dest: EU, CH, IND
EMS

Routeburn Walk Ltd.
P.O. Box 271
Queenstown, New Zealand 100
Dest: AA
MS

Sherpa Expeditions
Worldwide Trekking, Inc.
1440 Broadway, Rm. 1907
New York, NY 10018
800 431-1112
Dest: EU, IND, NAF
BS

Sierra Club Outings
530 Bush St.
San Francisco, CA 94108
(415) 981-8634
Dest: AA, EU, NAF, SAF, IND, SAM
MBS

Sobek Expeditions
P.O. Box 7007
Angels Camp, CA 95222
800 344-3084
Dest: NAF, AT, AA, IND, CH, SAM,
   IS, AF, EU
MBS

Tiger Paw Adventures
D-383, Defence Colony
New Delhi, India 11024
61637
Dest: IND
MS

Trek Nepal
7515 Goodman Dr., N.W.
Gig Harbor, WA 98335
(206) 858-3944
Dest: IND
MS

Voyagers International
P.O. Box 915
Ithaca, NY 14851
Dest: SAF
SB

Wayfarers
Chepynge House
22 Maltravers St., Arundel
West Sussex BN18 9BU, England
0903-882925
Dest: EU
EM

Wilderness Expeditions
P.O. Box H199 Australia Sq.
NSW 200, Australia
02-27-8744
Dest: AA, IND
MS

Wilderness Travels
1760 Solano Ave.
Berkeley, CA 94707
800 247-6700
Dest: AA, IND, SAM, EU, SAF
M

Womantrek
P.O. Box 1765
Olympia, WA 98507
(206) 357-4477
Dest: IND, SAM
MS

YHA Travel
14 Southampton St.
London WC2E 7HY, England
01-240-5236
Dest: EU
SB

APPENDIX C
WALKING CLUBS

THIS IS THE list of major sportwalk organizations (clubs, volkssport associations, tours and treks, and coaches and clinics). For more information check with the club nearest you or one of the national organizations. I have included hiking, racewalking, volkssport, orienteering, mountaineering, long-distance walking, and ski clubs (they often have walking divisions or outings). Telephone numbers are listed where available.

C = Coaches, Clinics	E = Event Organizer
R = Racewalking	T = Tours and Treks
M = Mountaineering	TR = Trail Association
H = Hiking	O = Outfitting or Bookstores

NATIONAL

The American Hiking Society
1701 18th St., N.W.
Washington, DC 20009

American Volkssport Association
1001 Pat Booker Rd.
Phoenix Sq., Ste. 203
Universal City, TX 78148
(512) 659-2112

American Walkers Association
6221 Robison Rd.
Cincinnati, OH 45213

American Wanderers Association
480 W. Lincoln Ave.
Myerstown, PA 17067

American Youth Hostels
National Campus
Delaplane, VA 22025

Appalachian Mountain Club
5 Joy St.
Boston, MA 02108
(617) 253-0636

Appalachian Trail Conference
P.O. Box 807
Harper's Ferry, WV 25425
(304) 535-6331

The Athletic Congress (TAC)
P.O. Box 120
Indianapolis, IN 46206

Federation of Western Outdoor Clubs
P.O. Box 548
Boseman, MT 59715

Long Distance Hikers Association
13220 Yates Ford Rd.
Clifton, VA 22024
(703) 830-9252

March of Dimes Walk America
1275 Mamaroneck Ave.
White Plains, NY 10605
(914) 428-7100

National Audubon Society
950 Third Ave.
New York, NY 10022
(212) 546-9202

National Campers & Hikers
  Association
7172 Transit Rd.
Buffalo, NY 14221

Sal Corallo
National TAC Racewalk Comm.
  Chairman
3156 N. Pallard St.
Arlington, VA 22207
(202) 357-6247

Prevention Magazine Walking Club
33 Minor St.
Emmaus, PA 18049
(215) 967-5171

Sierra Club
530 Bush St.
San Francisco, CA 94108

U.S. Orienteering Federation
P.O. Box 1031
Ballwin, MO 63011

Walkabout International
835 Fifth Ave.
San Diego, CA 92101

Walkers Club of America
445 E. 86th St.
New York, NY 10028
(212) 722-9255

Wilderness Society
729 15th St., N.W.
Washington, DC 20005

REGIONAL
NORTHEAST
Connecticut Chapter, AMC
P.O. Box 114
Salisbury, CT 06068

Green Mountain Club
P.O. Box 889
Montpelier, VT 05602

Maine Appalachian Trail Club
P.O. Box 283
Augusta, ME 04430

Northeast Volkssport
c/o Robert Holcomb
10886 Rock Coast Rd.
Columbia, MD 21044
(301) 992-9410

SOUTHEAST
Benton-MacKaye Train Association
P.O. Box 53271
Atlanta, GA 30305

Carolina Mountain Club
P.O. Box 68
Asheville, NC 28802

Florida Trail Association
P.O. Box 13708
Gainesville, FL 32604

Southeast Volkssport
c/o Sheila Taylor
5 Captains Dr.
Candler, NC 28715
(704) 667-5633
(704) 259-0742

MID-ATLANTIC

Adirondack Mountain Club
172 Ridge St.
Glens Falls, NY 12801

American Youth Hostels
75 Spring St.
New York City, NY 10012
(212) 431-7100

Finger Lakes Trail Conference
P.O. Box 18048
Rochester, NY 14618

Keystone Trails Association
RD #3, Box 261
Cogan Station, PA 17728

The Metropolitan Racewalkers
36 West 20th St.
New York City, NY 10011
(212) 675-3021

New York–New Jersey Trail
  Conference
232 Madison Ave.
New York, NY 10016
(212) 696-6800

SOUTHWEST

Colorado Mountain Club
2530 W. Alameda Ave.
Denver, CO 80219

Southwest Volkssport
c/o Doyle Piland
1910 Camelot Dr.
Las Cruces, NM 88005
(505) 523-7034

Texas Volkssport
c/o John Luther
2505 Briargrove
Austin, TX 78704
(512) 441-0748
(512) 442-3803

Walkabout Arizona
P.O. Box 17212
Phoenix, AZ 85011

MIDWEST

Buckeye Trail Association
P.O. Box 254
Worthington, OH 43085

Iowa Trails Council
1201 Central
Center Point, IA 52213

Mid-American Volkssport
c/o George Henderson
4864 Powell Rd.
Huber Heights, OH 45424
(513) 237-0553

North Central Volkssport
c/o Shirley Luther
1218 6th St.
Brookings, SD 57006
(605) 692-5159
(605) 688-5136

North Country Trail Association
P.O. Box 311
White Cloud, MI 49349

South Central Volkssport
c/o Tom Cabot
P.O. Box 145
Hermann, MO 65041
(314) 486-2747

NORTHWEST

Northwest Volkssport
c/o Charles Repik
P.O. Box 125
Tacoma, WA 98492
(206) 582-7474

Pacific Volkssport
c/o Ben Wilkes
P.O. Box 2461
Clearlake, CA 95422
(707) 994-4135

Sierra Club
730 Polk St.
San Francisco, CA 94109
(415) 923-5630

The Mountaineers
300 3rd Ave., W.
Seattle, WA 98119
(206) 284-6310

ALABAMA

CLUBS

Bartram Trail Conference
3815 Interstate, Ste. 202-A
Montgomery, AL 36109

Wanderers
Army Aviation Museum
P.O. Box H
Ft. Rucker, AL 35362

ALASKA

CLUBS

Alaska Wilderness Treks
P.O. Box C
Eagle River, AK 99577
(907) 694-9400

Mountaineering Club of Alaska
613 W. Sixth Ave.
Anchorage, AK 99501

South Eastern Alaska
Mountaineering Association
P.O. Box 1314
Ketchikan, AK 99901

TOURS AND TREKS

Alaska Mountain Adventures
3770 Terrace Dr.
Anchorage, AK 99502
800 544-2235

Alaska Travel Adventures
200 N. Franklin St.
Juneau, AK 99801
(907) 586-6245
800 227-8480

ARIZONA

CLUBS

Central Arizona Backpackers
   Association
2632 E. Glenrosa
Phoenix, AZ 85016

Southern Arizona Hiking Club
P.O. Box 12122
Tucson, AZ 85732

Walkabout Arizona
P.O. Box 17212
Phoenix, AZ 85011

TOURS AND TREKS

Grand Canyon Trail Guides
P.O. Box 2997
East Flagstaff, AZ 86003
(602) 526-0924

CLINICS AND COACHES

Gordon Wallace (R)
102 Aztec St.
Prescott, AZ 86301
(602) 445-5461

CALIFORNIA

CLUBS

California Alpine Club
562 Flood Bldg.
870 Market St.
San Francisco, CA 94102

City Sports (Hill Stride Series)
P.O. Box 3693
San Francisco, CA 94119
(415) 546-6150

City Sports (Los Angeles and San
   Diego Hill Strides)
1120 Princeton Dr.
Marina del Rey, CA 90291
(213) 827-4420

Pacific Crest Trail Conference
Hotel Green
50 Green St.
Pasadena, CA 91105

Southern California Trail Ramblers
P.O. Box 15582
Long Beach, CA 90815

Speedwalking
P.O. Box 6941
San Diego, CA 92106
(619) 224-9202

Edith Wyatt
Starlight Hikers
165 E. Milan
Chula Vista
San Diego, CA 92106
(619) 422-3321

Walkers Club of Los Angeles
110 S. Michigan Ave., Apt. 14
Pasadena, CA 91106
(213) 577-2123

VOLKSSPORT ASSOCIATIONS

Sierra Volkssport Club
1105 Spruce Ave.
Atwater, CA 95301
(209) 358-4540

CLINICS AND COACHES

John Allen (R)
1795 Pasqual St.
Pasadena, CA 91106
(213) 795-5935

Bob Bowman (R)
51 Chatsworth Ct.
Oakland, CA 94611
(415) 531-1427

Sue Brodock (R)
15362 Randall
Fontana, CA 92335

Tom Carroll (R)
2045 W. 230th
Torrance, CA 90501
(213) 532-2755

Bill Chisholm (R)
6315 Springdale Dr.
Bakersfield, CA 93307
(805) 831-5691

Ron Daniel (R)
110 S. Michigan, #14
Pasadena, CA 91106
O: (213) 577-9189
H: (213) 577-2123

Tom Dooley (R)
2250 Sherwin Ave.
Santa Clara, CA 95051
(916) 583-4072

Wayne Glusker (R)
20391 Steven Creek Blvd.
Cupertino, CA 95104
(408) 996-1272

Donna Gookin (R)
5946 Wenrich Dr.
San Diego, CA 92120
(714) 286-7958

Jim Hanley (R)
3346 S. Allegheny Ct.
Westlake Village, CA 91361
(213) 889-6729

Paula Kash (R)
1124½ Corning St.
Los Angeles, CA 90035
(213) 659-9772

John Kelly (R)
1024 Third St.
Santa Monica, CA 90403

Lori Maynard (R)
2821 Kensington Rd.
Redwood City, CA 94061
(415) 369-2801

Dan O'Connor (R)
7022 Main St., #20
Westminster, CA 92687
(714) 892-7258

Giulio de Petra (R)
P.O. Box 2927
Carmel, CA 93921

Murry Rosenstein (R)
8010 Fountain Ave.
Los Angeles, CA 90046
O: (213) 931-4727
H: (213) 656-3956

Harry Siitonen (R)
106 Sanchez St., Apt. 17
San Francisco, CA 94114

Elaine Ward (R)
358 W. California Blvd.
Pasadena, CA 91105

COLORADO
CLUBS

The Colorado Mountain Club
2530 W. Alameda Ave.
Denver, CO 80219
(303) 922-8315

The Rocky Mountain Wanderers
10175 W. Berry Dr.
Littleton, CO 80127
(303) 979-4674

CLINICS AND COACHES

Joseph Barrow (R)
675 Marion St.
Denver, CO 80218

Bob Carlson (R)
2261 Glencoe St.
Denver, CO 80207
(303) 377-0576

Leonard Jansen (R)
1776 E. Boulder St.
Colorado Springs, CO 80909
O: (303) 578-4500, ext. 3316
H: (303) 634-0517

Carl Schueler (R)
Olympic Training Center
1776 E. Boulder St.
Colorado Springs, CO 80909
(303) 636-9619

CONNECTICUT

CLUBS

Appalachian Mountain Club
Connecticut Chapter
c/o Jeri Lyons
535 Talcottville Rd.
Vernon, CT 06066

TOURS AND TREKS

Green Mountain Club
Connecticut Chapter
218 Jackson Hill Rd.
Middlefield, CT 06455

Machia's Outing Club
P.O. Box 1216
Weston, CT 06883
(203) 226-9771

DELAWARE

CLUBS

Brandywine Valley Outing Club
P.O. Box 7033
Wilmington, DE 19803

Wilmington Trail Club
36 Augusta Dr.
Newark, DE 19711

DISTRICT OF COLUMBIA

CLUBS

Potomac Appalachian Trail
  Conference
1718 North St., N.W.
Washington, DC 20036
(202) 638-5306

Wanderbirds Hiking Club
c/o Dan Risley
2939 Van Ness St.
Washington, DC 20008

CLINICS AND COACHES

Bill Hillman (R)
700 Seventh St., N.W.
Washington, DC 20024

Alan Price (R)
444 Lamont St., N.W.
Washington, DC 20010

FLORIDA

CLUBS

All Florida Adventure Tours
7930 N. Kendall Dr.
Miami, FL 33156
(305) 270-0219

Florida Trail Association
P.O. Box 13708
Gainesville, FL 32604

Hike-a-State
18600 S.W. 157th Ave.
Miami, FL 33187
(305) 231-0454

CLINICS AND COACHES

Henry Laskau (R)
3232 Carabola Circle, S.
Coconut Creek, FL 33066
(305) 975-3385

John MacLachlan (R)
1330 Sabal Palm Dr.
Boca Raton, FL 33432

GEORGIA

CLUBS

Benton-Mackaye Trail Association
P.O. Box 53271
Atlanta, GA 30305

TOURS AND TREKS

Wilderness Southeast
711 Sandtown Rd.
Savannah, GA 31410
(912) 897-5108

CLINICS AND COACHES

Wayne Nicoll (R)
3535 Gleneagles Dr.
Augusta, GA 30907

HAWAII

CLUBS

50th State Wanderers
2362 C Gemini Ave.
Honolulu, HI 96818

TOURS AND TREKS

Paradise Isles Adventures
501 Lilikoi Ln.
Haiku, Maui, HI 96708

IDAHO

Craters of the Moon National
   Monument
P.O. Box 29
Arco, ID 83212
(208) 527-3257

ILLINOIS

CLUBS

Prairie Club
6 E. Monroe St., Rm. 1507
Chicago, IL 60603
(312) 236-3342

VOLKSSPORTS ASSOCIATIONS

North Shore Wanderers
c/o Richard B. McFarlin
10093 W. Paddock Ave.
Waukegan, IL 60087
(312) 249-4813

CLINICS AND COACHES

Chuck Klehm (R)
1218 N. Rt. 47
Woodstock, IL 60098

INDIANA

CLUBS

Indianapolis Hiking Club
c/o Harrison Feldman
4622 Evanston Ave.
Indianapolis, IN 46205

CLINICS AND COACHES

Sam Bell (R)
Assembly Hall, Indiana University
Bloomington, IN 47401

IOWA

CLUBS

Iowa Trails Council
1201 Central
Center Point, IA 52213

CLINICS AND COACHES

Mary Adams-Lackey (R)
P.O. Box 165
Iowa City, IA 52244

Iowa Mountaineers
P.O. Box 163
30 Prospect Pl.
Iowa City, IA 52240

KANSAS

CLUBS

Kansas City Walkers
4500 W. 107th St.
Overland Park, KS 66207

Kansas Trails Council
1906 Jamaica
El Dorado, KS 67042

KENTUCKY

Fort Knox Volksmarch Association
c/o Ed Peterson
Outdoor Recreation Building
1060 Ireland Ave.
Fort Knox, KY 40121

LOUISIANA

CLUBS

Jim Bowie Wanderers
c/o John Gaustad
P.O. Box 1684
Opelousas, LA 70570
(318) 942-7193

Richard Charles
New Orleans Racewalkers
4236 S. Roman St.
New Orleans, LA 70125

CLINICS AND COACHES

Richard Charles (R)
4236 S. Roman St.
New Orleans, LA 70125

MAINE

CLUBS

Maine Trail Trotters
RFD #3
Winthrop, ME 04364

CLINICS AND COACHES

Larry Pelletier (R)
19 Juniper St.
Bangor, ME 04401

MARYLAND

CLUBS

Mountain Club of Maryland
802 Kingston Rd.
Baltimore, MD 21212
(301) 267-2831

CLINICS AND COACHES

Bob Lawson (R)
Halsey Field House
U.S. Naval Academy
Annapolis, MD 20403

Maryland Lupus Foundation Folk
  Walkers
c/o Linda Watts
12 W. 25th St.
Baltimore, MD 21218
(301) 760-9218

MASSACHUSETTS

CLUBS

Appalachian Mountain Club
5 Joy St.
Boston, MA 02108

The New England Trail Conference
P.O. Box 153
Ashfield, MA 01330

CLINICS AND COACHES

Betty Jenewin
Rec. Office, Channing St.
Worcester, MA 01605

Bob Kitchen (R)
122 Pine St.
Northampton, MA 01060
O: (413) 584-1325
H: (413) 586-0366

Brian Savilonis (R)
243 Mirick Rd.
Princeton, MA 02154

Steve Vaitones (R)
15 Chestnut St.
Waltham, MA 02154

MICHIGAN

CLUBS

Michigan Pathfinders
c/o Harold S. Vartanian
35220 Tall Oak Dr.
Sterling Heights, MI 48077
(313) 979-9193

CLINICS AND COACHES

Grank Alngi (R)
26530 Woodshire
Dearborn Heights, MI 48127

Jeanne Bocci (R)
1353 Grayton Rd.
Grosse Point Park, MI 48230

Frank Soby (R)
3820 Harvard
Detroit, MI 48224

MINNESOTA

Voyageurs National Park
P.O. Box 50
International Falls, MN 56649
(218) 283-9821

MISSISSIPPI

CLUBS

Sierra Club
Mississippi Chapter
P.O. Box 4335
Jackson, MS 39216

TOURS AND TREKS

Natchez Trace Parkway
RR #1, NT-143
Tupelo, MS 38801
(601) 842-1572

MISSOURI

Mr. Tom Cabot
Hermann Volkssport Association
(AVA 18, MO 1)
RR #1
P.O. Box 60A
Hermann, MO 65041

CLINICS AND COACHES

Joe Duncan (R)
2980 Maple Bluff Dr.
Columbia, MO 65201

Don Lawrence (R)
c/o Running Start
1655 N. Hwy. 67
Florissant, MO 63231

MONTANA

CLUBS

Montana Wilderness Association
P.O. Box 365
Helena, MT 59624

NEBRASKA

CLUBS

Omaha Walking Club
5238 S. 22nd St.
Omaha, NE 68107

NEW HAMPSHIRE

Dartmouth Outing Club
P.O. Box 9
Hanover, NH 03755

NEW JERSEY

CLUBS

Batona Hiking Club
301 Broadway
Westville, NJ 08093

Somerset City Hikers
Somerset City Park
P.O. Box 837
Somerville, NJ 08876

Union City Hiking Club
Union City Department Parks
Warincanco Park
Elizabeth, NJ 07207
(201) 276-9440

West Jersey Hiking Club
34 Laurie Rd.
Landing, NJ 07850

Woodland Trail Walkers
34 Hillcrest Dr.
Wayne, NJ 07471
(201) 472-4848

CLINICS AND COACHES

Eliott Denman (R)
28 N. Locust St.
Long Branch, NJ 07764
O: (201) 774-7000
H: (201) 222-9213

Ray Funkhouser (R)
37 E. Acres Dr.
Yardville, NJ 08620

Ron Kulik (R)
10 Cleveland Ave.
Nutley, NJ 07110

Alan Wood (R)
Regency House, Rm. 255
Pompton Plains, NJ 07444

NEW MEXICO
CLUBS

New Mexico Mountain Club
10212 Chapala Pl., N.E.
Albuquerque, NM 87111

VOLKSSPORT ASSOCIATIONS

Angel Fire Resort
Association Volkssport Festival
P.O. Box 252
Angel Fire, NM 87710
(505) 377-6062
(505) 377-3134

CLINICS AND COACHES

Gene Dix (R)
2301 El Nido Ct., N.W.
Albuquerque, NM 87104

NEW YORK
CLUBS

Adirondack Mountain Club
172 Ridge St.
Glens Falls, NY 12801
(518) 793-7737

Appalachian Mountain Club
24 East 38th St.
New York, NY 10016
(212) 684-3683

City Sports (Hill Strides)
140 West 22nd St.
New York, NY 10011
(212) 627-7040

German-American Hiking Club
Elfi Woschitz
1577 Third Ave.
New York, NY 10028

Metropolitan Racewalkers Club
36 West 20th St.
New York, NY 10011
(212) 675-3021

New York–New Jersey Trail
　Conference
232 Madison Ave.
New York, NY 10016
(212) 685-9699

The Shorewalkers
Cy Adler
241 W. 97th St.
New York, NY 10025
(212) 663-2167

Tramp and Trail Club of New York
229 E. 12th St.
New York, NY 10003

CLINICS AND COACHES

David Balboa
240 West 73rd St.
New York, NY 10023
(212) 799-4831

Richard Goldman
36 W. 20th St.
New York, NY 10011
(212) 675-3021

Howard Jacobson (R)
445 E. 86th St.
New York, NY 10028
(212) 722-9255

Gus Krug
3220 Perry Ave.
Bronx, NY 10467
(212) 652-1207

Bruce MacDonald (R)
39 Fairview Ave.
Port Washington, NY 11050
(516) 944-8905

Mort Malkin (R)
44 East 19th St.
Brooklyn, NY 11226
(718) 462-2212

Heliodoro Rico (R)
P.O. Box 1504
Ansonia Station
New York, NY 10023

Dan Stanek (R)
281 Meadowview Dr.
Williamsville, NY 14221
(716) 634-2634

Gary and Susan Westerfield (R)
P.O. Box 440
Smithtown, NY 11787
(516) 979-9603

NORTH CAROLINA

CLUBS

Carolina Hiking Club
P.O. Box 68
Asheville, NC 28802

CLINICS AND COACHES

Eric Bigham (R)
2511 Foxwood Dr.
Chapel Hill, NC 28514

OHIO

CLUBS

Buckeye Trail Association
P.O. Box 254
Worthington, OH 43085

Central Ohio Hiking Club
Central YMCA
40 Long St.
Columbus, OH 43215

Valley Vagabonds of Cleveland, Ohio
c/o Galen Cooleey
25316 Butternut
North Olmstead, OH 44070
(216) 777-5045

Zinzannati Wanderers
c/o Jerry Bocock
760 N. Hill Ln.
Cincinnati, OH 45224

CLINICS AND COACHES

Jim Janos (R)
3123 Mapledale
Cleveland, OH 44109
H: (216) 351-5786

Tim Melfi (R)
221 E. Home Rd.
Springfield, OH 45503

Jack Mortland (R)
3184 Summit St.
Columbus, OH 43202
(614) 263-8318

John White (R)
4865 Arthur Pl.
Columbus, OH 43220

OKLAHOMA

CLUBS

Oklahoma Trails Association
1821 Peter Pan St.
Norman, OK 73069

Ozark Society
2811 E. 22nd St.
Tulsa, OK 74114

Wandergruppe of Oklahoma City
c/o Leslie Weeks
2730 N.W. 20th St.
Oklahoma City, OK 73107
(405) 947-5152

OREGON

CLUBS

Mazamas
909 N.W. Nineteenth Ave.
Portland, OR 97209

Oregon TC Masters (R)
P.O. Box 10085
Eugene, OR 97440

Trails Club of Oregon
P.O. Box 1243
Portland, OR 97207

PENNSYLVANIA

CLUBS

Allentown Hiking Club
124 W. 16th St.
Allentown, PA 18102

Botana Hiking Club
c/o Oreste Unti
600 E. Phili-Ellena St.
Philadelphia, PA 19119

Horse-Shoe Trail Club, Inc.
c/o Mrs. Robert Chalfant
1325 Jericho Rd.
Abington, PA 19001

Keystone Trails Association
P.O. Box 251
Cogan Station, PA 17728

Lebanon Valley Hiking Club
c/o Emmett V. Mariano
RD #1
Bethel, PA 19507

Philadelphia Trail Club
1522 Huntington Rd.
Abington, PA 19001

Philadelphia Trail Club
c/o Elizabeth Perry
9 Hathaway Circle
Wynnewood, PA 19096

Reading Track Club
112 S. Sterley St.
Shillington, PA 19607

York Hiking Club
347 S. George St.
York, PA 17403

CLINICS AND COACHES

Dr. Howard Palamarchuk (R)
6357 Crescent Ave.
Cornwells Heights, Pa 19020
(212) 757-4350

RHODE ISLAND

CLUBS

Hikers Club of Rhode Island
c/o Dr. John Mulleedy
709 Hope St.
Providence, RI 02906

SOUTH CAROLINA

CLUBS

Palmetto State Pacers
c/o John D. Pollard
5812-B Popular Circle
Shaw AFB, SC 29152
(803) 499-2347

SOUTH DAKOTA

CLUBS

The Sierra Club
Dacotah Chapter
P.O. Box 1624
Rapid City, SD 57701

TENNESSEE

CLUBS

Smoky Mountains Hiking Club
c/o Richard H. Bolen
8001 Bennington Dr.
Knoxville, TN 37919

Tennessee Trails Association
P.O. Box 4913
Chattanooga, TN 37405

CLINICS AND COACHES

Hal Canfield (R)
502 Alandale Rd.
Knoxville, TN 37920

TEXAS

CLUBS

Colorado River Walkers
c/o John L. Luther
2505 Briargrove
Austin, TX 78704

Houston Hikers and Funrunners
c/o Gene Busic
1529 Wirt Rd., #21
Houston, TX 77055

Hucao Outing Club
c/o John Adams
5100 Hawthorne, Apt. 716
Waco, TX 76710
(817) 776-5597

Texas Trekkers of Dallas
c/o Jean Dewald
Hillcrest Dr.
Dallas, TX 75240
(214) 661-1279
(214) 521-7090

Texas Wanderers of San Antonio
c/o George H. Lewis
2915 Wacos Dr.
San Antonio, TX 78238
(521) 648-4040

West Texas Trail Walkers
c/o Thomas Spencer
P.O. Box 17126
Fort Worth, TX 76102
(817) 460-4889

CLINICS AND COACHES

John Evans (R)
5440 N. Braeswood, #945
Houston, TX 77096

Dave Gwyn (R)
6502 S. Briar Bayou
Houston, TX 77072

John Knifton (R)
12900 Catskill Tr.
Austin, TX 78750

UTAH

CLUBS

Wasatch Mountain Club
425 S. 900, W.
Salt Lake City, UT 84104

VERMONT

CLUBS

Green Mountain Club
P.O. Box 899
Montpelier, VT 05602

TOURS AND TREKS

Vermont Inn to Inn
Churchill House Inn
RD #3
Brandon, VT 05733
(802) 247-3300

VIRGINIA

CLUBS

Natural Bridge Appalachian Trail
   Club
c/o Edwin R. Page
2316 Glencove Pl.
Lynchburg, VA 24503

Old Dominion Appalachian Trail
   Club
c/o Nancy Lampert
P.O. Box 25283
Richmond, VA 23260

Roanoke Appalachian Trail Club
2416 Stanley Ave., S.E.
Roanoke, VA 24104

Tidewater Appalachian Trail Club
c/o Rees R. Lukei, Jr.
P.O. Box 8246
Norfolk, VA 23503

VOLKSSPORT ASSOCIATIONS

Gator Volksmarch Club
c/o Charles Seward
P.O. Box 14025
Norfolk, VA 23518
(804) 467-3959

CLINICS AND COACHES

Sal Corrallo
3156 N. Pollard St.
Arlington, VA 22207
O: (202) 357-6247
H: (703) 243-1290

WASHINGTON

CLUBS

Federation of Western Outdoor Clubs
4534½ University Way, N.E.
Seattle, WA 98105
(206) 632-6157

The Evergreen Wanderers
P.O. Box 85
Tillicum Branch
Tacoma, WA 98492
(206) 582-7474

Rainier Mountaineering
201 St. Helens
Tacoma, WA 98402
(206) 627-6242
(206) 529-2227
(304) 535-6331

The Mountaineers
300 3rd Ave.
Seattle, WA 98119
(206) 284-6310

The Northwest Trek (E)
c/o Evergreen Volkssport Association
Box 7458
Federal Way, WA 98003
(206) 838-6981

Pacific Northwest Association
P.O. Box 1048
Seattle, WA 98111
(206) 623-2314

CLINICS AND COACHES

Darlene Hickman (R)
1960 9th, W.
Seattle, WA 98101

Dr. Dean Ingram (R)
507 Cobb Medical Bldg.
Seattle, WA 98101
O: (206) 623-1920
H: (206) EM2-4862

Dan Pierce (R)
1137 N.W. 57th St.
Seattle, WA 98107

Martin Rudow (R)
4831 N.E. 44th
Seattle, WA 98105
O: (206) 623-3700
H: (206) 524-6081

WEST VIRGINIA

CLUBS

Appalachian Trail Conference
P.O. Box 236
Harper's Ferry, WV 25425

West Virginia Scenic Trails
  Association
P.O. Box 4042
Charleston, WV 25304

WISCONSIN

CLUBS

The Hoofers Hiking Club
University of Wisconsin–Madison
Madison, WI 53706

CLINICS AND COACHES

Mike DeWitt (R)
814 40th St.
Kenosha, WI 53140

Larry Larson (R)
909 Ostergaard Ave.
Racine, WI 53406
(414) 633-1943

WYOMING

CLUBS

Cheyenne High Plains Wanderers
c/o Ed Hazen
1132 S. Cribbon Ave.
Cheyenne, WY 82001
(307) 638-0924

AUSTRIA

Karwaendel March (E)
Innsbruck, Tirol BE2
Innsbruck-stadt, HSV
Horst Rauchdobler
A-6020 Innsbruck
Reichenauerstrasse 55

Organisation der International
Wienerwald-Wanderung (E)
Postfach 595
A-1011 Vienna, Austria

Osterreichischer Alpenklub (M)
Getreidemarket 3
A-1060 Vienna, Austria
(0222) 563 86 73

Osterreichischer Gebirgsverein (M)
Lerchenfelder Strasse 28
A-1080 Vienna, Austria
(0222) 52 38 44

Osterreichischer Touriskenklub (OTK)
Backerstrasse 16
A-1010 Vienna, Austria
(0222) 52 38 44

BELGIUM

Belgische Alpen Club/Club Alpin
  Belge (M)
Rue de l'Aurore 19
B-1050 Brussels, Belgium
(02) 548 86 11

B.L.O.S.O.
Kolonienstratt 29-31
B-1000 Brussels, Belgium
(02) 513 75 60

Club Alpin Belge
Section de Liege,
rue Caesar Franck 48
B-4000 Liege, Belgium
(041) 23 41 31

Conite National Belge des Sentiers de
  Grande Randonne
Boite Postale 10
B-4000 Liege 1, Belgium
(041) 23 99 60

Grote Routepaden
Van Stralenstraat 40
B-2000 Antwerp, Belgium
(031) 32 72 18

JH Kadee Bornem (E)
Dodentocht
Van Den Bossche Daniel
Aspergestraat 14
2680—Hing

Les Roses Noires (Paris-Tubize)
Wauters Raoul
Rue du Midi, 13,
1360—Tubize
021355 3166

CANADA

CLUBS

The Alpine Club of Canada
P.O. Box 723
Canmore
Alberta T0L 0M0, Canada
(403) 678-4134
(403) 678-5727

COMAX Vancouver Island Walk (E)
c/o COMAX Recreation Commission
1855 Noel Ave.
Comax, BC V9N 4X4
339 22 55

CLINICS AND COACHES

Roman Olszewski (R)
138 Indian Rd.
Toronto
Ontario M6R 2V6, Canada

CHINA

China Passage Inc.
302 Fifth Ave.
New York, NY 10001
(212) 564-4099
800 223-7196

CORSICA

Club Montagne-Corse
1 Boulevard Auguste-Gaudin
F-20200 Bastia, Corsica
(95) 31 71 59

DENMARK

Dansk Vandrelaug
Kultorvet 7
DK-1175 Copenhagen K, Denmark
(01) 12 11 65

Marchforeningen "Fodslaw"
Reberbanen 12
DK 8800 Viborg, Denmark
(06) 62 45 21

ENGLAND

The Alpine Club
74 S. Audley St.
London WlY 5FF, England

Backpacker's Club
20 St. Michaels Road
Tilehurst, Reading
Berkshire RG3 4RP, England
(0734) 28754
(0491) 680541, ext. 250

British Mountaineering Council
Crawford House, Precinct Centre
Booth Street East
Manchester M13 9RZ, England
(061) 273 5835

British Tourist Authority
680 Fifth Ave.
New York, NY 10019
(212) 581-4700

Coast to Coast Walk (315 km)
P. Campion
4, Ashford Close
Acorns, Aylesburg
Buckinghamshire HP21 7TW

Country-Wide Holidays Association
Birch Heys, Cromwell Range
Manchester M14 6HU, England
(061) 224 2887

Holiday Fellowship, Ltd.
142–144 Great North Way
London NW4 IEG, England
(01) 203 3381

Isle of Wight
Permanent Holidays Walks
Brookside Forge, Brookside Forge
Freshwater, Isle of Wight
(0983) 754644

Long Distance Walkers Association
Lowry Dr.
Marple Bridge, Stockport
Cheshire SK6 5BR, England

National Trust (Country Walks)
42 Queen Anne's Gate
London SW1H 9AS, England

Rambler's Association
1/5 Wandsworth Rd.
London SW8 21J, England
(01) 582 6878

YHA Adventure Holidays
Department HB, Trevelyan House
St. Albans
Hertfordshire AL1 2DY, England
St. Albans 55215

Mr. Colin Young (R)
55A Sackville Gardens
Ilford
Essex IGI 3LJ, England

FINLAND

Suomen Matkailutito
(Finnish Travel Association) (T)
Mikon Kutu 25
SF-00100 Helsinki 10, Finland

Keski-Suomen Matkutalito (TR)
Kauppakatu 22A
SF-40100 Jyvaskylaio, Finland
(941) 14720

FRANCE

Federation Francaise de la Montagne
7 rue la Boetie
F-75008 Paris, France
(1) 265 54 45

Federation Francaise de la Randonnee
 Pedestre
92 rue de Clignancourt
F-75883 Paris Cedex 18, France
(1) 259 60 40

GERMANY

Deutsche Wanderjugend
Hagberstrasse 11
D-7000 Stuttgart 1, West Germany
(0711) 46 60 05

Deutscher Alpenverein (M)
Praterinsel 5
D-8000 Munich 22, West Germany
(089) 29 30 86
info on hiking clubs
(089) 29 49 40

Verband-Deutscher Gebirgs und
 Wandervereine
Falkertstrasse 70
D-7000 Stuttgart 1, West Germany
(0711) 29 53 36

GREECE

Athens Olympic Marathon Walk (E)
Olympia Marathon Club
Thomas Papadakis
24 Patission Ave.
Athens 141

ICELAND

Icelandic Alpine Club (M)
Reykjavik, Iceland 36059

UTIVIST (Outdoor Life Club)
Laekjargotu 6
Reykjavik, Iceland 14606

IRELAND

C.H.A. Walking Club
2 Ardenza Park, Blackrock
County Dublin, Ireland

Castlebar's International Four Days
 Walks (E)
Courthouse
Castlebar, County Mayo, Ireland
(094) 21 0 33

Dublin International Two Days Walks
 (E)
61 Ardcollum Ave.
Artane, Dublin 5, Ireland
(01) 31 28-97

Federation of Mountaineering (M)
Clubs of Ireland
3 Gort na Mona Dr., Foxrock
County Dublin 2, Ireland

Irish Ramblers Club
20 Leopardstown Gardens
Blackrock, County Dublin, Ireland

Wayfarers Association (T)
"Athassal," Burnaby Road
Greystones, County Wicklow, Ireland

ISRAEL

Jerusalem Two Day Walk (E)
Israel Sport for All Association
Gonen Ilan
5 Varbourg St.
Tel Aviv 64289
(03) 29 6387

ITALY

Club Alpino Italiano (M)
Via Ugo Foscolo 3
1-20121 Milano, Italy

St. Georgen (Mountain Marathon)
Bei Bruneck—S. Giorgio/Brunico
Albert Steger
39031 St. Georgen bei Bruneck
Via Winkel-Weg, 8
South Tirol

Touring Club Italiano (T)
Corso Italia 10
I-20122 Milano, Italy

LIECHTENSTEIN

Liechtensteiner Alpenverein (M)
Ramschwagweg
FL-9496 Balzers, Liechtenstein
(075) 1 12 49

LUXEMBOURG

La Federation Luxembourgeoise des
  Marches Populaires
62 route de Luxembourg,
Rollingen/Mersch, Luxembourg

MEXICO

North Cascades Alpine School
1212 24th St.
Bellingham, WA 98225
(206) 671-1505

NEPAL

Himalaya Trekking Service
5730 Rising Sun Ave.
Philadelphia, PA 19120
(215) 342-8394

THE NETHERLANDS

Dutch Long-Distance Walking League
Voorkamp 2
Beets, The Netherlands
(02991) 17 34

Friendship Association of Individual
  Walkers
Postbus 909, NL-7301 BD
Apeldoorn, The Netherlands
(055) 23 22 96

Kononklijke Nederlandse
  Alpenvereniging (M)
Lang Voorhout 16
Den Haag, The Netherlands
(070) 68 25 68

Kononklijke Nederlandse Bond coor
  Lichamelijke Opvoedling (KNBLO)
Laan van Meerdervoort 440
Den Haag, The Netherlands
(070) 604141

Nederlandsw Bergsport (M)
Vereniging, Laan van
Meerdervoort 503
Den Haag, The Netherlands
(070) 65 52 37

Netherlands Christian Rambling
  Association
Corn. ten Hoopestraat 14
Midden-Beemster, The Netherlands
(02998) 15 02

Netherlands Rambling Association
  (Four Day Apeldoorn Walk)
Rubenslaan 123
Utrecht, The Netherlands

New Society for Rambling
Dahliastraat 175
Enschede, The Netherlands
(053) 35 36 11

North Netherlands Rambling
  Association
Den Loan 80 9
Uithuizen, The Netherlands
(05953) 12 99

Pied a Terre (O)
Singel 393
Amsterdam, The Netherlands
(020) 27 44 5

Strand 6 Daagse (Six Day Beach
  Hike)
H. Horsmann
Post bus 229
Den Helder, The Netherlands
(02230) 18 975

NORTHERN IRELAND

Irish Mountaineering Club
(Belfast Section)
82 Marlborough Park North
Belfast 9, UK

Ulster Federation of Rambling Club
5 Rowan Rd.
Ballyemoney, Antrim, UK

NORWAY

Den Norsk Turistforening
Stortingsgaten 28 III
Oslo 1, Norway
(02) 33 42 90

The North Cape Walk (E)
Nordmarksmarsjen
Oslo Gangkrets
Bjorn Thorstenson
Rugvn 29
0679 Oslo 6
(02) 26 5741

PORTUGAL

Clube Nacional de Montanhismo (M)
Rua Formosa 303
Porto, Portugal
28 3 23

SPAIN

Federacion Espanola de Montanismo
  (M)
Alberto Aguilera 3, 4 Izquierda
Madrid 15, Spain
(91) 445 13 82

SCOTLAND

Mountain Bothies Association
9 Drysdale Ln., Mickleover
Derby DE3 5PR
Mollison, 81 Dundas St.
Edinburgh EH3, UK
(031) 556 3536

Mountaineering Council of Scotland
59 Morningside Pk.
Edinburgh, UK

National Trust for Scotland
5 Charlotte Sq.
Edinburgh EH2 4DU, UK
(031) 226 5922

Scottish Mountaineering Club
22 Bonally Terr.
Edinburgh EH13, UK

SWEDEN

Svenska Klatterforbundet (M)
Box 14037
S-700, 14
Orebro, Sweden
(0586) 52 959

Svenska Turisforeningen (T)
Box 7615
S-103, 94
Stockholm, Sweden
(08) 22 72 00

SWITZERLAND

Berne Two Day Walk (E)
Fritz Hertig
Ob. Strassenackerweg 27
3067 Boll/BE
(031) 83 28 32

Romanshorn ITG (E)
Internationale Bodensee–Wanderung
Three Days-Three Countries
Hugentobler Alfred
Amriswiterstr. 28
8590 Romanshorn/TG

Schweizer Alpen-Club
Club Alpin Suisse (M)
Helvetiaplatz 4
CH-3005 Bern, Switzerland
(031) 43 36 11

TIBET

Western Heritage Tours
179 N. Main St.
Kalispell, MT 59901
(406) 755-8687

APPENDIX D
ALL-SEASON TRAINING
SCHEDULES

TOGETHER, THE SCHEDULES on the following pages constitute the year-round (52-week) GARY YANKER SPORTWALKING EXERCISE PROGRAM. These charts and schedules pull together the different types of sportwalk training in the four sample training weeks represented in the different seasonal periods: rest, build-up, transition, and sportwalking participation.

OFF-SEASON SCHEDULE
(NOVEMBER AND DECEMBER)

Exercises and Routines	Training Goals
Monday	
Light Calisthenics or Weight Training, Flexibility Exercises	Maintain Muscle Tone and Strength
Tuesday	
Walk/Bike/Run/Swim at 70%–75% Effort and Flexibility Exercises	Maintain General Endurance
Wednesday	
Flexibility Exercises, Light Calisthenics, or Weight Training	Increase Mobility
Thursday	
Walk/Bike/Run/Swim or Flexibility Exercises	Maintain General Endurance
Friday	
Rest/Stroll Day	Reduce Stress, Recreation, and Other Sports for Variety
Saturday	
¼- to ½-day walk at moderate pace or all-day ski	Maintain General Endurance
Sunday	
Longer distances: ½- to full-day walks (with frequent rest stops); X-C skiing or roller skating	Maintain General Endurance

Total Weekly Miles:* 15 miles (III) 21 miles (IV) 28 miles (V)
Total Weekly Hours: 4 hours (III) 6 hours (IV) 8 hours (V)
*It's very important to maintain minimum mileage or exercise calorie levels during off-season.

BUILD-UP PERIOD
(JANUARY THROUGH MARCH)

Exercises/Routines	Daily Hours III	IV	V	Training Goals
Monday				
Strength Training	¾	1¼	2¼	Increase Strength and Speed
Mobility Training	¼	½	½	
Speed Training	¼	½	1	
Tuesday				
Walking Training	1	2	3	Improve Flexibility and Technique
Wednesday				
Mobility Training	¼	½	½	Improve Flexibility and
Strength Training	¾	1¼	2¼	Technique
Speed Training	¼	½	1	
Thursday				
Walking Training	1	2	3	Increase General Endurance
Friday				
Mobility Training	¾	1¼	2¼	Maintain Flexibility, Reduce Stress, Recreation, and Other Sports for Variety
Saturday				
Walking Training Trial Event Walks	(training times vary according to short- and long- distance events)			Special Endurance
Sunday				
Walking Training at 70% to 75% effort	2	3	4	General Endurance

Total Weekly Hours: 6 (III) 10 (IV) 16 (V)
Total Weekly Miles: 35 (III) 50 (IV) 85–125 (V)

Pick at least one easy training or rest day, depending on your sportwalk schedule (usually Monday, Friday, or Saturday). Long-distance and hill walkers emphasize strength training with three sessions per week. Racewalkers emphasize flexibility and speed training three times a week.

PRE-EVENT PARTICIPATION PERIOD
(APRIL)

Exercises/Routines	Daily Hours			Training Goals
	III	IV	V	
Monday				
Strength Training	1	1	1	Maintain Strength and
Walking Training	½	2	3	Endurance
Tuesday				
Speed Training	1½	2	3	Specific Endurance aimed at
Mobility Training				Event
Walking Training				
Interval Walking				
Wednesday				
Walking Training	1	2	3	General Endurance
75% Effort				
Technique Exercises				
Thursday				
Walking Training	1	2	3	General Endurance
75% Effort				
Technique Exercises				
Friday				
Strength Training	1	1¼	2	Maintain Strength
Mobility Training				
Saturday				
Trial Walk	*	*	*	Test Performance
Sunday				
Trial Walks or	*	*	*	General Endurance
Walking Training				
75% Effort				

*For Short Distance: 2 miles (III) 3 miles (IV) 4 miles (V)
 For Long Distance: 3 miles (III) 4 miles (IV) 5 miles (V)

Total Weekly Hours: 6 (III) 10 (IV) 16 (V)
Total Weekly Miles: 35 (III) 50 (IV) 85–120 (V)

Note: You should be concentrating on the sportwalk training in the pre-events this month with one trial walk on the weekend (usually Saturday). Strength training is reduced to two sessions a week. You will continue with two full-length mobility sessions and shorter sessions with each sportwalk training session. Note also that daily allocation of walking mileages are not given. You must adjust your schedule for short, long, and racewalk events.

EVENT PARTICIPATION PERIOD
(MAY THROUGH OCTOBER)

Exercises/Routines	Daily Hours			Training Goals
	III	IV	V	
Monday				
Strength Training	1	1	1	Maintain Strength and
Distance Training	½	¾	1	Endurance
Tuesday				
Interval Walking	1	2	3	Maintain Speed
Wednesday				
Distance Training	½	1	1	Maintain Endurance and
Strength Training				Strength
Thursday				
Distance Training	½	½	½	Speed or Distance
75%–100% Effort				
Friday				
Warm-Up Walk	½	½	½	General Endurance
Saturday				
Warm-Up Walk	½	½	½	Special Endurance
	(1–10 hours)			
Sunday				
Distance Training	½	1	2	General Endurance
	(1–10 hours)			

Total Weekly Hours: 20 (III) 25 (IV) 35 (V)
Total Weekly Miles: 35 (III) 50 (IV) 80 (V)

Note: These totals include the mileage and hours spent participating in the events. Level V should cut back weekly miles to 80 or below, otherwise you'll wear yourself down unnecessarily.

INDEX

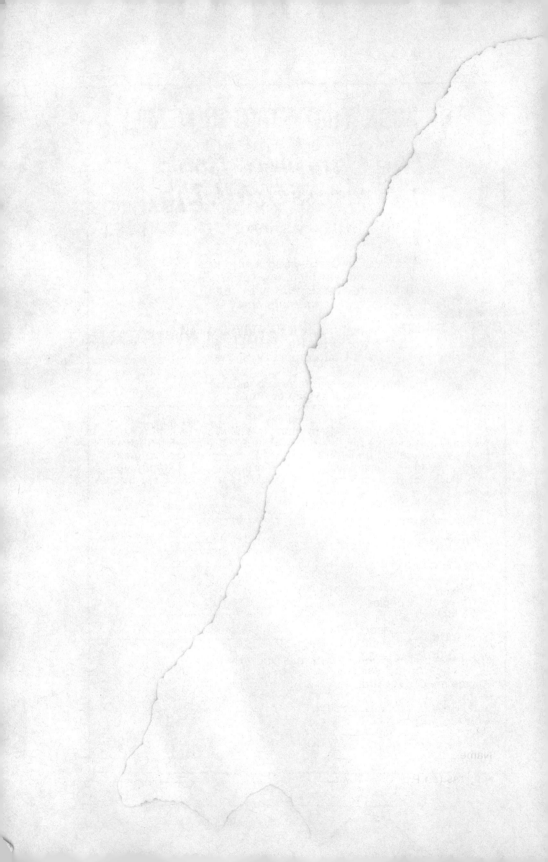